Rogue Diamonds

Rogue Diamonds

THE RUSH FOR NORTHERN RICHES ON DENE LAND

◆   ◆   ◆

ELLEN BIELAWSKI

Douglas & McIntyre

VANCOUVER/TORONTO/NEW YORK

03 04 05 06 07   5 4 3 2 1

Douglas & McIntyre
2323 Quebec Street, Suite 201
Vancouver, British Columbia
V5T 4S7
www.douglas-mcintyre.com

National Library of Canada Cataloguing in Publication Data

Bielawski, E.
  Rogue diamonds : the rush for northern riches on Dene land /
  Ellen Bielawski.

  Includes bibliographical references and index.
  ISBN 1-55054-950-2

  1. Tinne Indians—Land tenure—Northwest Territories. 2. Tinne
Indians—Northwest Territories—Treaties. 3. Diamond mines and
mining—Northwest Territories. I. Title.
KE7749.T56B54 2003   346.7104'32'089972   C2002-911501-9
KF8228.T56B54 2003

Editing by Lucy Kenward and Saeko Usukawa
Copy-editing by Naomi Pauls
Design by Val Speidel
Cover photograph © Galen Rowell/CORBIS/MAGMA
Maps by Stuart Daniel/Starshell Maps
Printed and bound in Canada by Friesens
Printed on acid-free paper ∞
Distributed in the U.S. by Publishers Group West

The publisher gratefully acknowledges the financial support of
the Canada Council for the Arts, the British Columbia Arts Council,
and the Government of Canada through the Book Publishing
Industry Development Program (BPIDP) for its publishing activities.

Owing to limitations of space, permissions to reprint previously
published material appear on p. 250.

◆　　　◆　　　◆

for my mother, Kay Bielawski,
who taught me to see;
for my sons, Connor and Adrian;
and for Łutsëlk'é

In Memoriam

Joe Bielawski

Joe Boucher

Zepp Casaway

Liza Casaway

Annie Catholique

Jonas Catholique

Judith Catholique

Terese Drybone

Emmy Lockhart Yamkovy

and

Kole Crook

　young friend, dancing partner, joyous spirit

Contents

◆   ◆   ◆

Sine—Summer

Xayt'às—Autumn

◆   ◆   ◆

Xaye—Winter

Xaluka—Early Spring

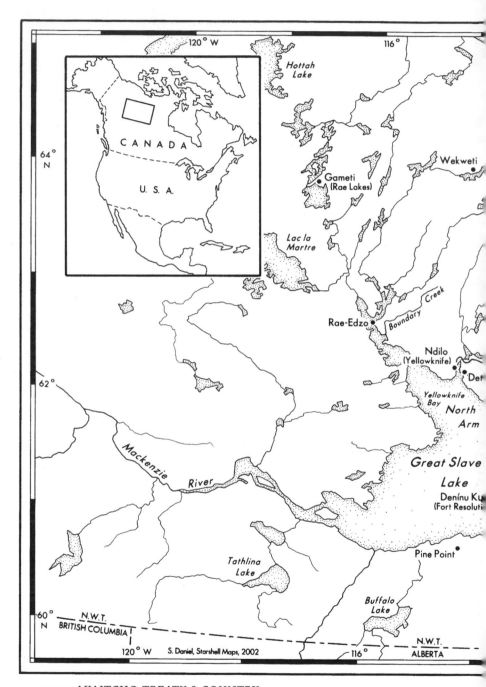

MAP 1: AKAITCHO TREATY 8 COUNTRY

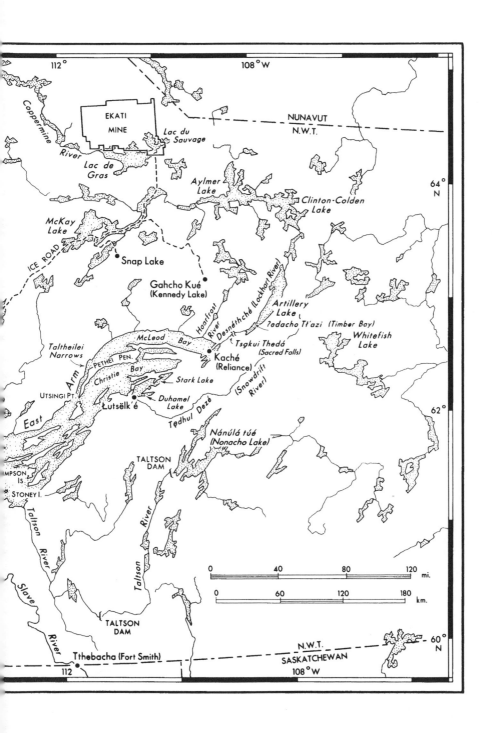

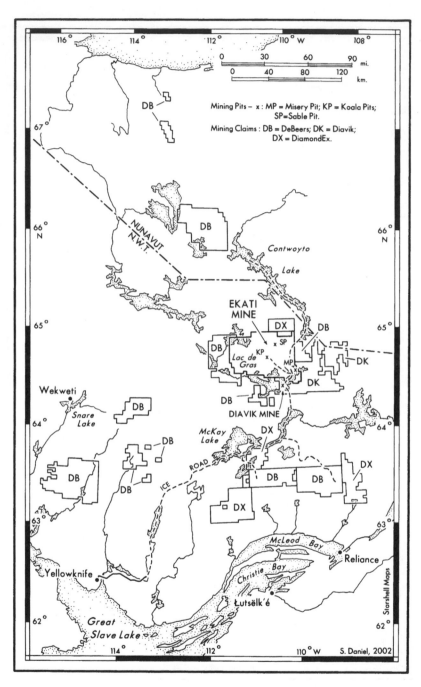

MAP 2: MAJOR MINERAL CLAIMS NORTH OF GREAT SLAVE LAKE

A Note on Language and Jurisdiction

◆　　　◆　　　◆

Dene is pronounced "DEN-ay." English speakers say "TLOOTsel-kay," stressing the first syllable, for Łutsëlk'é. Dëne Súłin yati refers to the language of the Dëne sułiné, known in English as Chipewyan people. Herein, I use Dene yati, a general term, when people speak in any of the Dene languages other than Dëne Súłin yati. Throughout the book, "Treaty 8" refers only to Treaty 8 in the Northwest Territories.

Prologue

◆　　　◆　　　◆

My friend and I would have these arguments about
what the most important elements of the world were.
I said "metaphor." He said "carbon."

—Carolyn Servid, "Matters of Fact, Matters of Faith,"
Sitka Symposium, 2000

"Are you going to walk to the falls?" I ask
Vicky Desjarlais as she turns over frybread in her skillet above the campfire. I've timed my visit well. The cooked side of her bannock is a perfect
golden brown, gently puffy. Mine never looks like that. Hers will break
open steaming and melt in the mouth. Mine will hold down a tent.

Vicky answers me, shaking her head. Her thick hair is the colour of
campfire smoke. "Me, I can't walk, I'm too old," she replies, "and my
kids need too much cookin' for . . . Those young guys, maybe some of
them will walk, but I'll go up with the elders on the plane."

As I walk on to Sarazin Basil's camp, compact sand gives way under
my moccasins. Fresh trout heads, split open, grill on her fire. Through

the tall spruce, Great Slave Lake is blue and still as glass. I pour myself a cup of old tea from the blackened kettle as Sarazin asks, "Are you going to walk up to the falls?"

"Yes. I want to walk, but I don't want to go alone."

"Yeah, walking's the best way to get ready for the Old Woman. I want to walk but I can't, my back is too sore."

In the ten days of the annual Spiritual Gathering, when the Łutsëlk'é Dene renew their life on the land, there is plenty of time for walking. I camp with the Dene at the mouth of Desnéthché, their sacred river, on holiday from my work for them. It takes a day to hike up to the falls, where the Old Woman sits. Maybe a day and a half, depending on whom you talk to and who you are. There is no trail. There are bears and caribou and moose and wolves. Bogs, lakes, dense spruce, mosquitos, blackflies. I don't know the way. I could follow the river, but that would take much longer than walking the great Precambrian granite ridges that lead to the Barren Lands.

In the end, only Henry Basil and I walk. Henry is older than I am, but much faster on foot. He shoulders his rifle and axe, saying, "We'll only be out one night. It'll be warm enough to sleep under mosquito netting."

Right. I pack my tent and sleeping bag. My fishing rod sticks up from my pack. We have dried caribou meat, oatmeal, some cheese.

At the last minute, Henry says, "Wait, I'm going to score some bannock from Sarazin." He slides her aromatic flat loaf into a plastic bag and places it at the top of his pack.

We walk over a rise. The tents and teepees disappear. We are in the bush.

We walk on old land, geologically the oldest on the planet. The bush seems endlessly wild, untouched by the surficial forces of modern life. Our feet cling to rock outcrops that are scored with the tracks of glaciers. The rock is rose-pink in colour, its pastel faces mottled with lichen and moss in every shade of green, grey, black and white. In its clefts and crevices, Labrador tea, blueberries and cranberries, even spruce find a foothold. To the impatient eye, the rock holds no trace of our passing. But if you look carefully, you see the worn patches. People have walked this way for centuries, if not millennia.

The Dene say that they will be able to live as they do "as long as this land shall last." It has lasted a long time already, almost four billion years. Older still is the light at this latitude, sixty-two degrees north. Before people, before caribou, before glaciers, even before diamonds, Earth floated on the axis that makes summer days here so long and winter days so short. All life here depends on the extreme seasons: the winter ice and the summer forest fires. With the light and the darkness flows all the history of the land: the heat that formed the diamonds, the eruptions that brought them near the surface, the glaciers that scattered them and the lakes that hid them from prospectors for so long.

Now the late-summer days are waning toward winter. The Spiritual Gathering is a brief respite for all of us. We hear more and more about the diamonds that lie underneath this land. The diamonds are about to be mined.

The summer's long light has ripened the cloudberries. We find them hiding under tussocks in a dim bog. They glow salmon-egg-orange when we lift the leaves. The berry taste glows as I swallow them, too. We find spruce gum, which is tart and full of vitamin C, of just the right consistency. I can chew this bit for hours, without cementing my teeth together, as I did once chewing unready sap. Soon Henry spots a low, small-leafed plant that he calls cedar. "This is the kind we use in ceremonies," he says. He lays his long frame on the ground and, holding a small plastic bag in his hand, gently gathers some of the greenery. He never takes the whole plant.

It is August, halfway between summer solstice and autumn equinox, so darkness does come. No more are the nights when the sun barely sets and the light hangs low to the north. We search in a gloomy dusk, peering through rain and mist and thick undergrowth for a place to camp. Henry makes fire while I pitch the tent. He casts for grayling from a bulge of stone in the river. I step past him to get water. He touches my arm, a silent caution on the slippery rock above the dark water. Later we eat dry meat in a watery stew, hunched near the flames.

"At the falls, you should offer women's things," Henry instructs quietly. "Maybe a needle, something that women use."

I think of what I have brought to leave at the falls. Just tobacco and wooden matches. These are not really women's things. Are they enough? "I have a needle in my pack," I offer.

"You should make it," he says, shaping something small in the air with his lean hands. "I have some caribou hide you can sew."

The night is opaque black around us, dripping steadily.

"You can sleep in the tent," I say, "but I'm not interested in anything but sleeping."

"I know."

In the morning, I hear light rain outside the tent and Henry saying morning prayers before he lights the fire. When I wade through the wet brush to pee, I see blueberries. Thousands of berries that were invisible last night now glisten with leftover rain as the sun breaks through low cloud. The droplets sparkle like diamonds, refracting sunbeams on millions of tiny green leaves. I pick and pick. My hands fill with cold water and berries. Soon my cap and cup are full. I push through the heavy wet bushes back to Henry, holding my offerings high in each hand. He is just pouring oatmeal into water boiling on the fire. We add the berries at the last minute, then a slice of butter as big as the hunting knife that cuts it. These are rich sweet tastes, made splendorous by morning sun after night rain.

Henry and I walk on. "Bear and wolf," Henry says as we follow a game trail northeast, "they're just watching us. They know we are here." We sit for a few minutes with our feet over the bluff, snacking on cheese, dry meat and the last of the bannock.

The day is perfect for hiking, warm but not hot. Soon we are at a place where the land drops so sharply that if I fell, I would tumble through the steep forest straight into the river where it gouges the bank. The water is so far below that I can hear but not see it. We go due east as the raven flies while the river curves away. We climb high rocky ridges. There are no trees up here, only scrub spruce in sheltered spots below. We are that close to the Barrens. I have the strongest sense of coming home, for I was born in country like this. Blueberry bushes cling to rock crevices, the first touch of auburn tinting their leaves.

Henry is far ahead, his long stride lengthening with excitement as we near the sacred falls. I am plodding through bog around two small lakes, trying to keep up. Late-afternoon sun brings a last burst of warmth and bugs as we reach the crooked lake where the plane will land tomorrow with the elders. We turn toward the river canyon, heading into tall spruce and growing shadows. It is cool in the forest, and tangy-tasting. As we near the river, high overcast dims the sun. At the canyon edge, Henry is silhouetted against the greying sky, thin and dark like the spruce around him. I follow to the rim and look down at the river racing and spraying far below.

Henry goes so fast now that I lose him amid the cavernous ups and downs of the canyon. It is late, and I'm cold and hungry and afraid I will stumble along the edge. Then I sight Henry standing on a high outcrop, looking at the river, then back for me.

Above the falls, the river boils out of the channel and rushes through the crevice that is the Old Woman's waist. Her white skirt spills full out of the ravine, cascading to the canyon floor. Spray drifts upward, opalescent blessings that wet my face. I wedge myself into a gap between boulders. Shield granite scores my back; ancient cold seeps into my bones. I feel Tsąkui Thedá, the Old Woman, flowing, falling icy from the Barrens down this undammed river to the sweat lodge at its mouth. When we return to the river mouth, we will pray in the sweat lodge, then immerse ourselves in the frigid waters, honouring the land.

We knew nothing of diamonds before they erupted into our lives. Above the falls, today, I wonder about gemstones and this land. The proposed diamond mine is Canada's first, the first on the Barren Grounds, the first this far north. We have learned that lavalike eruptions of something geologists call kimberlite carry diamonds from the Earth's mantle to its minable crust. We know that this land is that minable crust. What we don't yet grasp is the particular greed that diamond adoration inspires.

Sine
Summer

1. *The Diamonds*

◆   ◆   ◆

Both the Chipewyans and the Dogribs live a roving
life, according to the migrations of the game . . .
They obtain a precarious living by hunting and
fishing . . . The block of territory itself has no known
natural resources of sufficient importance to attract
people to the region . . . [Its] commercial possibilities
are small, and it is not likely to support any
population, except, possibly, such as might be
engaged in mining pursuits.

—George Camsell, An Exploration of the Tazin and Taltson Rivers,
    Northwest Territories, 1916

TALES of diamonds first came home to
Łutsëlk'é, Northwest Territories, with stakers, the men who mark the
boundaries of the prospectors' mineral claims on the land. One of these
able and fit men, wiry Frank Marlowe or gentle Peter Enzoe, would
stroll into the First Nation office for coffee in the morning, stir in the
sugar and whitener, light a cigarette and join the others on the hard-
wood chairs lined up against the walls of the common area. Desultory
conversation drifts here on good days, those without the routine upsets
of broken water trucks, delayed planes or impending deadlines suddenly announced by the federal government.

"You been workin'?" someone would ask.

"Stakin'," Frank or Pete would answer.

"Where?"

"Up near McKay Lake."

"What they lookin' for?"

"Diamonds."

"Diamonds?

"Diamonds."

"See any caribou?"

Almost always, the story teller and audience would speak in Dëne Súłin yati. A weathered brown hand, wafting cigarette smoke like the plume from a teepee in autumn, would show caribou herd movements across the map every listener carries in their mind. In Łutsëlk'é, people get excited about the caribou. In the fall when the animals return from the Arctic tundra, people ask, "How far are the caribou?" as they go through their days buying bread at the only store, driving the sewage truck, scraping and smoking hides, attending treaty negotiation meetings. By January, the airstrip condition reports faxed to Yellowknife daily caution pilots to watch for caribou on the runway.

About three hundred people live in this Dene (Athapaskan) community not quite two hundred kilometres east of Yellowknife. Here, on a granite point surrounded by Great Slave Lake, people hunt caribou, fish trout, gather berries, dry meat, make moccasins and collect welfare. This is a small place, where the quiet is broken only by the plane from Yellowknife once every day except Saturday, or the drone of snow machines heading out to traplines or for wood.

Most of the people here are Łutsëlk'é Dene súłiné. Some of us— maybe ten—are not Dene. Dëne Súłin yati (the First Nation language, called Chipewyan in English) does not translate he and she, so speakers of this language may call both men and woman "he" when speaking English. Most people here call us non-Dene "white guys." That is what

I call myself, one of the white guys. I've been here, off and on, for about three years. Sometimes I hear people talking about me in Dëne Súłin yati. They say *Ts'ékui Nánúlá túé,* which means "the woman who worked on Nonacho Lake." They are referring to the first community research I did with Łutsëlk'é in 1992.

Back then, I'd gone to the Spiritual Gathering to see if Łutsëlk'é was interested in collaborating on climate change research. In the dark of my first night there, as I walked toward the sound of the drum dance, I heard someone call my name.

"It's Felix," he said as he came out of the spruce forest. "So, what are your credentials?" His voice was almost harsh. Taken aback, I spoke the first words that came to mind, "I'm a person. And a mother, I have two young sons. I'm a northerner, I was born in Alaska and have lived all my life north of sixty. And I have a doctorate—" He interrupted this. "Oh. You *do* have credentials."

Not long afterwards, events led me to work with Łutsëlk'é for several years.

◆　　　◆　　　◆

DENE have watched the maniacal rushing of white people for minerals for a long time. There were rumours of gold in the 1890s, then the real thing at Yellowknife in the thirties; then uranium all along the Mackenzie River drainage; lead zinc in the fifties and tungsten in the seventies. So rumours about diamond prospecting at first seemed both fantastic and irrelevant.

Dene learned to take unusual rocks to outsiders for money when white prospectors first came to the Barrens over a hundred years ago. But these were never diamonds like those in India or Brazil, where rough gems washed out of alluvial soils. Nor like those that Boer farmers found when they tilled the soil of South Africa's Transvaal and

Orange Free State. Among the Dene, there is no tradition of digging into the ground for diamonds. Dene mined copper for its malleability and sharpness, so superior was it to chipped stone blades and projectiles. (It is from copper that the "Yellowknives" Dene get their name.) Dene quarried and traded for rocks that can be chipped and ground into tools, such as agate, chalcedony, obsidian.

 Diamonds could easily groove and cut antler, bone and softer stones. If the geology were different, if diamonds were not so rare, if cutting and polishing diamonds didn't require the only thing as hard as diamond—more diamonds—they might have been very useful to Dene before European explorers and whalers brought iron to trade. Instead, diamonds became the stuff of hierarchy and ornament, while the Dene lived as nomadic hunters in a land that required travelling light and moving often.

Prospectors now know that diamonds, some of the oldest rock on the planet, occur in the rare ore kimberlite. The name kimberlite comes circuitously to the treeless Barren Lands between Great Slave and Great Bear Lakes from American geologist Henry Carvill Lewis. He named the ore after studying a sample from the diamond rush settlement of Kimberley, South Africa. English prospectors had named the town after their own Earl of Kimberley, who was Secretary of State for the Colonies when the English annexed the diamond fields. The English wanted to impose order on the people and mining. Part of that order meant moving black Africans from prospecting their traditional land to working as diggers for white miners.

In the late 1860s a Boer farmer's son found a large stone weighing twenty-three carats, and a shepherd unearthed one of eighty-three carats. Buyers got hold of these gems, and prospectors from all over the world rushed to the area.

So many, in fact, that soon it was obvious that deposits along the rivers held disappointingly little. Fortuitous wanderings and "dry" diggings away from the rivers led some prospectors to discover that pans of yellow ground held diamonds worth digging for.

The first diggers called kimberlite "blue ground." It lay below the yellow ground. Strangely enough, although there was no water nearby, the dry diggings of 1869 in South Africa were richer in diamonds than any of the riverine deposits mined earlier in South America and India. At first, prospectors dug furiously through yellow ground recovering diamonds, stopping when they reached blue ground.

But kimberlite reaches the Earth's surface, where prospectors find it, in volcanic eruptions from near the Earth's core. The blue ground (yellow when dry, it turns out) is the molten river that carries diamonds to within reach of miners. When the kimberlite cools, it solidifies in the shape of a carrot. Geologists call these pipes. Barney Barnato, one of the self-made men behind the South African diamond trade, first surmised that diamonds came from a "tube in the earth."

Picture the Big Pipe at Kimberley, South Africa, mined out first by hand, later assisted with steam power, between 1871 and 1914. It is a giant, cliff-lined inverted pinnacle holding water far below its rim. This extinct volcano of kimberlite now has its own caldera, born of mining. The Big Pipe yielded much more than the 14.5 million carats of diamonds for which it is famous. Out of its depths came the colonial wealth and political power of the Cape Colony, later the Republic of South Africa. Diamonds and other minerals fuelled the founding of apartheid. By 1888, these riches, and the desire for more, drove the British to take control of Matabeleland and Mashonaland.

These tribal kingdoms are now named Zimbabwe and Zambia. The British called them Rhodesia, after the man who annexed them, Cecil Rhodes. Rhodes's real genius was figuring out how to control the market for diamonds, thus ensuring the value of gems. Controlling the market meant manipulating the people: Rhodes was a master manipulator of Africans, of the British Parliament and of his fellow colonists. He arrived in South Africa in 1870. He worked first with his brother in farming, which didn't pay. They moved on to mineral prospecting. Rhodes soon realized that the white diamond miners competing against each other prevented any of them from realizing wealth from their rocks. By 1888, the same year he succeeded in placing Matabele and Mashona lands under his control, Rhodes convinced other key South African diamond miners, including Barnato, to co-operate in negotiating prices with buyers from Europe and elsewhere. Thus was formed the DeBeers diamond cartel, which was named after two Boer brothers who owned the farm that became the Big Pipe. DeBeers, the dark power of the diamond world, completely controlled the global diamond market until the late twentieth century. It continues to exert massive influence on the trade. DeBeers is now poised to mine diamonds 135 kilometres northeast of Łutsëlk'é, only seventy kilometres north of Łutsëlk'é's sacred river.

◆   ◆   ◆

ON the Barrens, most kimberlite pipes are underwater. The massive ice sheets that once covered much of Canada expanded, retreated, expanded and retreated again. The ice scraped the Barrens down to the ancient, extremely hard Precambrian Shield. The glaciers also scoured out the softer tops of kimberlite pipes. When the glaciers melted, these hollows filled with water. Finding these pipes, and proving that they hold enough diamonds to make mining worthwhile, requires patience. The search may proceed as slowly as spruce grow at treeline, but investors are usually in a hurry to get rich.

These days prospectors look for geophysical evidence of kimberlite pipes, which they gather through aerial surveys and ground studies. So rare are diamonds that prospectors don't look for them, but for much more common minerals that occur with them. These indicator minerals have names as beautiful as the land that holds them: purple pyrope garnet, green chrome diopside, picroilmenite, chrome spinel. In the right places on the Barrens, it is possible to find these with little more than a rock hammer and an eye both well-trained and highly intuitive. But most of us would walk right over any diamond indicators.

Lots of Dene men know staking. Prospectors large and small have long relied on local labour to carry out the unskilled parts of the mineral exploration business. Many, like Frank Marlowe, are experienced, hard workers, and miners welcome their labour, their disinterest in the business and their lack of a union or expectation of anything other than seasonal employment. So far no stakers have been promoted to prospectors or developers, and least of all to owners in the mining business. Dene stakers aren't the men who threaten hostile takeovers or spy on the mining claims of people they aren't working for.

Not all the stakers were Dene during the 1990s diamond rush. The rush was far too big, needed far too many grunts for that. Its begetter, rogue geologist Chuck Fipke, is already a legend, a one-man story with all the right eccentricities and begrudged genius. For a time, the man became the story more than the gems. Briefly, Fipke and the diamonds, rather than the land that held them, were the only story.

Fipke, from Kelowna, British Columbia, first worked in New Guinea, South America and Africa for several of the world's big mining corporations. While overseas, he explored both foreign lands and innovative geochemical processes. Intensely curious, he gathered field data and pebbles of information from geologists wherever he travelled. While working in Brazil, he did his own geochemical experiments on his apartment balcony. He returned from overseas in 1977. With half his savings he patented the processes he had developed through experimentation. Marlene Fipke, who travelled the world with him, nursed him back from the near death of a tropical fever, raised their children and bought their first house with the other half of their savings. In 1977, when Fipke started C.F. Minerals Research Ltd., Marlene Fipke dried the company's samples in the kitchen oven. Fipke's eventual diamond strike relied on the labour of his wife, his sister and his eleven-year-old son.

Fipke found the diamonds after twenty years of studying both mutable landscapes and geochemical techniques for identifying diamonds. In 1981, Fipke and his erstwhile prospecting partner Stewart Blusson explored an isolated find near Blackwater Lake in the Richardson Mountains for a company called Superior Minerals. Fipke and Blusson found little except a large DeBeers exploration camp that one of their pilots mentioned. Fipke and Blusson promptly spied on DeBeers's activities. At the end of the prospecting season DeBeers left the area, convinced that their prospect was unworthy of further research. Fipke continued the search. Indeed, he welcomed DeBeers's dismissal of the area. Fewer geologists in the field, less industry attention to the area: both increased his chances of success in the diamond hunt.

Fipke was the first to put together all the subtle data that pointed to diamonds on the Barrens. In 1984, he added a critical secret from the diamond world to his own painstaking path through the detritus that melting ice sheets left behind. Geochemist John Guerney, a South African, had discovered a mineral that unerringly indicated diamonds. Guerney called it a G-10 garnet. Fipke tracked G-10s along the trail left when one ice sheet after another sheared the tops off kimberlite pipes and scattered the gems across the North.

By the winter of 1988–89, Fipke was getting samples from Lac de Gras, three hundred kilometres northeast of Yellowknife, that were loaded with diamond indicators. A Russian geologist had also discovered the G-10 indicator formula, as had DeBeers staff. It was only a matter of time before this information, combined with industry suspicion about Fipke's activity on the Barrens, would lead others there. Under cover of a small company expediting supplies to prospectors, Fipke claimed as much ground as he could afford to stake, then sought a development partner.

Fipke had to drill deep enough to prove he'd found enough diamonds to pay for the high cost of mining them. For drilling and bulk sampling, Fipke needed a big mining company with deep pockets. He found his partner in Australian mining giant Broken Hill Proprietary, known around the world as BHP. In September 1991, the partners found both kimberlite, the soft ore that holds diamonds, and diamonds under a small lake adjacent to Lac de Gras. Not just any diamonds, either. BHP and Fipke knew early on that their pipes held stones with three of the four "c's" that make diamonds into gems: colour, clarity and carats, or size. The Lac de Gras diamonds needed only cutting and polishing to compete with the most exquisite jewels on Earth. Despite the partners' desire to keep their finds quiet (the better to stake larger mineral exploration claims on more land) enough rumours spread that the price of stock in Fipke's exploration company, DiaMet, began climbing. BHP realized that the partners risked being accused of insider trading. As quietly as possible, they notified the Vancouver Stock Exchange and mining media of their drilling results. Fortune and fame had arrived faster than DeBeers could get back into the Canadian diamond play.

The announcement triggered what has come to be known as the biggest staking rush the world has ever seen—bigger than the California and Klondike gold rushes, bigger than the rush to South Africa for diamonds. No sooner did Fipke and BHP announce their find than stakers—any reliable able-bodied men who could walk the Barren Lands—were in demand by international and junior mining companies by the dozens. The world's diamond-mining high rollers figured that where there was one pipe, it was all too likely there would be several more. They sent crews to stake every possible tussock on the Barrens in the hopes of repeating Fipke's success. In helicopters and float planes, using Global Positioning Systems and computer mapping, more claims were staked faster than during the famed mineral rushes of history.

In 1994, Fipke and BHP drilled and sampled five kimberlite pipes. By late summer, people in the Northwest Territories knew that the scale of the work and BHP's plans to mine diamonds on the undeveloped Barren Lands would receive Canada's strictest environmental scrutiny, an environmental assessment review panel (EARP). In July, Minister of Indian and Northern Affairs Ron Irwin, who is originally from the mining town of Sault Ste. Marie, Ontario, requested that the Minister of Environment, Sheila Copps, appoint the panel of four. The panel members would distill the fact and fiction about diamonds and the North, then issue recommendations for Minister Irwin to use in his decision, yea or nay, as to diamond mining on the Barrens.

Meanwhile, back in Łutsëlk'é, and in the other tiny Dene communities on the diamond fields, people welcomed the stakers' wages. The money was the best Dene had seen since the fur market collapsed in the early 1980s. It went to groceries, boats and motors and snow machines, kids' winter clothes, ammunition and fishing gear. Some money moved around the community through gambling at the all-night card games in the villages or through bingo. Some disappeared into the bars of Yellowknife.

With their wages, the stakers brought home stories. At first, these weren't all that different from stories about gold or uranium or, even earlier, white fox furs. Those people down south wanted another commodity; there was money to be made procuring whatever outsiders wanted to pay for this time. But within a few years, diamonds would make an appreciable difference to people in Łutsëlk'é.

2. The Dene

◆　　　◆　　　◆

Hugh McLennan was incredibly naive when he wrote his book Two Solitudes. *He couldn't even begin to understand how many solitudes there really are.*

—Drew Hayden Taylor, *Funny You Don't Look Like One: Observations of a Blue-Eyed Ojibway*

*T*ODAY, sixteen Łutsëlk'é Dene and I are boating from Łutsëlk'é to Denínu Kų̀e, where the Yellowknives and Dëne sų́łiné made Treaty 8 with Canada back in 1899. On the shore where the grandparents and great-grandparents of today's Dene originally met the Crown's treaty commissioner and signed Treaty 8, about 200 people from the communities of Łutsëlk'é, Denínu Kų̀e (Fort Resolution), Ndilo and Dettah will attend the annual treaty celebration.

We glide most of the day southeast from Łutsëlk'é over water like glass. It is the kind of summer day when I imagine that paddling birchbark canoes on these lakes was uncommon ambrosia rather than cold risk. Even so, I am glad to be riding in a sturdy aluminum skiff powered by an outboard motor.

When we reach the easternmost tip of the Simpson Islands, we take a land break to make fire, eat and wait for one of the other boats that is travelling with us. Ernest Boucher points out the route we will take across wide open water to the Slave River Delta. Ernest is a hunter and trapper, respected by his peers as "a good man in the bush." Despite my efforts to pay attention, I have gotten completely lost in the maze of channels we have navigated from the eastern "neck" to the "belly" of the "goose" that is Great Slave Lake. Ernest squints for a time at the place where the sun's glare off the lake melts into a horizon of haze, then says, "I don' think the wind's gonna blow up . . ."

He gestures with a straight arm, his fingers and thumb together pointing straight ahead from the tip of the serrated rock where we are perched. "We go that way, then we go for a while and soon you can't see land behind, you can't see land ahead. So you go that way," he says, pointing farther in the same direction, "and then you see that land over there, Stoney Island."

Behind us, near the forest edge, our companions—Ernest's brother Albert; Pierre Marlowe and his family, in whose boat I am riding; Billy and Liza Enzoe and their youngest daughter; and various others—grill fish that we have pulled from the lake. All day we have been living in the Dene spirit of the treaty. The treaty states that Dene rights to hunt, fish and trap on their traditional lands will not be limited. Although I carry the required Northwest Territories fishing licence that allows me to catch two fish each day, the chiefs have told me I don't need to. "We'll give you a Dene licence," they say.

At last we hear an outboard motor, and soon a boat appears around the point of an island to the north and comes toward us.

"Not lost," the driver says, grabbing a mug of tea. "I went to see that other fish camp." Laughter erupts all around. It is true; the young people do not know the land as well as their elders.

We go then, across the open water while it is calm, or, calm enough. When we push off from shore, everyone offers something to the water for a safe crossing. On the trip between the Simpson Islands and Stoney Island, it is possible to believe that the land will last forever and the rivers will flow eternally. Out here, we cannot see any land. Only the water holds us. The skiff starts climbing waves then slamming into troughs, and I remember that Dene children are taught to "practise a method to calm the water." I've never learned what these methods are, and now I wish I had. Some great boatsmanship from Pierre and the other drivers at their outboard tillers gets us soon enough toward the shelter of the Slave River Delta.

In these shallow waters, Liza Enzoe, one of the most respected matriarchs and leaders in Łutsëlk'é, stands in the bow of the family skiff, poling and calling Dëne Súłin yati directions to her husband, Billy, over the head of their youngest daughter. Repeating ancient practice, the family is silhouetted against the silver glare of the choppy water. Slowly, oh so slowly, all four boats make it through the shoals.

Beyond this channel, we reach deeper water. By now it is evening, and we crank the motors to race through the maze of sloughs that are the Slave Delta. At full speed we whizz past a stripped birch sapling stuck in the river. Billy cuts his motor to idle, then waves for the rest of us to turn around. We've gone right past the marker for the channel that leads to Denínu Kų́e.

In the dusk, mosquitos rise out of the water and the marsh as soon as our boats slow. We speed up again, following a narrow twisting channel of inky-brown water.

A while later, we reach a sandy pullout where boats from Denínu Kų́e are beached. We are still some distance from town. Batting

mosquitos and spraying bug dope like firefighters at a blaze, we unload
the boats and wait for someone to come by road to take us into town.

Sometime after sunset my gear and I are finally dumped in a field on
the flat plain that is Denínu Kųe. After the noise of the outboard and the
jolting, dusty ride over ten kilometres in the back of a pickup truck, I am
lost in the evening quiet of a grassy field. And puzzled. I am supposed to
be in Tent City, but this is no tent city. I appear to be the only person
here, though idle young men driving pickup trucks occasionally cruise
the perimeter of the broad field like vultures. I am more than a little
nonplussed. All my friends from Łutsëlk'é have disappeared into the
houses of their relatives here in Denínu Kųe. My aloneness hits me hard.

By the temperature and the light I know it is somewhere between
about 10 P.M. and midnight. This matters only because I want to gauge
the amount of sleep I get. Treaty assemblies are long, often tiring
affairs. Pacing is important to stay awake for all the speeches on a hot
day then dance holes through your moccasins at night. Of course, it is
impossible to know when to get up in the morning, because starting
time is frequently flexible. Like most outsiders, I generally arrive too
early, then wear out before the climax of business.

I have dust in my mouth, my eyes, my nose, and very little water
left. There doesn't seem to be a water supply set up for the tent city, so
as I pitch my tent I ponder where to go for some. Before I finish setting
up, a pickup rolls across the field, then stops not too far from me. A
lone Dëneyu, middle-aged, climbs out with the stiffness of a long ride.
He starts unloading his gear. When he throws a tent on the ground, I
walk over to him.

He holds out his hand instantly and introduces himself: "Magloire."
"Ellen." We shake hands.
"Do you need some help?"
"I need some water."

"Oh, I've got the best water, got lots with me, right here."

He hauls out two five-gallon jugs. While he fills my small container, he says, "We got the best clean water. I brought that all the way from Fort Fitz, you know Tthebatthi over there? Good, clean water."

It is deeply refreshing.

As I drink the water, Magloire comments, "Not many people staying here." He suggests making coffee as he lights his Coleman stove and boils water.

I rustle through my grub box for mugs and instant. We pour two cups and sit on a low-post railing that edges the field. We relax into the calm, cooling evening. At first as we talk, it is hard for me to understand Magloire's clipped speech and his Dëne yati–accented English. I learn that he is the chief of the Tthebatthi contingent of the Salt River First Nation, based in Fort Fitzgerald, a tiny collection of houses a few kilometres from Fort Smith, called Tthebacha in Dëne Súłin yati. When I speak, I nearly have to shout in his good ear. Like many hunters he is hard of hearing, the result of exposure to frequent rifle reports. We tell each other where we came from that day and about our families.

Before long, a road-worn dusty van and two more pickups roll slowly over the uneven ground, throwing up soft dust from each tire. The van driver steps down next to us. It is Chief Darrell Beaulieu. Darrell is from Ndilo, the First Nation community now surrounded by the town of Yellowknife. Together, the communities of Ndilo and Dettah are the Yellowknives Dene First Nation. A troupe of young men—the Dettah Drummers—piles out with him, as do two of his sons. They set up tents and go off to scour the community, a search that yields some makeshift tables and some scrap wood to make more. In no time a fire and another kettle are going.

◆   ◆   ◆

To understand these diamonds, we have to look at the characters and action in the long-running drama of this land. The plot is quite simple. The land is the protagonist. The First Nations and the Crown, or Canada, are the antagonists. Diamonds are but the most recent of the bit players who cross the stage between scenes, each time in a different costume, saying the same lines. Diamonds are a good costume, drawing more attention than, say, tungsten or lead. Diamonds distract us from the plot.

Historically, the Treaty 8 First Nations lived from the land, hunting and harvesting. The Crown, later Canada, wanted the land not for hunting and harvesting, but for cash from its mineral resources and its fast-flowing water. Canada initiated treaties with First Nations to gain control of their land. Dene consider their treaties with the Crown to be treaties of peace and friendship.

To this day, the federal government seeks the denouement of this drama through "certainty." Certainty means that all parties will be certain of their rights, responsibilities, opportunities and profits. The feds believe that to achieve certainty, aboriginal title must be extinguished. The extinguishment "policy" is so rigid that it might as well be law.

Extinguishment. To First Nations, few words could be more harsh. Extinguishment is Canada's official policy on aboriginal peoples' connection to the land. First Nations recall their relationship with their land, including laws and moral codes, from time immemorial. British common law recognized that aboriginal people hold aboriginal title to their traditional lands in the Royal Proclamation of 1763.

But history diverges. There are two sources, two accounts, two rivers of memory. Dene hold Treaty 8 in their minds and hearts, in an oral account passed down since 1899 that is eerily consistent to those of us who grew up dependent on reading and writing. Canada relies on its written record, the hard copy ink and parchment treaty. Bolstering Canada's version are voluminous government notes, memos, minutes, orders and all the power that the written word holds in Western civilization.

In the Dene view, Treaty 8, an oral contract precisely documented by René Fumoleau and a team of Dene yati speakers between 1966 and 1973, is a treaty of peace and friendship. It frames coexistence between the Dene and the newcomers to their land. It neither extinguishes aboriginal title to the land nor cedes the land to Canada.

In Canada's view, Treaty 8 (and the 482 other treaties, adhesions and land surrenders that Canada entered into with the aboriginal people of North America between 1781 and 1902) extinguishes aboriginal title. Canada holds that in signing Treaty 8, the Dëne súłiné and Yellowknives ceded, released and surrendered all of their interest in the land and gave title to the Crown. This justifies Canada taking resources and profit from land within the boundaries of Treaty 8.

◆　　　◆　　　◆

THE first commodity that outsiders came north for—well before Treaty 8—was fur. Of all the riches outsiders have taken from the North, Dene best understand fur. From the time the Dene woman Thanadelthur met the English fur trader James Knight in the early 1700s, until the most recent collapse of the fur market in the early 1990s, Dene were the migrant workers of their hunting grounds. Drawn by the iron blades and needles, tobacco, tea, kettles, Western medicine (such as it was), sugar, flour, cloth and rifles they received as payment for furs, Dene shifted their usual nomadic travels to include an annual stop at trading posts. Gradually fur traders pushed farther and farther into Dene territory, often establishing their forts at well-used Dene gathering places. Today this legacy continues in the two names that many NWT communities bear: Denínu Kų̨e, or Fort Resolution; Tthebatthi, Fort Fitzgerald; Tthebacha, Fort Smith.

Other resources commanded attention briefly. Dene were well aware of oil seeps along the Mackenzie River, but before the invention of the automobile, the airplane and plastic, oil wasn't much in demand. In January 1899, rumours of gold in Łutsëlk'é country led prospectors to the east end of Great Slave Lake. Ottawa's treaty commissioner was not far behind. But these first rumours of gold in the Mackenzie faded quickly.

For the Dene, fur trapping remained. It grew more lucrative during the early twentieth century—so lucrative that individual white trappers made deep inroads into the trade monopoly that the Hudson's Bay Company had enjoyed since 1670. But the post-war fur market crashed in 1920, just as the influenza pandemic struck the Dene hardest. People remember that before the great flu epidemics, there were teepees all along the shore of Great Slave Lake; after, the people were much reduced in number.

Meanwhile, prospecting continued. White men who stayed in the North moved from trapping to mineral hunting. In 1920, outsiders discovered oil at LeGoline (Norman Wells) on Descho, the Mackenzie River. Flu decimated the Dene again in 1928.

In 1931, just in time for America's Manhattan Project to build a nuclear bomb, uranium was discovered on Great Bear Lake, at a place miners named Port Radium. Dene went to work moving burlap bags of radioactive ore on and off barges up and down the Mackenzie River, along what came to be known as the uranium road. Deline, where the ore was stockpiled on the river shore, is known as a community of widows, so high is the cancer rate among men. Uranium was also mined briefly on Stark Lake, just east of Łutsëlk'é. Łutsëlk'é Dene who worked at the small mine camped at the mine site with their families, who drank the water and breathed the dust. In 1993, Łutsëlk'é's cancer rate was three times what might be expected for a community of its size. In Denínu Kye, where barges bearing uranium often called, it is the same.

Researchers from Atomic Energy Canada found traces of radioactive ore among the beach gravels in 1992.

In 1933, it was gold again, at Ndilo. Dene call the new settlement that grew there Sambak'e, "place of money." It is also known as Yellowknife, where the definitive NWT gold rush began in 1934. Any gold missed in the tunnels below today's city was rapidly paved with streets. The old Giant Mine borders Yellowknife, with a wasteland of open pits and ramshackle buildings. Arsenic in Great Slave Lake, which surrounds Ndilo and the community of Dettah across the North Arm, is the profit Dene earned from Giant Mine.

Dene reacted in various ways to all this searching for and selling stuff that didn't move or grow. Old women at Ndilo tell a story about prospectors who needed their laundry done. They offered pittance to the women for washing. The women took time away from making dry meat out of fresh so it wouldn't spoil, from splitting and drying fish, from hauling water and nursing babies and sewing clothing for the coming winter. They washed the prospectors' clothes. They hung the clean laundry on their spruce racks, among the drying trout and whitefish.

The prospectors brought no more laundry to the Dene women. This may have been one of the earliest economic-development projects that outsiders tried with Dene. If so, its failure set a pattern that continued for several decades. Typically, white people offer something and believe that the Dene have failed to understand the worth of the offer. White people often believe that the Dene have not bothered to answer.

Oil, gold, uranium and lead, unlike fur, had no place in traditional Dene life. To trap fur one has to know the animals and the land very well. To appreciate hide and fur as a necessity, it helps to have walked a frozen lake in midwinter with the wind howling in one's face. Only a fur ruff keeps skin from freezing. Moosehide moccasins lined with rabbit fur keep toes alive. Moosehide mittens with the hair turned out are still the best protection for hands, no matter how cold the temperature and wind. Goose down keeps one warm at night, under a caribou hide tent or inside a dogsled upturned for protection from a blizzard.

Not until snow machines began to replace dog teams in the 1970s did an extractive industry send much back to the Dene way of life. Lack of interest in the product, however, did not keep Dene from working for the white people who looked for inedible riches. Since the first fur traders came into their country, outsiders have assumed that Dene should learn enough of their ways to provide what the outsiders are looking for. Practically, Dene are much more capable of taking on wage jobs in the mining industry than the average white person is of living within a Dene community. It is much less taken for granted that outsiders will learn the Dene way.

◆   ◆   ◆

TREATY 8 promises that land will be set aside for the Dene to keep for themselves, along with the right to hunt, fish, trap and gather as long as the land lasts. But for one hundred years after Treaty 8 was signed, no land was set aside for Treaty 8 signatories in the Northwest Territories. Throughout the twentieth century, the process of removing control of Dene land from Dene continued in different ways. It is now most commonly called the "land claims" process, a misnomer that implies Dene must "claim" back from Canada the land that they occupied from time immemorial.

Treaty 8 also means that the Crown will act as fiduciary, or "a person to whom property or power is entrusted for the benefit of another." But the Crown has not shielded any traditional Dene land from development since 1989. The right to live from the land is constantly limited through the creation of third-party interests. Treaty 8 is an agreement between the first and second parties, the Dene First

Nations and the Crown. Third parties are every mining company, dam builder, fishing lodge owner, road and airstrip builder. Even the Government of the Northwest Territories is a third party to the treaty. Contrary to what many Canadians may believe, Treaty 8 has never been fully implemented. Canada holds that when Treaty 8 is finally implemented in the Northwest Territories or replaced by a modern treaty, all third-party interests will be respected. For the last one hundred years, Canada has been completing the treaty by granting others permits and licences, creating third-party interests that it will respect, which remove land and water from the Dene, before the Dene can secure their portion of the land as the treaty allows.

Mysteriously, since the diamond rush began, negotiations to implement Treaty 8 have stalled. Canada has not yet appointed the new negotiator to replace the man whose contract the Crown "forgot" to renew. During the three days of Treaty 8 assembly business, I wonder when Canada will appoint a new federal negotiator for the Treaty 8 file. New mines are developing, and each will become a third-party interest. The exploration areas already *are* third-party interests. Canada will honour these if and when the Dëne súłiné and Yellowknives Dene (collectively known as Akaitcho Treaty 8 First Nations since they were brought together by the great leader Akaitcho, who made peace with the neighbouring Dogribs in 1829) ever get to choose land for themselves, finally fulfilling Treaty 8, which is already a century old. Intentional or not, Canada's delay in appointing a new negotiator to Treaty 8 is allowing the diamond miners to choose land before Akaitcho Treaty 8 does. Łutsëlk'é hired me to be assistant treaty negotiator to Łutsëlk'é's chief, Felix Lockhart. In the absence of the Crown and treaty negotiations, my job has become negotiating with diamond miners.

◆　　　　◆　　　　◆

THE evening before the last day of the assembly, I stroll away from camp around nine, leaving Darrell and Magloire and others chatting by the fire.

"You're going too early," someone says.

"Dance won't start for hours," comments another. But I want to get a seat on the bench along the wall so I can see the drummers, the dancing and the ever-changing flow of people into and out of the hall.

Beyond the fluorescent lights of the entryway, the dance floor is cavernous and full of shadows the plain ceiling lights don't dispel. Kids are running and shrieking in the big space as they always do before a dance. Some of the elders are already seated. Others, bent or shuffling with a cane across the dance floor, seek chairs. The old women wear Catholic mission skirts. The older men sport polyester slacks, western shirts, nylon jackets embroidered with "Pine Point Mine" or "Dene Nation" and baseball caps from the Edmonton Oilers or New York Yankees. The old people sit together. Every now and then one of them calls to a kid, hands over some money and instructions. The kid runs across the hall to the concession window, then returns with a cola or lottery tickets or tea.

The drummers arrive a few at a time. They gather on a low platform at one end of the room, where they light a Coleman stove over which they take turns warming their drums. Soon each of the twelve young men riffs a precursor rhythm, listening to the tone of the warming moosehide stretched tight over its circular wood frame. We hear the different drums rising and falling in the same irregular rhythm as air before it settles into a good blow: first come whiffles and stirs, then breezes, then gusts backing into a steady force. Gradually the drummers' individual warm-up rhythms come together—just a few times at first, then for longer and longer phrases, until what emerges is the solid trochee two-beat that is the bass line of Dene songs.

Meanwhile, the hall fills. People arrive, leave, then return with others. Each First Nation community gathers in a separate part of the hall, except for the elders, who mostly stay together to visit and relive their lifelong connections with each other. They talk about when they lived on the land and travelled to the summer gathering along the "three main roads" of lakes and portages that connect Łutsëlk'é, Tthebacha and Denínu Kų́e. When the hall is nearly full around midnight, some of the older men move to the stage and take drums from the younger drummers. Everyone stands: the drummers form a semicircle facing the hall, where the rest of us are crammed between benches and folding chairs. The dance opens with a prayer song, which is slow but deceptively powerful, like the current of swift water through a deep channel. The chief of Denínu Kų́e welcomes everyone.

After, the drumming begins in earnest. No one dances the first few songs. Then a few teenage girls—totally duded up in tight jeans, white runners and their best team jackets—line up one behind the other to form part of a circle. With their bodies close together, their feet move in perfect unison. Some elders join them, forming another fragment of the circle. They shuffle in small, perfectly precise steps. Above their white anklets and beaded moccasins, the old women's pleated skirts sway.

Finally, the chiefs lead a dance. Their solidarity draws others, and a full circle forms. Everyone dances one behind the other, turning in the circle of the drum, always in the direction that the sun moves. By then the hall is stifling. People peel off jackets, strip down to T-shirts and get down to serious dancing. I am lost in the rhythm of the pounding drums, in the community, in the circle, as we stomp round and round and round, the singers' high wailing cascading like the rapids on the rivers over the drums, the rumbling of deep water around boulders.

This is the Dene. This is the people, this unending unity of the circle, round and round as the sun goes, as long as the rivers flow, the sun shines and the land lasts. This also is the treaty, of peace and friendship, among the Dene and with their neighbours, people like me who come to them, people from the rest of the world out there beyond their traditional borders. Each dance is a prayer, each step a renewal of spiritual strength, a recognition of human unity with all other living things and the land itself.

3. The Deadline

•   •   •

In the Band office, never plan. You'll live longer.

—First Nations staff motto

O<small>N</small> August 8, 1996, a familiar voice on the CBC news startles me awake. Northwest Territories Premier Don Morin is speaking from a press conference in Ottawa. He is with Canada's Indian Affairs Minister Ron Irwin. Irwin is granting Canada's first diamond mine conditional approval. It is subject to "significant progress in sixty days" on agreements between mining giant Broken Hill Proprietary (BHP), the Dene First Nations, the Inuit and the Northwest Territories.

It has been at least 3.5 billion years since the diamonds formed deep in the Earth's mantle. Łutsëlk'é ancestors arrived in this land between four thousand and eight thousand years ago. One hundred years ago, the Crown took control of Dene land and resources through Treaties 8 and 11. It has been five years since geologist Chuck Fipke discovered the diamonds up at Lac de Gras. Now we have only sixty days to reach agreement with the diamond miners.

Stunned, I lie between clean sheets thinking about Irwin's statement. Only yesterday, I was in the bush at the annual Spiritual Gathering, where most of the Łutsëlk'é Dene are missing this announcement of a deadline for their future. I can still smell woodsmoke. I picture the campfires, teepees and tents among stately spruce in the early morning. I hear the quiet cadence of Dëne súliné voices, drifting about the encampment with the smoke.

◆   ◆   ◆

OUR journey to the gathering at Desnéthché began as it always does. I'd tidied my desk in the First Nation office, leaving it as clear as it could be in the midst of treaty negotiations and proposals for diamond mines. I'd called my sons in Edmonton to say I'd join them for our holiday soon. Then I left my home in the village, hitched a pickup truck ride to the shore below the old white-steepled church and waited with my gear—my grub box, groceries for ten days, my tent—for my boat ride. I never know quite when we'll leave, which way we'll go or how many boats will travel together.

When the hot day cooled at last, Antoine Michel pulled up in his pickup truck. Antoine was chief of Łutsëlk'é when I first came here three years ago. I worked most closely with him on Nánúlá túé, and he remains one of Łutsëlk'é's leaders. Chief Jonas Sangris sat in the cab, a pack of boys in the box. Jonas, chief of Dettah, had offered me a ride in his large, comfortable boat, which was a generous offer, given that a few nights ago during the fishing derby I'd navigated it into rocks off Dog Island.

Jonas's genial manner, marked most often by a broad grin full of white teeth, and his Dene yati–accented English can mislead outsiders. He's a businessman, husband, father, hunter and chief. To watch him run his council meeting, speaking in his own language until he changes to English for the younger people, is to see a delicate diplomatic dance by a body built for defensive hockey, which he plays as devoutly as he attends the Roman Catholic Church every Sunday. Jonas is a warm, barrel-shaped man with completely black hair although he's over fifty. "They don't call him *sans gris* for nothing," a colleague once observed.

As he stashed bug dope and cassette tapes under his boat's dashboard, Jonas mentioned that we'd head to Christie Bay first. This was opposite to the way we needed to go to reach Desnéthché. He and Antoine are good friends, and Antoine wanted to stop at his cabin on the way. Both Jonas's and Antoine's boats are too big for the portage between Christie and McLeod Bays, so from Antoine's cabin we'd backtrack southwest to Utsingi Point, then turn sharply northeast through Taltheilei Narrows, then back along the East Arm.

"Sounds good," I replied, though inwardly I was thinking that it could be at least two days before we reached the gathering. If we left tonight. If we didn't get windbound. If we didn't decide to build a new room onto Antoine and Mary Jane's cabin before going on to Desnéthché.

But the following afternoon, we paid the water with tobacco as we turned almost 180 degrees below the steep granite wedge of Utsingi Point. After we'd travelled east, through Taltheilei Narrows, we sighted Chief Darrell Beaulieu in his boat with his three sons. We formed a flotilla and late in the day, we reached a small island opposite a waterfall on the north shore of McLeod Bay. We set up tents, grilled fresh fish and I fell into the deep sleep I only sleep in the bush.

I woke early and walked to the far side of the island seeking that rarest of pleasures, a frigid Great Slave Lake bath. I found a double-wide

Precambrian bathtub floored with soft sand whose creamy colour rippled below sunlight-fractured water so clear I could see individual grains. The wave action was just enough to douse my shoulders and agitate the village dust out of my hair.

By eleven, even as we broke camp, the weather was blowing up. We passed the windbound day on shore, then loaded the boats and tried to push off again in the evening. (We ignored the evidence of the lowering sky.) Beyond the lee of the shore, the swells proved too much, and we rapidly sought refuge in the next sheltered cove.

Anchored there was Premier Morin's cabin cruiser. We tied our three skiffs together in a raft alongside his, then crawled gratefully out of the elements into Donnie's warm, dry palace. With loaves-and-fishes magic, he and his wife, Gladys, fed all nineteen people who jammed aboard their boat, while the storm grew outside.

Jonas and Darrell discussed the best places to go to shore and make camp.

"No way," boomed Donnie in the crowded wheelhouse. "Stay here, we've got plenty of room." He looked gleeful at the prospect of hosting such a large group.

Several people followed Gladys below to sleep. Darrell and his youngest curled up in sleeping bags on the wheelhouse floor. Donnie brought me a blanket, and I stretched out on the bench where I'd been sitting. Jonas and his sons crossed our flotilla to his boat, where the canvas cover kept out the storm. Everyone left over squeezed into sleeping bags under canvas on the aft deck. All night we dozed and listened and rocked while the storm waxed and waned.

By daybreak, grey and misty though it was, we crossed McLeod Bay to the Reliance side. Everyone but the drivers and me—acting as ballast in one of the lighter boats—rode in the shelter of Donnie's boat. The trip across was a kaleidoscopic vision of our open bow crashing through glacial green waves roiling with white foam. By the time we reached the far side, we'd lost sight of the other boats. But when we pulled through the narrow rock gap between Reliance and Desnéthché, we saw the larger boats and regrouped near the shore. "How was it?" Jonas called from his boat.

"Rough, not too bad," I called back.

"You're all wet."

"Been wet before."

When the last boat came through the gap, all the boats headed northeast on the last, short leg to the Gathering campsite.

It was good, like nothing else is good, to reach Desnéthché. I carried my gear to a small treed alcove, the same place I camped every year. Jonas often repeated a story about my early wanderings, in the years before I felt comfortable in Łutsëlk'é.

"One day I see her go this way. Then next day, back that way, and dragging her tent! I thought she was lost." Without family, clanless, I was ripe for alliance, if not adoption or bride service. I got unlost the day I found this sheltered copse not far from the shore. I made my camp. After the long boat ride and the exposure to the elements, my mind was clear, scoured of abstract schemes to manage the environment. My spirit was ready for renewal from the land.

◆   ◆   ◆

FOR some time we have surmised that the diamonds will be mined whether we like it or not, despite the appearance of industry and government consultation with us and neighbouring First Nations. First, international diamond-mining conglomerates—like BHP and Kennecott-Diavik and DeBeers—staked huge claims on the Barren Lands during the diamond rush in the early 1990s. Then, in 1994, came the first steps to approve BHP's mine: the environmental assessment review panel (EARP) was appointed. Irwin received the EARP report on

July 21, 1996. This sixty-day deadline is just the next step, though its timing has come as a surprise to all of us, including Premier Morin, who abruptly left the Spiritual Gathering yesterday to join Minister Irwin in Ottawa. But why only sixty days?

Thinking it through at a before-coffee pace, I realize the minister did not set the sixty-day time frame—the land did. Irwin not only wants the diamond mine to be approved, but he wants construction to begin this year. If he can approve the mine by Thanksgiving, BHP's construction materials will roll up the ice road as soon as it is frozen solid, perhaps as early as mid-December. Without a deadline, the mine approval process might drag on until it is too late to supply the next construction season. The ice road is unsafe after mid-March; the only other supply route to the diamond fields—by air—is prohibitively expensive.

Minister Irwin's deadline sets off the last charge in the environmental review epic. The EARP made 28 detailed recommendations. Irwin wants "significant progress" on a myriad of agreements that the panel recommended. All are to interlock as seamlessly as Liza Enzoe's stitches hold together moccasin soles and uppers. The deadline means squeezing complex negotiations into the equivalent of a geological nanosecond. No engineer, scientist, aboriginal elder or politician will be able to predict diamond-mining consequences with any reliability under such pressure.

One of these agreements will set environmental standards specific to BHP's operation, because this diamond mine will be Canada's first. This agreement will stipulate a specific agency to "watchdog" the new mine. The agency will be a first-time addition to the usual land-use permits and water licences that mines legally require.

In the Environmental Impact Statement that BHP presented with its applications for permits to mine, the company tried to sell diamond mining as a clean process. No chemicals are required to isolate the mineral from its matrix. Mining diamonds at Lac de Gras, BHP argues, is a simple matter of draining water from the top of kimberlite pipes, digging the kimberlite out, trucking it to an ore processing plant and separating the diamonds from the ore. This is a mechanical process that mimics nature; it seems benign, as mining goes.

Of course, the company mentions, a few small matters might cause concern. Parking a thousand people on the Barrens to build the mine. Draining the kimberlite pipes, otherwise known as the lake homes for waterfowl and fish. Releasing not just the diamonds from the crushed ore, but other chemicals and minerals as well. We have little information about what might leach out of the crushed ore once the miners discard their tailings. Building roads, quarrying gravel, diverting water, hauling diesel fuel . . .

BHP must also reach agreements with five groups of people: the Inuit living downriver from the mine, the Metis with interests in the diamond fields, the Dogrib Treaty 11 First Nations and the Akaitcho Treaty 8 First Nations. The last agreement will be with the Government of the Northwest Territories (GNWT) on behalf of the public. Many people in the NWT, like myself, are not members of any aboriginal group. GNWT is a public government without its own revenue base, and it is determined to get as much benefit for all NWT residents as it can.

Agreements between aboriginal groups and BHP will be contracts, essentially, allowing BHP to take diamonds from the First Nations' traditional land. These agreements are called impact and benefit agreements (IBAS). The agreement between BHP and GNWT will be called the socioeconomic agreement.

The EARP also recommended that the government complete its "protected areas strategy." When in place, the strategy should protect enough habitat to support the caribou herds forever, even if they are migrating over diamonds.

Two of the agreements fall in the terrain where I work: the Akaitcho

Treaty 8 IBA and the environmental agreement. I work on treaty negotiations; the treaty rests on the land. The IBA might pay for some use of, and resources from, the land. Obviously, the land is the key to the environmental agreement, so it, too, will become part of my job.

"Our granny at the falls, she will look after the land and look after us," say the Dëne súłiné. But they are surrounded by a world whose interest is not in how the land looks after people, but in how people can make money from the land.

I get out of bed, then, fast, and go to work on the minister's "significant progress." Making coffee, I reach for the phone. I don't know when Łutsëlk'é chief Felix Lockhart will return from his honeymoon in the bush. Or when I will be able to reach the rest of the First Nation councillors. I try various phone numbers for Chiefs Sangris and Beaulieu. Neither is answering. Leaving messages across the North, I check the calendar. In the context of all the other First Nations deadlines, sixty days is precious little time to make informed decisions about diamond mining.

Xayt'as
Autumn

4. *You Got the Gold, We Got the Shaft*

◆　　◆　　◆

The combination of numerous lakes, acting as reservoirs,
with waterfalls in the streams, makes the whole Taltson
River system an excellent one for the development of
water powers.

—George Camsell, *An Exploration of the Tazin and Taltson Rivers,*
Northwest Territories, 1916

N o diamond dust rises in the days immediately after Ron Irwin, federal minister of Indian Affairs and Northern Development, sets the sixty-day deadline. Summer torpor lies on the land. It is forest-fire hot. Many people—from the Dene communities, from Yellowknife, from Ottawa—are on holiday. Northerners drive pickup trucks and families to Edmonton, where they shop for back-to-school clothes, bulk groceries, boat and snow machine parts. This is the time to enjoy the brief summer and get ready for winter, for the weeks when the highway between Yellowknife and Edmonton is closed. By December, prices in Yellowknife will skyrocket because ice forming on the Mackenzie River is a hazard to the ferry, but not thick enough to form a bridge. Pragmatic concerns obscure even diamonds.

The minister's deadline ticks away unnoticed until August 27, or Day 19 of 60, when Łutsëlk'é receives a letter from a Crown representative inviting the leadership to a meeting on August 29. On the agenda are possible changes to the extinguishment policy. Our First Nation administrator, Jackie Coulter, calls me in Edmonton, where I am getting my two boys ready to go back to school. Jackie reads the letter to me over the phone.

"Someone's got to go," she says.

"I know," I mutter, thinking hard. Chief Lockhart had a hunting accident on his honeymoon; the councillors are all out on the land. I calculate the cost of a one-day flight to Yellowknife versus the logistics of finding some of the councillors and getting them to the meeting. I say to Jackie, "I could get a ticket, see Felix at the hospital, then go. I'll call you back. I need to find someone to look after the boys." I do, book a ticket and catch the dawn jet north.

As we descend over Yellowknife Bay, I see the green of summer turning to the amber of early autumn. I drive directly to the hospital, where Chief Lockhart has been for a week. He looks dreadful. I haven't seen him since the nurse in Łutsëlk'é medevaced him to Yellowknife. Even now, after the treatment has taken hold, I can see why she did. Blood poisoning from a hunting knife is the Western diagnosis. Bad medicine is the Dëne súłiné interpretation. Felix was butchering a bear and some of its blood got into a small cut on the middle finger of his left hand. He became increasingly ill and risked losing at least a finger, if not his hand. When oral antibiotics didn't work, the nurse switched him to intravenous antibiotics and put him on the plane. Now his hand is still grossly swollen, his face pallid. Odd on a Deneyu.

I greet him, then get straight to the point: "Felix, I'm leaving every other file outside the door. But the feds called this meeting to get our response to possible changes in the extinguishment policy. I need your direction."

We review Canada's latest moves on extinguishment and the recent Supreme Court decisions on aboriginal title. Eighteen months ago, the Minister of Indian Affairs sent one "fact-finder" across Canada to discuss certainty and extinguishment with First Nations. On page 100 of his 1995 report to the minister, A.C. Hamilton wrote, "Rather than extinguish, treaties should recognize the existence of Aboriginal rights." Felix gives me clear, minimalist instructions for the meeting.

I bump over the twenty-kilometre road around Yellowknife Bay to Dettah, where the rest of the Akaitcho Treaty 8 leadership has agreed that we will meet with Canada. None of the Akaitcho Treaty 8 people are in the interior of the old school where the feds wait. It is dim after the brightness outside, and I retreat to the First Nation office next door. There, Chiefs Beaulieu and Sangris and several of their First Nation councillors are talking over Canada's letter. I describe my meeting with Chief Lockhart and his brief direction.

Our meeting with Crown officials proceeds slowly, uncomfortably. We are only here because we know that if we hadn't attended, the feds could have interpreted our absence as an expression of "no concern" on the issue. Yet they may well consider this one meeting as an actual "consultation" with Akaitcho Treaty 8. We state that this meeting has been called on ridiculously short notice during a week when most people are out on the land. The leaders have had no time to consult with the people. The chiefs reiterate that Treaty 8 did not extinguish aboriginal title to their land, nor cede it to the Crown. I listen, contributing only Chief Lockhart's regrets, his request that aboriginal and treaty rights be affirmed, and his statement that Łutsëlk'é's position is the same as that of the Yellowknives.

Chiefs Sangris and Beaulieu remind the lone Crown representative that Akaitcho Treaty 8 negotiations with Canada have been stalled for some months now, and that the land is under a great deal of development pressure due to the diamond discoveries. They respectfully request that Canada appoint its new negotiator for the Akaitcho Treaty 8 file so that negotiations can resume. Following Chief Lockhart's direction, I emphasize the urgency of that request. Canada's representative says he is just here to gather information. The meeting ends, inconclusively. I fly back to Edmonton that night.

We don't think about diamonds or the deadline over the Labour Day weekend. However, early on September 4, Day 27, I fly north to Yellowknife again. I join a day-long strategy session of First Nation community representatives about the impact and benefit agreements (IBAS) with Broken Hill Proprietary. Although individuals are fairly clear on what the communities need to benefit from the mine, as a group we are unclear about how to proceed with negotiations. We want to present a clear position to the company, not simply react to formulaic offers that BHP sets out. At the end of the day, we still lack clarity.

Most of the IBA negotiating team will prepare through Thursday for our first meeting with BHP since Irwin set the deadline, scheduled for Friday, September 6. But I fly with Chief Lockhart—his healing hand held rigid in a brace—to Fort Smith to appear before the Northwest Territories Water Board about Nánúlá túé. It is telling that the only thing to supersede diamonds this week is a festering conflict born from mining on Dëne súłiné land.

On the plane to Fort Smith, lulled by the vibration and thrum of the propellers, I shift my mind to south of Great Slave Lake. Nánúlá túé, or "islands across the water," is a large lake in the Taltson River drainage. This flight, with the plane's shadow dancing on the land and water below, makes me see how clearly what happened when the river was dammed shapes Łutsëlk'é's perception of diamond mining. In November 1992, when diamond rumours were only beginning to reach Łutsëlk'é, trappers Morris Basil and Morris Klutzie broke through ice upstream of a dam and drowned. Łutsëlk'é's shock and grief fuelled the First Nation's long-standing belief that two dams on the Taltson River, built during the 1960s, changed the water flow through one of Łutsëlk'é's prime living and trapping areas.

Like much industry in the NWT before the Mackenzie Valley pipeline controversy of 1975, building began on the Taltson dams without consulting the people of Łutsëlk'é, or the other First Nations that lost land and water to the hydro system. In fact, Łutsëlk'é hunter and trapper Pierre Marlowe, who had lived on Nánúlá túé with his family, found out about the dam only when he drove his dog team down there one late-winter day. Near the lake's outlet, much to his surprise, he came upon a crew of men dynamiting rock to create a spillway around the falls called Deschoe, "the boiling water."

The Taltson drainage was dammed in order to provide electricity to Pine Point Mine, a lead-zinc operation located seventy kilometres west of Denínu Kųe, which opened in 1965. The mining company also built a road to Denínu Kųe, where it sought unskilled labour. The dam, the mine, the road. Before the mine and the townsite closed down between 1986 and 1988, it paid $100 million to the government-owned power company that built the dams. It paid $176 million in taxes to Canada. It paid $339 million in dividends to its owners and shareholders. Not one cent went to the Dene First Nations.

What did the Dene inherit? After two dams and spillways were completed, the ice cover, essential to winter travel, became unpredictable and unsafe. The dams raised the water level so much that traplines and travel routes flooded. Rotten trees, both standing and floating, made boating dangerous. Fish became soft, diseased, inedible. People abandoned most of their trapping cabins in the area.

In Denínu Kųe, the road brought access to temporary wage jobs at the mine. The road was supposed to make it easy for men from Denínu Kųe to work at the mine. It did. It also took them away from honing their land skills, speaking their aboriginal language and spending time with their families. It brought alcohol in abundance to offset the mind-numbing boredom of low-paying wage work timed to an industrial clock.

It is this history that has all of us negotiating on the diamond mines worried. Although the diamond mines will receive much more public and government scrutiny than the Taltson dams did, past experience demonstrates that even when the First Nations deliver a message clearly, the Crown rarely listens. When I first arrived in Łutsëlk'é, people told me about the years when there had been "big meetings" about Nánúlá túé with government representatives, who licensed the Taltson dams  years after their construction. "We told them, again and again, about the mess the dam made, that the land was ruined and the fish were bad. They never done nothing." After Morris Basil and Morris Klutzie died, people said, "They should have something posted out there, about the water behind the dam and how it's not safe."

Over the winter of 1992–93, I followed the paper trail on the case after the Royal Commission on Aboriginal Peoples funded our small research team—Łutsëlk'é First Nation, Dene university student Barney Masuzumi and me—to investigate the damage on Nánúlá túé. Henry Basil, who had driven his dog team around Nánúlá túé and photographed much of the damage, helped me find records that were stashed in every nook and cranny of First Nation offices chronically strapped for space. One day I was up in the dusty loft of the Łutsëlk'é office, going through box after box of documents that no one had had time to look at in years. Flipping up the cardboard flap of a grocery box, I saw at last the records I had surmised must be somewhere in storage. The busyness of the office below me faded as I read.

The paper trail showed clearly that policy directives from the federal government had shifted seemingly at whim over the years, making it difficult for the First Nation to keep up with events. I sought and found the first water licences issued to the hydroelectricity company that built the dams. I found the transcripts of all the previous public hearings—the "big meetings"—on the water licence applications.

Until it was superseded by environmental legislation specific to the Mackenzie Valley in the late 1990s, the Northwest Territories Water Board held some of the strongest powers for regulating development in the North. Although a new board holds these powers, the licence requirements have changed little. Industrial projects such as dams and mines that cause significant change to the environment must have a Class A water licence to operate. Unlike Class B licences, "A" licences require public hearings on the project and must be approved by the Minister of Indian and Northern Affairs.

The Taltson case has been dragging on for thirty-three years without resolution. Tomorrow, Thursday, September 5, Chief Lockhart and I, along with others, will spend the day discussing compensation for the Dene and their land. As we negotiate the diamond mines, we do not want a repeat of the Taltson debacle, which prompted former chief of Denínu Kų̀e, Don Balsillie, to quote an old country-and-western song over and over again to federal negotiators about Pine Point: "You got the gold, we got the shaft." No matter that the mine produced lead-zinc, not gold. Chief Balsillie, an astute businessman, understood that the real money from Pine Point flowed south. The damage remained behind with the Dene and their land.

◆　　　◆,　　　◆

Two days later, Day 29, early in the morning, I fly back to Yellowknife on Ptarmigan Air's "suicide tube," as many frequent flyers call the skinny, claustrophobic craft that none of us trusts. My brain is as opaque as the thick cumulus clouds over Great Slave Lake. The plane is cold and cramped. Almost everyone on board was at the Taltson hearing last night. Today I am on my way to Dettah and the first IBA negotiation on the diamond mining since Irwin imposed his deadline. Our two meetings with BHP last summer yielded nothing of substance. I'll taxi the twenty kilometres around Yellowknife Bay because everyone else is already at the meeting. I'll be late.

I walk in on the pleasantries we exchange at the beginning of each session. My Dene colleagues are the most unfailingly courteous people I know, no matter who their adversary. The table in the Dettah council chambers is long, oval and very narrow, but as solid as Precambrian granite. Across that table, the negotiators are in each other's faces, swivelling in big, imposingly comfortable chairs. Today BHP's negotiators have the view of the lake through the big windows. I join the Akaitcho Treaty 8 group opposite BHP—Chris Knight, who will be chief negotiator for the IBA, Chief Beaulieu and several First Nation councillors. The light is shining on BHP representatives David Boyd and Jerry Bair.

David, or "Die-vid," as he pronounces it, is one of BHP's point men for community relations. We call him the Australian demolition man. He became well-known early in the EARP hearings for his oft-stated solution to the "fish problem" in lakes the miners want to drain. Dynamite. Quick and simple.

I think of Jerry as the long, tall Texan, though he isn't particularly Texan except in speech. He isn't outstandingly tall, either, but quite tall enough to tower over me. Meeting for the first time, we shake hands as I ask him, "You're the one from Texas?"

"Yes," he drawls.

"I'm from Alaska, and I think that gets us into trouble right away." Texans still resent Alaskans for usurping "biggest state in the union" status back in 1959.

The day turns out to be another preliminary session in which we get to know each other and discuss the negotiating process. The slowness of this meeting astonishes me now that we are working under Irwin's deadline. In the end we don't reach agreement on anything but dates for the next meeting. It's all part of the posturing, I suppose, on a tired Friday. I leave the meeting already thinking ahead to Monday morning, when the Water Board will begin publicly reviewing BHP's application for a Class A water licence.

5. Water—First Rapids

◆　　　◆　　　◆

All treated effluent will report to Kodiak Lake.

—John Witteman, environmental manager, BHP

M ONDAY, September 9, Day 32. The Explorer Hotel is a white multi-storey edifice perched high on rock at the edge of "downtown" Yellowknife. It sits like an albatross over the plebian grocery store and gas station that locals frequent. The hotel is the venue for the Northwest Territories Water Board public hearing on Broken Hill Proprietary's application for a Class A water licence. Today is the first public discussion of the diamond mine since Minister Irwin set his deadline. Right now, the water licence remains the strongest regulatory instrument that exists to limit, to delay or even to prevent opening the mine.

Inside the hotel, moveable walls have been configured to form one of the largest rooms in the city. Crisp September air rushes into this big space every time the double doors open. Low morning sun spills through the wide doorway at the front of the room, where the board members are arrayed in a semicircle facing the audience. Presenters and intervenors are gathering in their factions, but small-town cordiality prevails among the northerners. No matter the outcome, we will all still be here, jump-starting each other's frozen cars in winter.

As we gather on this fresh Monday morning, voices murmur, spoons clink against coffee cups, people open briefcases and unpack stacks of technical reports. About one hundred people will attend the hearing. Nearly forty will present information or question the presenters. Sound technicians speak "test, test, test" into microphones and tape thick black cables along the floor. I pick up a headset at the interpreters' table, then click the dial onto each channel. Dogrib, Inuktitut, English. No Dëne Súłin yati. Before I can find out why not, Gordon Wray, chair of the Water Board, speaks at the front of the room.

"Before I make my opening remarks this morning, there is an issue I must deal with." Last week, the Dogrib Treaty 11 council requested that this hearing be postponed, citing their concern that Wray himself could not chair the hearing impartially. The Dogribs also feel that there has not been enough time for them to address the complex issues in BHP's application.

The Dogribs requested Wray's resignation because of what he said to the press last week. "If we postpone the hearing, it would in all probability shut [BHP] down." The board has discussed the Dogribs' request but voted (with Wray abstaining) to begin the hearing as scheduled. Down comes Wray's gavel: the board isn't about to let its control over the hearing be diminished.

Wray then calls the hearing to order with the standard preamble, delivered in his trademark, no-nonsense Scots brogue. Like many non-Native northern men, he first came to the Northwest Territories as a "Bay boy"—an employee of the Hudson's Bay Company, descendant of the first fur-trade monopoly. "Some twenty years ago, Canadians began to take a new and real interest in the environment in which we all live and work. In reponse to this heightened awareness, Parliament enacted several new environmental laws. One of those was the Northern Inland Waters Act designed to help protect the environment north of sixty degrees. The act created the Northwest Territories Water Board and directed it to hold public hearings like this one . . . Water is the only business of the board. The board's mandate is to provide for the conservation, development and utilization of waters in a manner that will provide the optimum benefit therefrom for all Canadians, and for the residents of the Northwest Territories in particular."

Water may be the only business of the board, but water is life. It connects everything. Dene know this. European explorers knew this, too, when they followed rivers and lakes deeper and deeper from the oceans into what they perceived as wilderness North America. We are here to discuss water, but it will be impossible to avoid all the life that water makes possible.

Wray continues, outlining the tightly scripted hearing procedure. He leaves no doubt that he is in charge here. Presenters and questioners will address the board, not each other. He, as chair, will recognize each speaker before they may speak. BHP will present its application to the board first. Then the board will question the company. Next, intervenors—the First Nations, special-interest groups such as the Northern Environmental Coalition and individual members of the public—will question BHP. Then intervenors will present their comments and recommendations on the company's application to the board. Intervenors will include three federal government departments with jurisdiction over fish, environment, "Indians" and economic development. The hearing is scheduled to run today, tonight, tomorrow and tomorrow evening if necessary.

Wray spells out the steps BHP's application will go through after the hearing. The board members and the water experts who make up the board's Technical Advisory Committee will study all the material presented at this hearing. The board will draft a licence and circulate it to all the intervenors for comment. The revised licence will go to the Minister of Indian and Northern Affairs for his signature.

"The minister can accept or reject the licence, but cannot change the conditions it sets. No major water-use proposal can lawfully be put into operation until the minister's approval is given. The public hearing today is a vital part of the licensing process because the board is particularly concerned to hear from the people who use water resources to support their particular way of life," Wray concludes.

The Water Board had already scheduled this hearing on BHP's application well before Minister Irwin set his sixty-day deadline. But what Minister Irwin has not done is explain to anyone—his own staff in Yellowknife or the public or the First Nations—how his sixty-day deadline is supposed to fit in with the process for granting the Class A water licence and land use permits necessary for BHP to build and operate a mine. It will become clear during this hearing that no one knows, yet, what law or regulation—the standard water licence and land use permits, or a first-time, as yet unwritten, environmental agreement—will prevail when it comes to monitoring and controlling the company's impact. So BHP's standard applications to use water and land are moving on a path parallel to negotiations on the environmental agreement. No one is quite clear where these parallel paths will come together, in law or in application.

All we know—the negotiators and regulators on the ground, so to speak—is this: the Water Board hearing is the last chance, the waist of the hourglass, to make arguments about mining diamonds, for and against, in a public forum. All other discussions will take place in closed negotiations or within the government bureaucracy.

◆   ◆   ◆

THE mixed crowd—engineers and attorneys in ties; Native elders in moccasins; reporters, generic consultants and advisors in jackets and jeans; BHP's public relations guru in a suit—settles in for a long haul. Most of us have notebooks open and translation earpieces dangling around our necks. The public hearing is akin to trucking heavy equipment over the ice road: slow and deceptively smooth. Concentrating on the presentations is essential, otherwise interminable boredom might blind you to sudden hazard.

Six people sit at the presenters' table for BHP. Dan Johnson, project manager for BHP mine development, introduces himself and the others. He leads off with an overview of the company's corporate assets, then describes the NWT Diamonds Project, as BHP calls its future mine, illustrating the company's work with beautiful slides of the proposed mine site on the Barrens. He concludes with a list of the water uses that BHP's licence application covers: water to drink at three mining camps; water to wash the diamonds out of the ore; water that will become "waste" as it travels through the waste rock from the kimberlite pits; other waste water from treated sewage. He describes water diversions around two lakes that will become open pits, and diversion berms for what is now Long Lake and what will become the Long Lake Tailings Containment Area. Last he states BHP's intention to "dewater," essentially drain, six lakes. Five will become open kimberlite pits. One will provide construction materials for roads and dams.

From his presentation it all sounds quite straighforward, a subtle brew of elegant engineering and well-oiled obfuscation. BHP's speakers explain how this water use will happen, how the mine's environment will change, how the structures to use and hold water will be engineered, how the whole operation will be monitored and managed, and how BHP figured all of this out. The quality of the company's research will prove to be one of the weakest parts of its application.

In hearings like this, Inuktitut, Dogrib and Dëne Sų́łiné interpreters who translate simultaneously have the most difficult journey. Although the interpreters grew up on the land, the language used in the hearing makes the land and water under discussion infinitely abstract. The rules, the acronyms and the technical jargon of the hearing are nearly incomprehensible to the average person, even those of us who speak English as a first language.

Don Hayley is the BHP engineer responsible for the dams that will prevent polluted waste water from flowing down the Coppermine River drainage. He is precise, dedicated and enthusiastic about the structures, called frozen-core dams, he designs. They use the natural cold of the North and just the right combination of moist fill to make a firm, safe barrier—one strong enough to serve as a road area. With overhead projections Hayley tries to show us what he means: "The thermal response of our typical embankments is shown by the predicted position of the minus-two-degree isotherm immediately after impoundment . . . The thermosyphons serve their function of enhancing freezeback of the thawed zone below the outlet dam within three years after construction . . . You can see this initial thaw-frozen bulb . . ."

Wray cautions the presenters. "I would really like to stress that the submission is highly technical in nature and by its very nature, it's difficult for the interpreters to follow. So I would ask that you slow down your presentation."

But John Witteman, environmental manager for BHP, continues in Hayley's manner when he describes maintaining the best possible balance between acidic and alkaline environments (measured with an indicator termed pH) in waters that the mine will disturb: "Freshly crushed kimberlite is normally alkaline with a pH above 9.5 . . . The pH drops as CO_2 is dissolved in the water and forms carbonic acid, which brings down the pH . . . The pH effluent requirement requested is 6.0 to 9.5." Later he adds, "The processing plant will use 58,000 cubed metres (of water) per day. Tailings will discharge 9,000 cubed metres. There will be makeup water reclaimed from the tailings area in the order of 8,275 cubed metres."

And so on. At mid-morning, Chairman Wray announces a short break, adding, "We also have to do some shuffling of chairs because we are running out of room." We stand, stretch, stream for the coffee and tea stations. I exchange waves with David Boyd and Jerry Bair, who are observing from the back of the room. After the break, BHP answers questions on its application.

Chairman Wray questions the security BHP will provide to pay for returning its mine to something resembling the pre-mine environment. "You reference the fact that BHP employs sixty-five thousand people in fifty countries, you have assets of thirty billion dollars, your annual revenue is eighteen billion, and you have net profits of a billion. I quote your words, 'These factors are relevant for today's hearings in that the company's assets, profitability and reputation are consideration in determining the requirement and extent of security deposits associated with a water licence.' I take it then that your position is that BHP is a big company with lots of assets and therefore it's not necessary to require an unduly large security deposit?"

Dan Johnson replies: "I think the point we tried to make, Mr. Chairman, is that we do have a large asset base and the company, BHP, is not a one-mine operator and is not going to walk away from any of its obligations on the project."

Wray: "Would I be correct in assuming then that BHP Diamonds Inc. is a Canadian corporation that was incorporated on July 15, 1994;

it has two directors who are resident in Canada, and eight of nine officers are resident in California?"

Johnson: "I believe that to be the case, yes."

Wray: "I take it, then, that this applicant that we are dealing with today does in fact not employ sixty-five thousand people or have thirty billion dollars in assets, and that the applicant's main asset is its mineral claim in the Northwest Territories . . . Then I would also be correct in assuming that once the mine has reached the end of its life cycle, your assets are also gone. In that case, if BHP Diamonds Inc. does not properly reclaim the project and there is a shortfall in security, there would be no realistic recourse against a now empty company."

With Wray's prodding clarification, BHP agrees that its parent company, the large international conglomerate it described in its opening presentation, would be responsible for any "shortfall and costs" referred to in the NWT Water Act.

Then we reach the question that troubles so many of us. Arthur Pape, legal counsel for the Dogribs, asks it. "It is my understanding from the materials in the application that these diamonds have been in the ground some fifty million years . . . It's my understanding that these diamonds are not about to go away. It is not as if they should be mined on an urgent basis or else somehow the deposit will become inaccessible. It is also my understanding that the end product of this project is to produce gemstones, that is, a product to be used for conspicuous consumption, not for the health and safety or immediate foods and shelter needs of anyone anywhere in the world. And so, I do not understand there to be urgency about the project from the point of view of the end result." Pape also asks about BHP's ability and willingness to provide a security deposit against accidental damages and for mine site reclamation. He wants the company to state what priority it gives to protecting the aboriginal, land-based economy in the Lac de Gras area.

Dan Johnson punts. "Obviously, many of the questions [Pape] raised I think we went through in quite a lengthy environmental review process. I will ask Karen Azinger, manager of external affairs for BHP, to try to give an overview in terms of some of the questions raised in regards to schedule and in regards to long-term planning."

Azinger reviews all the work, over many years, that it took first for Fipke and Blusson to find the diamonds, then for BHP to prove mining will be commercially viable. She explains that the company has spent $200 million to date and she reminds us that BHP has already, willingly, gone through the highest level of environmental review. She states that thousands of people have applied for jobs in the mine and they want those jobs now. Gaining momentum, she continues, "For the Government of the Northwest Territories, this project over its life will contribute $2.5 million to the gross domestic product of the NWT. We will be the largest single purchaser of supplies and services in the North, outside of the government, and we will be the largest employer in the North outside of government. For Canada as a whole, the project will contribute $6.2 billion to the GDP of Canada over the life of the mine. It will also contribute $2.5 billion in direct revenues in terms of taxes and royalties."

As her voice crescendos, I imagine Ms. Azinger as a dark warrior princess waving her sword over her head. "So what are we waiting for?" she cries. "Well, why wait? The longer the mine waits, the longer the delay in any of these benefits for northerners, for aboriginal people and for Canada as a whole. Thank you."

Pape comments on Azinger's answer then asks: "What would be the effect if in fact the regulatory process said we don't have enough information, we need more time?" Secondly, "What has the company done in regards to any potential environmental effects on the land-based economy as it relates to the use of water by both people and animals?" He asks for BHP's response.

Dan Johnson tackles the first question: "There is a demand for high-quality gemstone diamonds that we project to produce out of the operation. The market for that demand is currently very high. So again, delays of this project, as alternative operations come in, could again have impact on whether investment proceeds or not."

Ah, the threat of "alternative operations." He means the competition—Kennecott-Diavik, DeBeers. We've heard this line before. It is trotted out in the IBA negotiations whenever Akaitcho Treaty 8 digs in its moccasins over getting better benefits. Essentially, project delays mean higher project costs. Although the market for gemstones is, at this moment, very high, the company, of course, cannot guarantee that this will continue. "Do it now, do it our way, or we will pull out and you will have nothing" is the underlying message. I deduce that BHP wants to be first to realize profit from Canadian diamonds. The company needs to cut into DeBeers's control of the global diamond market.

John Witteman handles Pape's environmental question. Before he joined BHP, Witteman worked for the Department of Indian Affairs and Northern Development (DIAND) for several years; he even chaired the Water Board's Technical Advisory Committee. He is responsible for BHP's continuing research into the environmental changes that will be wrought at the mine site. He replies, "Although we are strictly dealing with water at this point here, this is work that BHP will be carrying out itself . . . to ensure that our operations don't impact adversely on the land-based economy and the peoples that use it." He asks Azinger to talk about the "socio," or human, aspects of the question. She proselytizes until Wray interrupts to bring our focus back to water.

Discussion continues about current and future markets for diamonds. Then technical questions and explanations resume. Finally Pape, thorough, ponderous and well aware that the pace of the hearing will favour his clients, queries BHP about "dewatering" lakes.

Dewatering is not in my dictionary. For a long time I puzzled over the unnaturalness of the verb. To Dene elders, it is incomprehensible.

Among miners, dewatering, or draining water from lakes and rivers, is both accepted parlance and practice. Oddly enough, when they wish to do this, either to mine lake bottoms or to create tailings ponds, the Department of Fisheries and Oceans (DFO), not the Water Board, makes the rules. Confused? You aren't alone.

Before a lake can be dewatered, it must be defished, or fished out. Pape continues: "I understand that the company has entered into one or two contracts, and one has in fact been carried out, to fish out a lake? The contract's been let, and I gather it has been carried out, or just let?"

Dan Johnson replies: "The contract has not been carried out. That is correct."

Pape: "But the contract has been entered into?"

Johnson: "Yes, it has."

Pape: "And the implementation of the contract, is that contingent on a licence being granted from this board?"

Johnson: "That's on authorization from DFO." Mysteriously, the Department of Fisheries and Oceans is absent from the hearing. Some consternation ensues.

Pape: "So DFO could authorize the fishing out of one of these lakes even before this board decides to grant an "A" licence for the project. That is your understanding?"

Johnson: "That would be my understanding. Yes."

Pape: "That is what you call integrated resource management."

Wray: "No, you call it the federal government."

So there you have it. The Water Board is responsible for the water, but the Department of Fisheries and Oceans is responsible for the fish. DFO can allow BHP to dispense with the fish before the Water Board decides how to conserve the water and the life it supports. Intervenors, perhaps naively, perhaps because there is no other forum for the question, have brought this matter to the Water Board.

Arthur Pape addresses BHP's Witteman: "So I take it, sir, that you would agree with me that under the Fisheries Act there is not a public hearing process, and no licensing process analogous to the process before this board under the NWT Water Act?"

Back and forth they parley, until Witteman summarizes: "We expect the Water Board to address those issues that are in front of it, that are within its jurisdiction. We expect the same of the Department of Fisheries and Oceans."

The questions and answers then turn to compensation for people who fish the lakes that will be dewatered. (See how quickly that word comes to seem an acceptable action?)

Arthur Pape addresses BHP: "I understand that it is common ground that a number of fisheries are going to be destroyed by this project, never to be rehabilitated. Specifically, I understand that seven lakes which are fish-bearing lakes are going to be lost permanently—Long Lake, Airstrip Lake, Willie, West Panda, Northwest Lease, South Fox and Fox 2; and that another five lakes will be virtually destroyed as fisher lakes as well—Panda, Koala, Leslie, Fox 1 and Misery . . . I ask that because the Dogrib are one of the aboriginal peoples who are users of these fisheries . . . I know that there are other aboriginal users as well, but I haven't been able to locate anything in the materials which indicates what the proponent [BHP] suggests and I don't understand that."

Dan Johnson responds: "As part of the lakes that bear fish that will be taken out of existence or destroyed, as you put it, I believe the numbers and list you had were correct. We have, at least with the federal government, talked compensation for loss of fish habitat with the Department of Fisheries and Oceans. In respect to instream users of these fisheries, *we have no evidence of specific use of these specific fisheries for the lakes in question*" (italics added).

Pape: "Has BHP never been told by any aboriginal peoples that they either independently, or in the course of caribou hunting, fish these lakes? Surely you have heard that. I would like to know what inquiries you have made and what efforts the company has made to find out if there were instream users?"

Wray: "We all would."

Johnson again: "To the best of my knowledge, through all of our discussion with traditional users of the area, there were no specific references to fishing in these specific lakes."

This statement contradicts what Karen Azinger said only hours earlier: "Another thing we did in the project was we took into consideration traditional knowledge. This was the first time that any mining company had been asked to give due consideration to traditional knowledge in the development of a modern mining program." I shake my head. Yes, the environmental assessment review panel (EARP) required BHP to include aboriginal knowledge of the land in its assessment of how its mine would affect the environment. That BHP requires specific naming of several lakes in order for the "aboriginal fishery" to be recognized there only shows how poorly the company understands Dene and Inuit knowledge. Science splits nature into smaller and smaller categories. Traditional knowledge (the official designation that the Northwest Territories government uses for Dene and Inuit knowledge) is holistic. It interprets species, places and seasons and their connections through time and space. BHP has concluded that because no Dene they talked to specifically mentioned fishing in the lakes we are discussing, that the Dene are not concerned with these lakes.

But water connects everything.

◆   ◆   ◆

THE day passes quickly for me. I admit to myself a deep fascination with what the miners do. I am intrigued by the extremes these engineers, biologists and chemists will go to in order to get rocks out of the ground. Their competence, their technical language, their tribal code has a beauty all its own. Some part of me is as tempted by the secret of the G-10 garnet and the integrity of frozen-core dams as by the beauty of the Barrens. I am as curious as the undergraduate I once was, drawn both to engineering and to neuroscience. I opted to study human behaviour. When that pointed toward a career running rats through a maze, I got outdoors again as soon as I could. I chose people and land. But the scientific secrets of life and technology fascinate me equally. I just wish we could balance science and technology with people and nature, better than we are in this hearing. Does good government have to be so turbid?

Chairman Wray breaks the hearing for supper around 5:30 P.M. "In deference to the elders," he says, he has set aside 7 P.M. for the Yellowknives and Łutsëlk'é elders speakers to present their concerns with the mine to the board. Members of Łutsëlk'é's Land and Environment Committee, and two elders, flew into Yellowknife earlier today to make this presentation. My job all day has been to observe and record the technical discussion so I can help bridge the gap between the elders' knowledge of the area and what BHP wants to do to it. Archie Catholique, who will be both interpreting and presenting Łutsëlk'é's recommendations to the board, sits with me for some time over the supper break so I can brief him.

When Wray calls the hearing to order again, Judy Charlo of the Yellowknives Dene begins. She speaks in Dene yati. We listeners don earphones. I leave my right ear open to the Dene yati cadence as the English translation rises and falls in my left ear. As if to highlight Johnson's comment about the lack of references to fishing in these specific lakes, elder Charlo says, "There are a lot of people who used that Lac de Gras area out in the Barrens. People used to go for muskox, the white fox . . . There are a lot of people who used to jig and fish there in the winter months with hooks."

When she finishes, Isidore Tsetta, a Yellowknives elder who is also on the community's Land and Environment Committe, speaks at length: "Without water I know for a fact that you would not be able to build your mine. And us, we the Dene too and us humans cannot drink contaminated and polluted water . . . Maybe sixty years ago there was nice clean, unpolluted water here in Yellowknife Bay. As of today it is contaminated and polluted. Just like this water right by the Bay of Giant Mine . . . I know that we know that we don't get any compensation for having our environment contaminated, for the pollution. I used to go to Ottawa. I used to be a chief . . . I have been to Montreal and I have been to most parts of the country. I have seen a lot of contaminated and polluted area. But this uncontaminated area up north, I am pretty sure it will get contaminated and polluted if we don't take care of it."

When Tsetta finishes, Fred Sangris, land and environment coordinator for the Yellowknives Dene, introduces the First Nation's legal counsel. He requests that the Water Board adjourn this hearing for four weeks, because the Yellowknives have only this week received funding that will allow them to properly review BHP's licence application. Wray says the board will consider the request.

It is Łutsëlk'é's turn at the presenters' table. Elder J.B. Rabesca concentrates on water: "The water that you are talking about, you are going to dewater, drain the water to another lake. If that happens, the fish are also going to be damaged. That is what happened to a place near where I am from . . . Nánúlá túé is one example . . . We looked at the fish today and nobody can eat it . . . The river [referring to the entire Lac de Gras drainage] flows to Ptarmigan Lake and from Ptarmigan Lake to Artillery Lake, then from there it flows down the Lockhart River to Great Slave Lake . . . Nánúlá túé, the damage around that area we have never been compensated for . . ."

Archie Catholique then takes the microphone to say, "As a Dene person I do have respect for this land where I come from. I have been taught that way, and also to respect the water . . . Some of the people that come into our lands come here to take the things that we have and are not worried about what happens to the people that use this land . . . I am not saying that I am against this development. All I want is that what happens out there is not being destroyed, that it is being done the right way so that we can benefit from it . . . I have some recommendations that I would like to put forth, if I can do that right now?"

Chairman Wray: "Yes, by all means, go ahead."

Like the Yellowknives and the Dogribs, Łutsëlk'é recommends that the hearing adjourn until we have enough funding from DIAND to intervene properly. Łutsëlk'é also requests that the Water Board not issue a licence until Akaitcho Treaty 8 reaches an impact and benefit agreement with BHP; that Minister Irwin not sign a licence until the Crown resumes treaty entitlement negotiations; that any licence last only three years; and that BHP be required to research the drainage from Lac de Gras to Artillery Lake, then to Great Slave Lake down the Lockhart River, "recognizing and acting on the traditional knowledge our elders described."

After Łutsëlk'é's presentation, Rachel Crapeau, a young Yellowknives woman, brings one more of the elders' concerns before the board: "So the elders of the Yellowknives Dene First Nation have some concerns about the stability of the underground geology of the area. The elders know that tremors have been felt in the area of Lac de Gras . . . They wonder what will happen to the frozen-core dams in the event of a severe tremor. I was wondering if you thought about tremors or earthquakes and what the effect would be on this area, the waste water and all that?"

Wray calls a short break after the Yellowknives and Łutsëlk'é finish. Queries about BHP's application from the audience begin. Besides the question of where Lac de Gras drains, which begs the question of just how thoroughly BHP has "taken on board traditional knowledge," several other issues demand attention. We are in the warm, full room long after darkness falls, although when he closes the hearing for the day, Wray exhorts us to "start fresh tomorrow morning."

We do, at 9:15 A.M., Day 33. DIAND, the two-headed beast with conflicting mandates, is at the presenters' table. Specifically, DIAND is responsible for encouraging, monitoring and regulating the miners. It is equally charged with acting as fiduciary for the First Nations—a legal trustee that acts in their "best interests."

Wray queries the department's representatives: "What support has DIAND provided to the First Nations to review the application and intervene in the public process?"

Yes, the procedures for notifying the First Nations about the application have been followed, although only the Yellowknives Dene office, not the Łutsëlk'é or Denínu Kye First Nations, received copies of BHP's water licence application. Yes, the First Nations have applied for funding from DIAND to prepare interventions. No, no money has yet been advanced to Akaitcho Treaty 8.

As the hearing progresses, innumerable questions remain unanswered. Worse, some of the answers are truly alarming. When Witteman speaks on restoration and abandonment of the pits left after kimberlite and diamonds are removed, he says, "There is no prediction as to what life will exist in the open pits after they fill." He cites research from south of the sixtieth parallel that suggests some biological community will re-establish itself.

Some of the kimberlite that BHP will excavate is dangerously acidic. David Jessiman, the industrial coordinator for DIAND's Water Resources division, answers questions about "acid-rock drainage" and metals that leach from waste rock. "Waste rock leaches metals regardless of the pH levels in various conditions . . . Yes, there could be instances where the rock could be above licence limits if allowed to discharge if uncontrolled."

Kitikmeot Inuit Association's Jim Cunningham raises the spectre of cumulative effects that many of us saw well before BHP applied for its water licence and land use permits. We know if this mine proceeds, others will follow. But the EARP was not allowed to look at the cumulative effects of mining, only the effects of this one mine. No one knows just how the minister's environmental agreement is supposed to mitigate the effects of even one diamond mine on the Barrens in the face of all the uncertain predictions and leachings. Board member Bob Overvold asks DIAND: "Could you give us an example of what may be contained in such an agreement? Does the federal government anticipate that there may be others party to the agreement, in particular, aboriginal First Nations?"

It has been thirty-two days since the minister set his deadline. His staff has no more than Ottawa's press release of August 8 to quote regarding the proposed environmental agreement.

What we don't know, what BHP does not know, clearly outweighs what we do know about the proposed mine's impacts.

Two precious autumn days, each several minutes shorter in daylight than their predecessor, fly toward winter outside the Explorer Hotel. We are two days closer to Minister Irwin's deadline. Inside the hearing, we haul our legal loads over the interminable adverse terrain that leads only to compromise. At last, on the afternoon of the second day, Wray calls a recess for the board to confer. When the board returns, he addresses the room. "The board is concerned that in the past, development has proceeded in the Northwest Territories without its residents having a say in the development or even understanding the development. Despite the procedures set up for public hearings, history appears to be repeating itself . . . Although BHP's application is very extensive, it is, with respect, directed to a technical audience—not a public audience . . . It is the board's belief that the elders who spoke last night are having difficulties understanding BHP; and it is also the board's opinion that BHP is having difficulty understanding the elders."

Wray announces that the board has decided to extend the hearing. The Technical Advisory Committee to the Water Board will consider the last technical submissions in meetings October 8 and 9 (just at and past Irwin's deadline). Technical work must be complete by October 14. Today we will complete this phase of the hearing, then reconvene on October 21. I don't know whether to laugh or cry.

So we continue, until almost ten o'clock at night. Dr. Ian Gilchrist of the board speaks last. "I will be very brief as I know everyone is tired . . . The whole purpose of the Water Board is to ensure that water is conserved, used properly and protected for people. I have a sense that often in these deliberations, people get forgotten. I think we were all reminded of real people during the presentation from the elders yesterday. I would like to ask the applicant if it is familiar with the makeup of this board? Who are the people who are on the board? I am sure that it is, but I would note that among the people on the board are those representing health. I would like to ask the applicant if it is aware of the fact that human health is the fundamental reason for existence of the board and this process? I would like to ask the applicant if it has a definition of health that it has used in its planning process, and if so, what it is? I would like to know if the applicant is familiar with the World Health Organization definition of health as a state of complete mental, physical and social well-being? . . . The board has heard quite detailed presentations of the physical and chemical issues of rocks and water . . . Also, I think it has been clear that there has been a lot of review of costs and money and benefits. Nothing seems to have been presented on how people—local or imported, and who are surely the most important matter here—are going to be affected . . . What well may be the impacts of changing the land and of changing people's way of life? . . . Has the applicant employed the same calibre of social scientists, as it has employed of natural scientists, representing sociology and history and anthropology and culture? What have been the reviews of partnerships with the affected people, and where are the results? The changes that have come from this project, whether for good or for bad, are changes that are forever. So surely, it is important to know who the people are, and how they were, and how they want to be, and how they will be as a result of this project . . . I think that they are matters that ought to be addressed also by the regulators and the intervenors; because I think that in the end, nothing matters more than the impact of what we do on the people we affect."

6. *Ever Lotta Berries*

◆   ◆   ◆

I don't care precisely when spring becomes summer, or autumn becomes winter. It is not the standing still of the sun's arc in the sky that is significant, but the change in the trend of the days, and the shift of the year.

—Dave Oleson, *North of Reliance*

DAY 34, September 11. "The sweat will be ready about four," Archie Catholique says on Wednesday afternoon. He calls my office from his house after he and some other young men have returned from upriver with rocks for the sweat lodge. They unload the big cobbles in a pile on the shore in front of J.C. and Hanna Catholique's house, beside the sweat that J.C. built a few years ago. I am housesitting there for the winter because J.C. and Hanna have taken their kids to Fort Smith for school.

Archie and I and the others flew back from Yellowknife at midday. Gilchrist's comments replay in my mind while I struggle to write a plain-English summary of the Water Board hearing. People are what it is all about here. They stick their heads in my door and ask "How'd it go?" when they come to the First Nation office with queries on housing, welfare or to see the chief. "The elders told them the way the water flows from Lac de Gras, BHP has a lot more work to do, and there will be another hearing" is my first-draft answer.

The sweat is one way people attend to what Gilchrist called their health: a state of complete mental, physical and social well-being. The sweat will be a blessing after the long hours and debate of the hearing.

I walk down to the point, where several people are already gathered in the afternoon sun, feeding wood to the fire. When the rocks are hot enough, the men strip to shorts, the women to shorts and shirts or longish gowns. The domed frame of saplings is covered with thick layers of blankets and sleeping bags and a blue plastic tarp. We file inside, bending low through the entryway, turn left, then move around the central pit following the direction of the sun.

Archie is leading today's sweat. He sits opposite the entry, facing east. After we are all seated, cross-legged on the ground, the last person in brings hot rocks from the fire on a shovel, which he slides through the low entryway. Archie uses small logs to move the rocks off the shovel into a deep hole in the centre of the floor. Sparks fly as the rocks collide on their way into the pit. The last man pulls the hot shovel out of the lodge, then ducks inside and brings the coverings down, sealing the base of the doorway. It is pitch black, and instantly, intensely hot.

Archie opens the sweat with his prayer. Each of us follows, one by one around the circle. The heat builds. We pray for the land, for the people, for our families, for our enemies, for ourselves. While the sweat pours off our bodies, we speak or sing as the leader tells us to, "in the best way you know how." When the heat sears our skin and the air is almost too hot to breathe, Archie ends the round. The entrance is opened, and we leave the lodge to rest and cool ourselves in the breeze off the lake. By the time we close the sweat at the beginning of the last round, the fire that heated the rocks outside the lodge has sunk to a caldera of coals. When we emerge the last time, people gather their clothes and water bottles in the darkness.

A few people come into the house to drink water and change into dry clothes. Archie covers the entrance to the sweat lodge. We say quiet good nights. The others walk off into the night, and I make my weary way upstairs to bed.

◆   ◆   ◆

EARLY the next morning I walk to the First Nation office. Set on the south shore of the point, it is a low log building, beautifully incongruous among the standard blocks of government-supplied houses. The entrance opens into a common area, its south wall floor-to-ceiling glass with a view of the small bay. The floor is great slabs of East Arm stone. To the left, the common area opens into the council chambers, two stone steps down. I go right, through another log-and-glass door, into the work area. Here, about sixteen people, sharing small offices that have just enough room for two desks and three chairs, run all of the programs of the First Nation and community—everything from water delivery to elder care through reviewing land use applications to treaty negotiations.

I haven't actually seen my desk for weeks. It was buried in paper when I left, and the stacks of documents are piled higher now. I triage the paper on my desk and from my jammed in-box. The chief's box, next to mine on the wall, is worse because he has been sick for so long. I have two high-priority stacks: anything related to Broken Hill Proprietary and Canada's current deliberations on extinguishing aboriginal title to traditional lands. Most of BHP's multi-volume Environmental Impact Statement is stored up at the community hall because we don't have room for it in the office. I keep a few volumes here, along with copies of the environmental assessment review panel report and recommendations, the minister's information package about the mine, and drafts of the impact and benefit agreement (IBA). I read everything that comes in related to indigenous peoples and mining, water quality studies, and caribou and toxins.

Looking out the window, I keep an eye on the morning light changing over the lake, the glowing yellow birch on the far shore. Sun falls on the log wall of my office, and my illustrated periodic table of the elements shines brightly, ready for reference when people ask about the chemicals in water from mines.

I sieve faxes from law firms and chiefs and consultants and researchers down south, who want facts checked before they publish. Legal bills go to Rachel and Stephan in accounting. I make an "urgent" pile to go over with Jackie, the First Nation administrator.

We have two goals right now: to get an agreement with BHP and to meet all deadlines on other applications for development. If we miss a federal deadline for stating First Nation concerns with outsiders' activity on Łutsëlk'é land, the Crown decides we have "no concern" and issues the permit. The diamond rush started with small exploration permits. In fact, each third-party interest on Łutsëlk'é land started with a permit application. Daily we receive more applications to review. At the same time that we are trying to work with BHP, we are trying to hold back a flood of development. Much research and planning that we need to do—East Arm tourism, environmental research proposed for Great Slave Lake and east to the Nunavut boundary through the Thelon Game Sanctuary, the cancer epidemiology and uranium mining study, the Stark Lake fish quality study, the Nánúlá túé water licence renewal—all are shelved for now. Their piles of paper sit, mute, gathering dust and mice turds.

At 9 A.M., Dora Enzoe, our never-misses-anything receptionist, arrives to answer the phone. It has already been ringing non-stop for the past fifteen minutes. I lean against the frame of my doorway then, sipping coffee, mindful of the sharp caribou antler door handle at my hip. I am right next to the administrator's office and two feet from Dora's desk. Between us the chronically overloaded fax machine beeps and jams. Across from me, social worker Addy Jonnasson sees a steady stream of people who need welfare checks, counselling or subsidies to pay young men to get firewood. Addy came home after almost thirty years away and keeps her balance better than almost anyone here.

I will see more First Nation members here this morning than I might in a week of information sessions. Few people in Łutsëlk'é read much, so I tell them as much as I can of the draft agreements, proposals, even the rumours that fly about the diamond mine. I try to displace the rumours, to provide facts and options that people need to know to make informed decisions. Most of the people who do read work for the First Nation or the Northwest Territories government, in offices within fifty feet of mine. To them, I deliver copies of key documents. If I have time, I write a plain-English summary to go with them.

Around mid-morning, Liza Enzoe comes to see me. An elder and First Nation councillor, my friend and teacher, she sits down in my chair. Her waist-length hair, streaked with less grey than mine although she is possibly ten years older than me, is twisted up in a clasp. Her face and her hands are land weathered. Cancer has left its mark, too. She has a smile to die for, missing teeth and all, especially when she is trying not to laugh outright over something—the ignorant comment of an outsider or the vagaries of one of her many children. Then she places a hand over her mouth, but the smile escapes up around her seamed fingers, leaking until it floods her eyes. I lean against the desk and we are knee to knee. There is one other chair in the office and no room to move. I step around Liza's legs to get tea for her, then review for her my previous week's work. Dora, who is Liza's daughter, leans in between answering phone calls, translating some of what I say into Dëne Súłin yati. Liza's English is very good, but Dora learned hers through an English-language school curriculum and she has the better grasp of technical words. We discuss the meaning of terms and proposals; Liza helps me understand how my words in English will be understood in Dëne Súłin yati. When we are satisfied with her grasp of my briefing, she coaches me in explaining it clearly for translation.

A bit past noon, when everyone goes home for lunch, I head home myself. The house is bright now and eerily quiet after the office. I stoke the fire, put a stew pot on top of the wood stove, chop the vegetables I brought from Yellowknife. They are barely fresh, but they are vegetables. I cut the caribou meat that I removed from the freezer before going to work into semi-frozen chunks. It all goes into the stew pot. No matter what time I finish formal work today or who comes to eat or work here tonight, there will be food. Hanna has a bread maker, too, which I fill with ingredients for a loaf. Then I set the timer. If visitors don't eat this bread, I'll freeze it for when our negotiators come to stay during meetings.

At one o'clock, I go to the Co-op store. On the south-facing steps, some of the elders and several young men rest in the weak sun, out of the north breeze. I sit for a while too, telling people the latest on the diamond mines. I spell out where things stand with BHP, fill them in on what the elders said to the Water Board about how we are trying to get BHP to address Łutsëlk'é's concerns, especially with the water flow southeast of Lac de Gras into the Lockhart River drainage. The younger men ask, as they always do, about jobs, whether the company has agreed to pick up employees from Łutsëlk'é rather than require them to fly to Yellowknife. I say we are still working at that through the IBA negotiations. Eventually I go inside, empty my mailbox and chat with Mary Jane Michel, who keeps the store accounts. She is married to Antoine, past chief and one of the leaders of the community's Land and

Environment Committee, which reviews all of the applications for land use permits. I buy fruit juice and head back to the office, stopping to tell Alfred Catholique—also a member of the Land and Environment Committee—about the Water Board hearing, while he pumps Marie-Louise Nitah's water tank full from the big truck. He translates for me when I speak into her wizened face and nearly deaf ears: "Marie-Louise, is Freddie here? I need a load of wood. Tell him I'll pay $40."

Around four o'clock, Antoine calls to ask about the diamond mines. He says, "Tell me everythin' that's goin on."

"You comin' over, or you want me to come there?"

"I'm headin' out, up Stark Lake for moose."

"Can I come? I'll brief you there."

An hour later, Antoine, Mary Jane, two-year-old Brendan and I boat far up Stark Lake in the perfection of the evening. The air is tart but still amazingly warm when the wind dies. The aspen are at the brief height of their yellow. Red fireweed and cranberry bush leaves carpet the ground. As the sun goes down, the aspen seem to glow from within, in bright contrast to the dark green spruce around them. The lake reflects the evening sky: it is a clear aquamarine blue where calm, a darker royal blue where wind ruffles the surface. We see no moose.

On a sandy beach, we make fire on the edge of an aspen grove. Mary Jane brought ducks her older son shot earlier that day. She plucks one and I do the other, my soft office-work fingers aching with the unaccustomed tugging. Antoine splits the ducks for the grill. I wrap blueberry bannock I've taken from my freezer in foil and place it on the grill.

Long cirrus streaks, lit sunset pink, arc across the sky as we talk around the fire. I review all of the meetings and the status of the negotiations. Antoine probes for details. Mary Jane listens while we talk. When we finish, her questions highlight details Antoine and I have missed. I've been very concerned that all of the negotiations, and the

Water Board hearings, are taking place in Yellowknife, so that the impact the diamond mine will have on the small communities falls to the bottom of the agenda. In other negotiations, like those about treaty land, the First Nations take turns hosting the sessions. This rotation helps keep the process open to the First Nation members. Antoine, Mary Jane and I toss around the idea of moving the IBA negotiations to Łutsëlk'é for one session. Would this help keep Łutsëlk'é's concerns higher on the IBA agenda?

We return to Łutsëlk'é after darkness falls on the land, but the water still reflects light, first from the sunset, then from the stars. We come downriver slowly, Mary Jane in the bow watching for rocks in the channel. The motor stalls, and we drift home on the current with only ripples against the metal skiff to break the stillness.

The next morning, in the common room of the First Nation office, I tape flip-chart paper to the walls. On them, I outline summaries of the IBA negotiating points and the Dene concerns with BHP's water licence application. I spend the morning briefing First Nation staff and every-one else who comes to do business, visit, drink tea or smoke, explain-ing the issues in the clearest language I can muster. The big wooden chairs on the flagstone floor, where everyone proudly points out the imprint of a caribou's hoof in the rock, remain full all morning. The faces come and go. There is good debate, in English and Dëne Súłin yati.

"We should go for those diamonds," one young man says. "The jobs will be really good money."

"But you don't know," answers one of the elders. "Look what they did to Nánúlá túé for that mine at Pine Point. Those diamonds are up on Uncle Noel's trapline, and that water runs into Desnéthché."

Alice Michel leans over to Annie Catholique. Auntie Annie is one of the oldest elders, a tiny stalwart woman as solid as Shield rock. Alice is much younger, still spry, out and about in the community, but old nev-ertheless. Alice takes Annie's gnarled hand and places Annie's finger on her own, where she wears a synthetic ruby set in a gold ring. With her other hand, Alice points to the stone in the ring. In their language Alice is telling Annie where these stones that come out of the sacred land will go. To jewellery that people wear on their fingers.

Another young man speaks: "It's gonna happen anyway. So we might as well get what we can from it. We want some jobs and money for a healing centre on the land and something for the elders, something for the youth . . ."

Mary Rose Enzoe asks, "What happens next?" I draw a calendar on the flip chart and list the meetings, public hearings and decision dates between now and October 8. Over and over again I say, "Tell the chief and council what you want. That's our negotiating position."

In the afternoon, people drift in and out of my tiny office. Such a personal business this is, building the wishes of the First Nation out of their statements one question, one conversation at a time.

Just as I am ready to leave the office, Chief Don Balsillie calls from Denínu Kų̀e, which is even farther from the action in Yellowknife than is Łutsëlk'é. When he first took to calling me in Łutsëlk'é about treaty issues several years ago, I underestimated his capacity for hearing, recalling and synthesizing detail. Now I move step by step through all the facts, figures and intimations of the negotiations that I can muster. We're on the phone a long time.

Don understands more deeply than I do that both the federal government and BHP will try to cut Denínu Kų̀e out of any agreements with Akaitcho Treaty 8, and thus further divide Treaty 8 along the comprehensive claim lines that Canada prefers. Like Antoine, he understands the importance of moving the negotiations away from Yellowknife.

Saturday afternoon I resolve, again, to get out of the office. I take out my bike and sling a berry bucket over the handle. I ride uphill, over sharp gravel and through dust. Facing the wind toward the airstrip, bumping along below the rocky promontory that overlooks the community, I leave the little point of land that is Łutsëlk'é behind me. The road curves past the dump to the end of the airstrip. There I turn left past the stop sign that the government installed last winter, per airport regulations. Someone promptly ran into it. Now it juts out of the ground at a forty-degree angle, pointing downhill toward the river. It bounces in the wind, a lethal object born from a safety regulation. It might take the bureaucracy three years to remove the sign, but long before then a hunter will probably impale himself on it racing up from the river in a whiteout carrying home fish or caribou.

I glide down this pretty track now—an old trail widened to accommodate pickup trucks, not the straight graded roads that planners insist on carving through the community. It leads to First Rapids, where the Snowdrift River reaches Great Slave Lake. Another track leads off to the graveyard. I ride down to the rapids in the clear fall air and roll my bike well into the trees, so any kids who come by won't borrow it. It's a long five kilometres back to town.

I start up the path by the river, looking for cranberries. Some places are picked clean, but patches thick with berries still remain. I can't pick nearly as fast as the old women. Their brown weathered hands, fingers slightly spread like a bear's claws or a berry scoop, clean a hillside faster than a bulldozer strips topsoil. I don't need a lot of berries. I just want enough for Thanksgiving cranberry sauce, and also for cranberry breads. I haven't mastered cooking fish or caribou in any of the Łutsëlk'é ways, but people actually ask me now if I'm bringing "my" cranberry bread to community feasts. A few quarts for the freezer would be nice. But I'm here to enjoy the afternoon.

I face the wind and sun on my knees. There is nothing like this feeling on a fall day to take away all my tension, my pain, my worry. I am instantly content, though the half-frozen ground beneath my knees thaws to a frigid damp in the time it takes me to pick a patch. My hands are cold. I can hear the river rippling and burbling. The wind is a sigh through the spruce now that rustling aspen and birch leaves are falling.

Gradually I crawl and walk toward Second Rapids, then I pick a last patch at Third Rapids, where this short stretch of the Snowdrift River drains forty-eight-kilometre-long Stark Lake. In a few weeks when snow falls, everyone will ride snow machines out here to picnic, catch whitefish and trout, and grill it over campfires in the dusk of early-winter afternoons. But today this stretch of the river is deserted. Everyone must be out in skiffs, going far for sustenance on this last sunny Saturday of autumn. Although the wind is brisk, it is not a storm wind. It will be cold in the boats. But it is so clear that you can see forever across Great Slave Lake from the high land at Third Rapids.

I wander slowly back downriver toward my bike. I push it out of the alder into the clearing at First Rapids, where Vicky Desjarlais, Mary Rose Enzoe and Emily Kailik have made a fire. I can smell fish and meat cooking. Their huge berry pails—commercial buckets from Kentucky Fried Chicken in Yellowknife—are full to the brim. The women's burnished faces crease in warm smiles as we greet each other. I lean the bike against a tree and sit opposite Vicky at the weathered picnic table someone banged together out here last year. The cold has made me hungry. Suddenly the smell of their cooking food makes my stomach rumble and my mouth water.

"Aren't you afraid of the bushman, wandering around in the woods alone like that?" asks Vicky. Mary Rose listens from the fire, where she turns caribou on the grill with a barbecue fork.

"Nah, bushman's not interested in skinny white women like me," I reply.

They laugh. It is commonly thought that I don't eat enough, that I work too hard and that I spend too much time alone—lacking, as the older women constantly tease me—a good man.

"You walk out from town?" I ask.

"Yeah, picking, picking, picking. Ever lotta berries . . . need lots."

Mary Rose hands me a large chunk of dripping moose on a fork. I slice it into manageable strips with my pocket knife. It tastes hot, juicy, fresh—quintessentially delicious, a rich but subtle contrast to the pungent scent of decaying leaves around us. I could wolf down much more than I do, but I remember a story another Łutsëlk'é woman once told me. Do not eat too much or all that is offered, she cautioned, lest your gluttony be the cause of others' hunger. And always, when you eat, feed some of the food to the fire.

I've brought nothing in my pack except a few dry cookies, almonds and chocolate. These I put on the table with the freshly cooked meat, fish and bannock. The women look at my skimpy offerings as if I am daft or a child.

"You can't live on that stuff! Eat some real food!"

I change the subject. "How you gonna get home?" I ask, eyeing their full berry pails, knowing Emily's bad leg and Vicky's age.

"You're gonna find us a ride," Vicky answers.

"OK, I'll ride in and send someone for you with a truck," I reply, happy to have something to give them.

When I pedal up to the flailing stop sign at the turn, Vicky's son Tommy is just turning the corner in his pickup truck. We both stop. I pass along the word about the women at the river needing a ride home. Just as I top the rise before heading into town, the pickup passes me. In the box, Vicky, Mary Rose and Emily sit, backs against the cab, buckets full of berries between their knees. We all wave, laughing, as the pickup dust wafts over me.

7. *Insignificant Progress*

◆　　　　◆　　　　◆

What do they want those rocks for, anyway?

—Dene elder to environmental assessment review panel

MONDAY evening after work I stay out on the lakeshore for a long time. The wind is strong and steady, warm from the southwest. Beneath the storm-dark sky, the air is charged with energy. I am not. Tomorrow I must return to Yellowknife. My stay at home has been too short. I don't feel grounded, or connected enough with people here to go out with their instructions again so soon. I have not been in town nearly long enough to catch up on routine work, much less update everyone on the various negotiations. I collect the small trampled leavings of summer gatherings on this point—candy wrappers, pop cans, sharp slivers of caribou bone—while my mind trips through the sixty-day schedule. Blue-black clouds smudge the western sky—stormy weather over Yellowknife. But when the setting sun breaks through at the horizon, all the earth and water glow beneath the heavy sky.

On Tuesday, September 17, Day 40, I fly to Yellowknife and go directly to the gathering of people from several aboriginal organizations and the NWT government. We are getting our first look at the ephemeral environmental agreement. Minister Irwin announced on August 8 that there would be an environmental agreement specifically for BHP's mine. The only information we have on its contents, so far, is in the press packet Irwin's staff released that day. It says that a single environmental agreement, negotiated between Canada and Broken Hill Proprietary, will address at least six recommendations from the environmental assessment review panel (EARP). Each of these recommendations deals with an aspect of environmental conservation that is not covered in the land use permits and water licence that the company requires for its mine. Two of these recommendations are concrete to Łutsëlk'é. One calls for monitoring the health of the caribou herd that migrates annually across the diamond fields. The second recommends that water quality issues that may not be covered in BHP's water licence be dealt with in this new environmental agreement. More abstract recommendations, but equally important, propose annual and long-term monitoring and analysis of environmental changes at the mine site.

Once again, the federal government has structured the agenda by calling for the agreement, then drafting it. Now we have a black-and-white draft document in front of us. We begin by reacting to the federal draft, trying to insert our interests into Ottawa's legal language. But the minister has made it clear that these negotiations are between BHP and Canada; the aboriginal groups and the Government of the Northwest Territories are only here for discussion. Consequently, we aim to structure the agreement so aboriginal people have more responsibility for monitoring BHP than the first draft allows. This is going to be another long, slow effort.

On Wednesday, Day 41, Akaitcho Treaty 8 meets again with BHP for impact and benefit agreement (IBA) negotiations. Our IBA negotiating team is beginning to gel. In previous meetings, we have had different members of each First Nation participate. Now each First Nation has delegated one or two people to see the negotiations through.

Yellowknives Chief Darrell Beaulieu, a business visionary, is the person most prepared for these negotiations. He has done extensive research on what diamonds might bring to Akaitcho Treaty 8. He's travelled to South Africa to visit the mines, to Belgium to see how the diamonds are marketed, to Israel to see the diamond-cutting industry there. But the chiefs delegate the nuts and bolts of negotiations to others. Among them, Darrell is the most directly involved in the developing IBA. Our team will meet with all the chiefs frequently during the negotiations; from time to time the chiefs join us at the table. The chiefs' words, judgements and decisions—not the recommendations of negotiators—are especially important to the elders. The chiefs are both our principals and our chief negotiators when they join a session.

Chris Knight, a Victoria, B.C., consultant new to Akaitcho Treaty 8, will lead our negotiating team. He brings training in land claims negotiations and a coordinating presence to our somewhat eclectic group. We have each worked on different environmental and economic issues for the Akaitcho Treaty 8 First Nations. I will be at all of the meetings for Łutsëlk'é, getting direction from and reporting to Łutsëlk'é's chief, council and elders. My job is, essentially, to translate their interests into language that BHP can deal with—and pay for. Łutsëlk'é has also brought in Nick Poushinsky from Whitehorse, for financial expertise. He is the only one among us who has prior experience with agreements between miners and First Nations, mostly in Yukon. He and I met several years ago when the Dene Nation put us together for work with the Assembly of First Nations and the feds on revisions to environmental assessment legislation. Last winter, he called me frequently with steady reminders that Łutsëlk'é needed to prepare for these IBA negotiations. So Łutsëlk'é hired him to review agreements that First Nations had made with mining companies elsewhere. His discussion paper, which includes evaluations of how well these agreements are working, is Łutsëlk'é's wish list.

Avi Isackson is a management consultant who has worked with the Yellowknives' economic development corporation for several years. Jerome Slavik is legal counsel for Akaitcho Treaty 8 negotiations, with a strong background in oil and gas revenues for First Nations in Alberta.

We are a mostly compatible group, although we tire of each other's company after several twelve-hour workdays that all seem to begin and end with strategy sessions over greasy restaurant meals. Only Darrell lives in Yellowknife. The rest of us live the road life (or the air life), days and nights of work and restaurants and hotel rooms. I'm spared the latter, with their ever-present, too-intimate soundscapes, because I have friends to stay with in Yellowknife. I sleep on their spare bed in the cheerful clutter of a kids' playroom, but I leave so early and return so late that I hardly ever see my friends or their children.

Negotiations are taking a long time because we have two major stumbling blocks. First, BHP has a template for an agreement. The company is insisting on the same framework for each of the four aboriginal groups it is negotiating with. In other words, accepting the template means allowing BHP to structure the agreement before we even have our interests on the table. The company wants to begin the negotiations with its template. Chris Knight wants to begin the discussions talking about money. We have been stuck there for a long time. Most of the meetings revolve around what-if scenarios, such as "If you accept the template, we will offer this" versus "If you remove the template, we want this and would accept this."

Nothing is moving.

The second negotiation cul-de-sac is First Nation membership. BHP keeps suggesting that Denínu Kųe First Nation should not be included in the negotiations. The company argues that Denínu Kųe will not be affected by the mine and should therefore not be included in an impact and benefit agreement with Akaitcho Treaty 8. BHP is playing this game just like the federal government, trying to tell the Dene who the Dene are. What it wants is a lower head count of First Nation membership. Like the Crown, BHP calculates benefits on the basis of the First Nation census, a formula that has been flawed since Europeans began claiming Dene land. Canada wants to "pay" per person for the land it claims because the land supports only a sparse human population. But Canada calculates the value of the land for itself in terms of the "value-added" profits its resources generate. So the federal government's "take" is much greater than its payment. If BHP can cut Denínu Kųe out of the IBA negotiations, the company's benefit payments to Akaitcho Treaty 8, for land its members hold title to in common, could be reduced by a multiple of 651, the number of members in Denínu Kųe First Nation.

We are quite sure that BHP isn't trying this tactic with the Dogribs, who have four villages in their Treaty 11 tribal council. The company *needs* the Dogribs to sign an impact and benefit agreement. BHP only *wants* Akaitcho Treaty 8 to sign. If BHP can reach agreement with the Dogribs, who have already agreed to negotiate their land claim with Canada in the way Canada prefers, Minister Irwin might well decide this is all the "significant progress" he needs. If Irwin approves the mine because the Dogribs and BHP make a deal, then Akaitcho Treaty 8 might not get any benefits from the mine.

♦   ♦   ♦

A perverse combination of greed and fear drives the process. I am quite sure only greed drives the miners; I recall one of the elders asking, "What do they want those rocks for, anyway?" No one needs these diamonds.

Everyone else—the First Nations, the Government of the Northwest Territories, the business community in the North, all the prospectors still looking for diamonds—seem driven by a fear of being left out of almost unimaginable riches. I am caught up in this fear, too. Fear that Akaitcho Treaty 8 won't get benefits at least as good as any that go to the Dogribs, even though Akaitcho Treaty 8 already shares impacts to the land with the Dogribs. Fear that if we don't have an agreement by the deadline, there will be no agreement. Fear that even within Akaitcho Treaty 8, Łutsëlk'é's interests will not be addressed equally with those of the Yellowknives. With Yellowknife as BHP's point of hire for the mine and locus for business operations, the Yellowknives can more easily take up the employment BHP will offer and the business opportunities that will flow through Yellowknife. The Yellowknives, I know, fear more the direct impacts that diamond mining will bring to Yellowknife. More people will be using the Yellowknives' traditional land for recreation. A new but likely itinerant population will squeeze the ever-tight housing market. As always during a mineral boom, there will be more crime, more drugs.

So we work, uneasily around the table, with much of this unspoken. At best, we address these things only abstractly in the language of BHP's template for an IBA.

Greed, fear, will. Strong wills, to be exact. On our negotiating team, we each have our way of advancing and defending the interests we hold. Chris prefers a very structured discussion, one sequential point checked off at a time. Darrell has a clear vision of where we should be going, but his job as chief requires him to delegate many of the steps to the negotiating team. He is in and out of the sessions but he never misses a thread in the negotiations. He requests, and attends to, updates and briefings in the most minute detail. I think he'd like to be doing these negotiations full-time himself.

Jerome's will is present, front and centre, but he knows when an issue under discussion moves off his turf. (Like all successful attorneys, he interprets most issues so they are part of his turf.) He and I work well together, though. And his manner is hilarious, especially during our internal sessions. Late one night in an empty restaurant, he mimics his classmates at the Harvard Negotiations Project, using their strengths and his weaknesses to demonstrate what we should be doing with BHP.

At the table, Nick is serious, steady, always to the point, realistic and creative—anything but linear. He proposes that BHP contract Akaitcho Treaty 8 directly for certain services to the mine, without putting the contract out to tender. Not possible, BHP says. OK, then, unbundle the contracts, Nick replies. Break them down into parts so that First Nation businesses can bid on small parts of the work successfully. If BHP has to tender, then provide information to the First Nations in advance of the tender. Um, not sure we can do that, says BHP. Well then, counters Nick, we need to establish a joint business opportunities committee of BHP and Akaitcho Treaty 8.

Away from the table, with us or with the BHP negotiators on a smoke break, Nick is self-deprecating and off-the-wall funny, a big, laid-back man in jeans with the precise mind of a Treasury Board banker. One moment he's joking about some personal business disaster, the next he's nailed BHP with a question about First Nations earning equity in the company as payment for a service they provide.

Avi is a mensch, warm and fast-talking. He leans into each discussion, sleeves rolled up, collar open, as if his exuberance and determination alone will take us to agreement. Ideas bubble out of him. Often they have little immediate bearing on the clause we are discussing. The way Avi works, that doesn't matter. One never knows where solutions will come from.

My hard edge emerges when people—on our team or with BHP— gloss over the hard realities of life in the small communities. I bristle when people speak of mine royalties twenty-five years from now but skip over immediate questions. How much wage money will actually make it to families when workers have to overnight in Yellowknife on their way home from the mine? Why can't BHP agree to fly the workers directly to and from the mine rather than through Yellowknife? The latter route adds another night away from family and community to a multi-week shift. The focus on Yellowknife as the point of hire and locus for business opportunity makes me think that it would be a good idea to have at least one round of these negotiations in Łutsëlk'é so that the company can understand the realities of living in a small community.

During a break, I call Chief Lockhart to discuss the idea. He tells me to suggest holding negotiations in Łutsëlk'é to our caucus and, if the caucus is in favour, to invite BHP. We want to demonstrate Łutsëlk'é's need for workable employment practices—which will help, not harm, the community—as well as investment opportunities.

◆   ◆   ◆

THURSDAY, September 19, Day 42, those of us on the IBA team who are involved in treaty negotiations take time out from diamonds to meet with a Department of Indian Affairs and Northern Development guru. Senior bureaucrat John Sinclair from Ottawa will be overseeing land negotiations and wishes to meet the leadership of Akaitcho Treaty 8 First Nations. A professional, bright and pleasant man, he faces several of the Akaitcho Treaty 8 chiefs, prepared to listen to their treaty history and find out how they want treaty negotiations to proceed. The topic of diamond prospecting, claim staking and mining comes up. The chiefs ask: "When, in the permitting process for mining, is a new third-party interest created?" In other words, when does the prospector or miner's investment in a claim supersede aboriginal title to Dene land? The gentleman from Ottawa, loosening his tie, squirms so subtly that I almost miss his discomfort.

"Well," he clears his throat, "I know you don't have much previous experience with mining . . ." I think of Liza hiding her laughter behind her hand as he says this.

It is refreshing to hear Chief Don Balsillie present the issues in his clear, precise but forceful way. I think, listening, if one just remembers the simple framework of the treaty and keeps BHP and other third-party interests in that framework, then what needs to be done is quite straightforward. Treaty 8, a bilateral, nation-to-nation agreement, needs to be fulfilled before any more development can proceed.

Lawyer and Queen's Counsel Tom Berger was right. Back in 1977, reporting the conclusions of the Mackenzie Valley Pipeline Inquiry, he recommended a ten-year moratorium on major development so that Native claims could be settled and the northern economy diversified beyond major resource extraction. His words ring true today: "Native people desire a settlement of native claims before a pipeline is built. They do not want a settlement . . . that will extinguish their rights to the land. They want a settlement that will entrench their rights to the land and that will lay the foundations of native self-determination under the Constitution of Canada." His vision of the journey we are on was prescient: "To develop a diversified economy will take time. It will be tedious, not glamorous, work. No quick and easy fortunes will be made." We are still on that journey. Ten years was not long enough to settle all of the aboriginal claims in the Northwest Territories. And Canada still clings tenaciously to negotiating agreements that require Dene to extinguish title to the land. That "extinguishment" split the Dene Nation and its claim to all of the Mackenzie Valley in 1989. And the glamour and temptation of quick fortunes to be made with diamonds are splitting people still.

◆   ◆   ◆

ON Friday, Day 43, we are right back into the risky business of negotiating cash benefits from BHP in return for their exploitation of the land,
before we know the consequences. Yesterday's Ottawa man never did
answer the chiefs' questions about exploration permits creating third-
party interests. Minister Irwin has said BHP must reach agreements with
aboriginal people. But he hasn't said what effect—legally, what "preju-
dices"—the impact and benefit agreements might have on treaty entitlements or land claim settlements. I am not the only one who fears
that, when we get back to treaty negotiations (whenever the federal
government appoints its new negotiator for Akaitcho Treaty 8), we will
be told, "Land? What land? You took money from the diamond miners
for your land, and that's all you get."

8. *The Perfectly Useless Product*

◆   ◆   ◆

Every day of the year another 328,000 carats come out of the ground, and someone must buy them. The ingeniousness of DeBeers' marketers lies in having forged a link between something people do not need, diamonds, and something they do need, love.

—Mathew Hart, *Diamond: A Journey to the Heart of an Obsession*

SEPTEMBER 29, Day 52. Another dawn flight from Edmonton via Yellowknife to Łutsëlk'é. I take advantage of my four hours in Yellowknife to meet with Christina Ishoj of the Yellowknives environmental staff. Over coffee we discuss the research necessary for the second round of Water Board hearings. Then we spread out the sixty-some pages on her kitchen table and go through the environmental agreement carefully, listing questions for Chris Lemon, Akaitcho Treaty 8's new legal counsel. The chiefs retained him after the Water Board hearings on September 9–10, to work specifically on the environmental agreement and Water Board preparations. I met with Chris during a quick trip to Vancouver last week; Christina has been getting to know him over the phone. We are both pleased with his approach, glad to have his expertise to draw on.

From Christina's I drive to the airport and leave my car on gravel across from the Air Tindi hangar. Inside, the flight agent hangs my car key on a pegboard with many others, each identified with a luggage tag for the community where the owner lives. The waiting room is warm and smoky. Packed into this small space are boxes and plastic bins of groceries, along with awkwardly shaped bundles like brooms, unassembled baby cribs and the ubiquitous snow machine parts. As always, this Sunday flight is overbooked with people who want to return home after a weekend in Yellowknife. Those who are wait-listed for the Twin Otter's thirteen seats stash their boxes to one side and teasingly beg confirmed passengers to give up their seats.

One of the young men interrupts the flow of conversation to ask, in English, "Where you been, this time?"

"Working here in Yellowknife on getting you benefits from the diamond mine, if it goes ahead. Then I went down to Vancouver. Conference there on some ways the law might help you look after the Treaty 8 land," I explain as briefly and clearly as I can. Then I add, "The BHP negotiators are coming to Łutsëlk'é to meet with us. We'll have lots of people in town this week, the chiefs too. Minister Irwin will decide in ten days if the mine goes ahead. So you can talk to all of them, about the mine and what you want in an agreement with BHP." A small circle of people listens, their bundles stacked on the floor around them. Some ask questions, translate for others. Discussion begins in both English and Dëne Súłin yati. People nod.

One of the young men asks, "When can I go to Vancouver?"

"As soon as you are ready to take over this job," I say with a laugh. "Please, make it soon!"

When the flight finally lifts off, my heart lifts too. After city hustle, even in smaller Yellowknife, departure is a relief. This flight, crammed full of people who know one another, is the familiar road home. Everyone with a window seat watches the land below, intently. Each season, each sign—caribou tracks in winter, ice breakup in spring—is noted. When we land in Łutsëlk'é, everyone will ask what we saw.

Autumn is windy on the big lake, and freeze-up—these next six weeks—is one of the worst times to travel, by boat or by air. Today is no exception; it is gusting and the Twin Otter bumps and lurches. Some on board use the airsick bags. I'm all right, because I can see out a window to the islands and trace our fifty-minute flight path toward Łutsëlk'é. I follow my own map of the land. There's where Raymond shot the moose in the water one July night. We'd taken the boat out to escape the heat, but that moose swam right into our path. There's the narrow point where we butchered it, cooked it, ate it. There's where Addy and Jerry took me for a picnic one September evening. Jerry, who maintains the diesel power plant, looked across the water to Łutsëlk'é at dusk to make sure the lights came on. There's the place where three islands come together. Ronnie, J.C., Stephan and I followed skittish caribou through there until finally shooting three late one bitter January afternoon.

After landing, we all unload the plane together, dumping luggage, boxes and groceries into the beds of about ten pickup trucks, pretty much every vehicle in town. I throw my duffle and boxes into the First Nation's truck. Outgoing passengers load gear, then board the flight. I hitch a ride with Sabet, Air Tindi's agent in Łutsëlk'é. We stay on the strip until the outgoing plane takes off.

Sabet drives over the hillock into the community, where she stops at several houses to drop off freight or people riding in the back of the truck. She pulls up in front of J.C. and Hanna's house, out on the point, last. I am home.

◆   ◆   ◆

Monday, September 30, I am at the office early, thinking about self-government. When First Nations regain self-government within Canada, they will need local capacity to govern. Today my job is to support the many attention-to-detail tasks that successful leadership requires. The chiefs and the impact and benefit agreement negotiators are scheduled to arrive at midday on Tuesday. We will work out our strategy that afternoon and evening. BHP's negotiators will arrive Wednesday morning. As the meeting host, Łutsëlk'é First Nation must make sure that the meetings run smoothly, and that the guests—all of them—are well looked after in the community. This is Łutsëlk'é's chance to observe the discussion of mining royalties, aboriginal employment targets and conditions workers will face at the mine. First Nation members will be able to ask their questions directly to BHP's businesspeople.

I think about where to house everyone. Łutsëlk'é's public accommodation is called the "hotel from hell." No one who knows the village ever stays in its trailer bunkhouses. Outsiders who do only advertise their ignorance. Most of our negotiating team will stay with me, at J.C. and Hanna's house. Others will stay at Bernadette's Bed and Breakfast, one of the only entrepreneurial enterprises to make it here. Bernadette is both a savvy businesswoman and the best rabbit snarer in town.

BHP has asked that its people have a private place to stay, with access to a private phone line and fax. I've arranged for the company to use the First Nation administrator's house while she is away. Although the house has both phone and fax lines installed, no one can guarantee that Łutsëlk'é will be connected with anywhere else when BHP needs to be—satellite phone connections being beyond our control.

My next task is to try to summarize the latest version of the environmental agreement for the Lands and Environment Committee, a group of skilled hunters who cannot read English, much less a legal document that has grown to over sixty pages. The draft now includes provision for establishing a "public watchdog agency" to monitor BHP's operations. At issue now is how it will be structured, who will fund it and who will control it. Before I can begin, Lucy Sanderson, the First Nation coordinator for these meetings, stands in the open doorway of my office.

"I got the creamer and the sugar, but the store is out of coffee," she says.

"Did you ask the store manager if any more is coming on the plane?"

"No. Also, there's no one ready to make bannock."

I think for a moment. "Call Nick in Whitehorse," I reply, handing her a scrap of paper with his phone number. "Tell him to pick up ten pounds of coffee."

Lucy walks off to make the call, and I turn to my paperwork. The "watchdog" will be called the Independent Environmental Monitoring Agency (IEMA). No mine in the NWT has ever been monitored so closely as this one might be. Akaitcho Treaty 8 will have a seat on the board of directors, as will the Dogribs. This we know, but there are still many questions to be answered. How many board members will there be, and what will the balance be between aboriginal groups, government and others? Will the aboriginal members on the board, or their representatives, have any real power?

Lucy returns, asking, "Should I ask Nick to bring doughnuts since we won't have bannock?"

"Good idea. Tell him we'll reimburse him. If we freeze them overnight up at the hall, they won't be too stale for the meetings." Then I add, "Did you get the truck reserved so you can pick up all the elders for the public meeting?"

"Yeah."

Lucy goes to call Nick again, and I return to the agreement. If the IEMA is going to work, it needs secure funding. If it is going to communicate well with aboriginal people, interpretation and translation funds are essential. How much of the agency's translation costs should BHP pay?

I hear Lucy on the phone outside my door and jump up. "Lucy, do we have new batteries for the interpreter headsets?"

"Don't know."

"Ask Nick to bring a dozen nine-volts. You know how the store is always out of them when we have a big meeting."

I go back to my work. If the IEMA is a public watchdog, who does it report to and how? Who oversees it? Should its work emphasize studies of the ecology around the mine site or more communication with the public? What power will the agency have, if any, to make BHP meet the environmental standards set for it?

I muddle through these questions until around five, when I pack up some of the paper. At home I put clean sheets on the extra beds, make another stew, set more bread. I'd like to spend the evening stretched out on the sofa reading a novel, but it is a large dose of legalese that puts me to sleep.

At 11:30 on Tuesday morning, I ride up to the airstrip in the back of the First Nation's pickup truck. It is a cold ride at this time of year, but not impossible. Chiefs Sangris and Beaulieu are first off the plane. Then Chris Knight, stepping carefully off the plane's short ladder to the ground. Then Nick jumps down, with Avi following. They each envelop me in a bear hug. Last is Sarah Plotner, who works for the Yellowknives economic development office. She will look after our record of these negotiations. I am glad to see her because she is the only other woman routinely part of the negotiations.

On Wednesday morning, Day 55, Nick comes down the stairs to breakfast wielding a pineapple. He plants it in the centre of the table, then grabs one of J.C.'s big meat cleavers. Whack! The pineapple is splayed in wide sections on the table for me, Avi and Sarah.

"Power food?" I ask.

"Nah, it's just that you always ask me to bring fresh fruit, and this was the easiest to carry."

Around mid-morning, we hear BHP's chartered plane buzz the village. Shortly after noon, Akaitcho Treaty 8's negotiators sit opposite BHP's in the council chambers. This session is open to the community to observe, but not for questions. For Łutsëlk'é, Chief Lockhart has asked two of the First Nation councillors to join him at the table, Emily Saunders and George Marlowe. BHP has sent Jim Excell, the mine project's director; Jim Bergelsman, legal counsel from BHP's San Francisco office; John Bekale, a Dogrib Deneyu who was formerly a land claims negotiator, now working for BHP; and Jerry Bair. First Nation employees and several others, mostly the community's working adults, watch and listen. Archie Catholique and Bertha Catholique, our two best interpreters, take shifts translating throughout the negotiations. There are fresh batteries in each of the headsets. It is a still, grey day outside, and chilly in the chambers. The meeting is like that, stiff and formal all afternoon.

At the hall that evening, the community attends. The Dene question BHP, but the questions are not specific to the negotiations. Instead people bring up the same questions that they have yet to hear answered. Why these diamonds? Why here, why now? What about the treaty? When is the government going to set aside land just for the Dene? Why is the mine going ahead when people don't have their treaty lands yet? Why isn't there an agreement to set aside some land, to protect it, until the treaty is fulfilled?

The BHP men grow increasingly frustrated, as does our chief negotiator. Nick intervenes and proposes a closed negotiating session as the public meeting winds down.

I'm helping elder Annie Catholique into her jacket when I hear Nick ask, "Where?"

"My place," I suggest. "I mean, J.C. and Hanna's. It's big enough, it's quiet. We don't have to worry about keys or locking up, like we would here or at the office."

There is swift agreement. I give the BHP men directions, although you can practically see the house from the hall. But it is October, and we have only a few street lights to lessen the black-velvet darkness.

Nick and I walk against the wind back to the house. Inside, we ready the oval table for the two negotiating teams.

"Lots of problems have been solved or at least grieved around this table," I say to Nick as I wipe coffee stains off the plastic tablecloth. "It's a good place to do this."

Who in the community hasn't sat here, in person or through a family member, for sustenance of all kinds? I usually sit at the table with my back to the wood stove, a seat so hot most people can't stand it. From there I look through picture windows west across the big lake, watching the sun light the islands as it rises and silhouette them as it sinks. I see people come and go to the sweat lodge down by the water or the teepee north of the house. Tonight no boat or snow machine lights shine in the blackness beyond, and I leave the curtains open. I add wood to the fire, then damp the stove down for a slow, steady burn during the meeting. The overhead light, while not bright, will do. On the other side of the wood stove, the worn couches draped with Southwestern-motif blankets stay in deep shadow. Nick makes a pot of coffee.

Avi and Chris arrive, and we gather chairs to place around the table. Counting, we are short one. I bring my bush cooler in from the porch to sit on.

While we wait, Nick and Avi drop into their usual shoot-the-shit banter. I fidget around the room, cleaning this, moving that. Something's missing. Finally I go upstairs to the large bedroom where I sleep. It's J.C. and Hanna's, and their young children sleep there too. I take a large braid of sweetgrass off the wall and bring it downstairs. I place it high on the meat-drying rack above the wood stove, just east of the table.

Finally the BHP group arrives.

We gather around the table, tightly. It's barely big enough for the eight of us. The discussion is calm, wide-ranging, humorous, its purpose for staff to be open, out of the eye of our principals. Not that any of BHP's principals are here—the nearest board member is in San Francisco, and most are in Australia. The Akaitcho Treaty 8 chiefs, on the other hand, are in nearby houses. The Łutsëlk'é people are all around. I feel them surround us, invisible.

Because I am sitting on the cooler, my head is well below those of the others. Even John Bekale, no taller than I am, looks down at me from his seat next to mine. At one point he turns directly to me and makes eye contact; this is decidedly un-Dene. His question is a less-than-subtle ploy to bait me.

"Someone like you, what do you want us Dene to do? Are you one of those people who thinks we should just to go back to living on the land?"

"Nope. I'm one of those people who think what people have to do is make hard but well-informed choices about how they're going to live in the world today. I don't see how the people I work for can make informed choices when they don't have all the information about what this mine, and those that follow, will do to their land. They don't even know what part of their land they will be able to keep—because the Crown hasn't implemented Treaty 8. I realize that isn't BHP's responsibility. But you have to realize that what you offer has to be really good, because these people don't know what any of the consequences will be when it comes to setting aside land for what they, not you, want to do with it."

Bekale points out that people shouldn't need to wait until the treaty is settled to get good jobs. I agree, and we move on to number-crunching how many Akaitcho Treaty 8 people BHP can fairly be expected to hire, and when.

Nick and Avi handle the business parts of the discussion: royalties, production costs, training costs, aboriginal employment targets, profit percentages, multi-year payouts and signing bonuses. Chris keeps the discussion moving when one or the other of us starts to dig in. The acrid smell of coffee burned to the bottom of the pot pervades the air.

Jim Excell pleads for us to recognize the worth of BHP's "revegetation research." BHP is required to produce a restoration plan for the mine site. As the company uses, then abandons, locations throughout the life of the mine, it must return the landscape to something resembling its natural state. BHP has gone to great lengths to advertise its intent to regrow natural vegetation at Lac de Gras, based on its experience restoring areas where it has strip-mined coal in Arizona. Eighteen months ago, Luci Davis, a revegetation specialist hired by BHP, spoke in Łutsëlk'é's council chambers about the Navajo experience revegetating mined land. "I think," she said, hands dug into her jean pockets, blue denim work shirt setting off black Dene hair, "I *think* we can do it." She suggested that BHP might be able to repeat some of its Arizona mine revegetation success up here on the Barrens. Now, as Excell reiterates the restoration plan, I struggle to stifle my frustration. It can hardly be argued that a restoration plan for land that doesn't need to be destroyed in the first place is a benefit from the mine. But this blatant attempt to garner goodwill is crazy.

I blurt out: "Do you know how slowly things grow up here? Your Navajo mine is thirty degrees of latitude *south* of Lac de Gras. Up here there are miles and miles of eskers, Jim. It takes decades, centuries, for a Barren Lands plant community to establish itself. Even without wind-borne air pollution from mine excavations."

I'm thinking, too, about the drained lakes. And Long Lake, which will be dammed into separate cells for holding mine effluent. I find it hard to visualize how long it might take for dwarf willow, which will flourish into shoulder-high groves in sunny, sheltered spots on the tundra, to soften the edges of one of those exposed giant pits. Excell asks for patience, for time for BHP to show what it can do on the

Barrens. I ask that they consider revegetation a responsibility that will be covered in various environmental agreements and stop trying to sell it to us as a benefit of the mine.

About midnight BHP's contingent leaves. We agree to meet again in the morning. I follow Nick and Avi's lead in believing the session was really worthwhile because we were all honest. Because we removed an overlay of posturing and laid bare what they need and what we need to reach agreement. But we still haven't managed to get around the issue of BHP's template agreement, we've heard no dollar amounts, and BHP still wants Denínu Kų́e out of our IBA.

◆　　　◆　　　◆

THE next morning Nick, Avi, Sara and I are just finishing breakfast when Chris arrives. We feed him and drink coffee at the table, which is now lit with watery light from a high-overcast day. Chiefs Beaulieu, Sangris and Balsillie soon follow. The eight of us plan what to do in our next session with BHP, but time passes and no one arrives or calls. We'd set no meeting time, but it is getting late and we start to second-guess what BHP is planning. Then, as we toss around strategies, the porch door opens and shuts. We hear people removing jackets and boots in the entryway. Voices in the hall. The inner door swings open with its signature squeak, and John Bekale and Jerry Bair enter, sidle right into the living room and settle comfortably on the sofas with us. I get up to make fresh coffee and hand it around.

Nick, Avi, Jerry, John and Chris skirt the key issue: BHP's template agreement and our unwillingness to use it as a starting point. We want BHP's financial offer up front before we negotiate the agreement laid out in the template. Eventually even I sense why only two BHP negotiators have come. John and Jerry have been dispatched to tell us that unless we agree to discuss the template, the negotiations can go no further. Everyone chews on this for a while, then Nick and Jerry go outside for a cigarette. Chris, John and Avi continue to circle the issue.

Sick with now-stale hot air, I go outside to find Jerry and Nick. As I round the corner of the house to the lake side, I walk straight into a cold, early-winter gust. It is the fall wind bringing the first snow—snow that may come this afternoon, or not until next week. Snowflakes bounce off Jerry's red BHP Arctic parka. Others disappear into the yellow stubble at our feet. Waves crash on the shore. Nick, his open jean jacket pressed tight to his spine by the wind, faces Jerry. Nick's right hand is pressed against the wall over Jerry's shoulder. His left hand stabs the air with a dead cigarette. Jerry cups his own cigarette, trying to keep it lit.

I lean next to them, letting their bodies break the wind. To me, they look exactly like what they are: two well-matched opponents who respect each other's skill. I stifle laughter at the way Nick has backed Jerry against the proverbial log wall in the most congenial, friendly manner. Standing chin to chin, they talk, their words bouncing on the stiff breeze. I listen. Over and over again, Nick repeats ways that the company could, and should, direct benefits to the community that will hardly put a dimple in their bottom line. Jerry is frustrated. He understands Nick, even agrees with some of what he is saying. Yet he cannot, or says he cannot (in fine negotiator style) agree to anything for Akaitcho Treaty 8 that he has not agreed to for the others—the Dogribs, the Metis, the Inuit. This is the company's mantra.

Our job is to craft benefits that will work for Akaitcho Treaty 8 people. We are being forced to do this within a foreign framework developed at other negotiating tables, not our own. But our strategy is paying off, and Jerry knows it. He stands, freezing, a Texan out of heat, back against the wall. He wants to go inside where it is warm and rejoin the other member of his negotiating team. Nick and I won't let him.

We calmly repeat the same points in a different form. Jerry looks cold, then colder, his face pinched against the wind. Nick and I enjoy Jerry's discomfort, teasing him.

"Up the signing bonus by a million, and we'll let you go inside." I add, "We can make sure your plane never comes. We can offer you a winter in Łutsëlk'é. You can set nets for fish below three feet of ice, hunt for caribou at forty below. You, too, can line up each week at the First Nation office for welfare payments."

Ten minutes pass until we relent and retreat to the south wall, which is sheltered from the wind. There, pale sun sends some warmth through the overcast. Sparse snowflakes blow past us, but the ground still smells like autumn. Avi calls us inside with the news that BHP has decided to cancel the rest of the negotiations scheduled for today. Excell and Bergelsman have called their charter aircraft. It will arrive to take the four BHP representatives back to Yellowknife at midday. Bergelsman is on the phone proposing one final meeting with only our chief negotiator present. We decide to send Chris and Nick in one hour. Apparently Bergelsman wants to summarize how far we've gotten.

Back outside, Nick and I discuss BHP's moves while he helps me stack wood, which Freddie Nitah brought sometime last night.

"So did we get anywhere?" I ask, pitching a log, hard, against the wall of the house. "Just when we start to get to the heart of matter, they pull out."

"I'm not surprised," replies Nick. He changes the subject. "Who sold you this wood?" Nick is disgusted at how much I paid.

"But it's fall," I say. "The guys can't use snow machines yet and it's tougher and tougher to get wood by boat. The loads will increase when they have snow and can pull wood sleighs."

"Doesn't matter," he says. "They charge you for a cord, they should bring a cord—and of decent wood, not these spindly sticks."

"OK, OK," I say, "just help me get it stacked. And next time I need wood, I'll hire you to negotiate the price."

He walks off up the gentle slope to meet Chris at the First Nation office. Avi and I wait, and wait. I pack my battered duffle bag with a few clothes, books, lots of files. I know we'll be on the afternoon flight to Yellowknife, after BHP.

"Some brief meeting," I mutter.

"Awfully quiet," Avi declares.

"You're right." I phone the First Nation office.

"Better come over," Dora says.

Avi and I walk fast across an eerily quiet Łutsëlk'é. No trucks, no kids, no unemployed young men walk the roads waiting for freeze-up. There's no one outside the office either, no traffic in or out of the doors. We step inside, right into the overflow of people from the council chambers. Most of the First Nation is there, along with Chiefs Balsillie, Beaulieu, Lockhart and Sangris. The four BHP men sit at the council table, facing the crowd. Somehow they got themselves cornered, probably while arranging their ride to the airstrip. Word must have spread quickly through the community. Like Avi and I, most of the town figured out "something's happening at the office." It is very quiet. Then Bergelsman speaks. He says the BHP negotiators are leaving because it is impossible to do anything here, that BHP has too much to do, too many other people to satisfy before October 8. They cannot stay any longer in Łutsëlk'é. His words fall like pebbles into the still room. They ripple through the crowd slowly while young people translate for their relatives. As if they have summoned it, the company's Twin Otter flies low over the village. They stand, gather their bags and briefcases, file out to where the Co-op truck waits for them. Over the hill, they disappear in a cloud of dust and snowflakes.

9. *The Minister's Significant Progress*

◆   ◆   ◆

Native people have this wonderful respect and love for
the land. They believe they are part of it, a mere link
in the cycle of existence. Now as many of you know, this
conflicts with the accepted Judeo-Christian, i.e., western
view of land management. I even believe somewhere in
the first chapters of the Bible it says something about
God giving man dominion over nature. Check it out,
Genesis 4 ( ): Thou shall clear cut.

—Drew Hayden Taylor, *Funny You Don't Look Like One:*
Observations of a Blue-Eyed Ojibway

October 4, Friday, Day 57, in Yellowknife.
It is like a southern fall this morning as my boot heels snap on Yellowknife's pavement. Everything is frosty and cool, but nothing is cold.
Bright yellow birch leaves hang rigid in the still air. The big lake and even
some of the small lakes are open. In the old days, the big lake froze fast,
hard and early. In 1981 I lived in a shack on Yellowknife Bay. One day the
still lake was clear. The next morning, a solid skim of ice covered it. The
next day, a few inches. Soon it was thick enough to walk on. Then, snow.
And that was that, for winter.

Now it is different. Whether you call it global warming, climate
change, climate variability or just "Should be five chops. S'only three

chops," as Chief Felix Lockhart said one October morning in Łutsëlk'é. He'd come to my place for coffee. Minutes earlier I'd seen him on the lake below his house, chopping through the ice with his axe.

Chris, Avi and I are on the way to our early-morning meeting with Peter Nixon, the special representative to Ron Irwin, federal minister of Indian Affairs and Northern Development. He has come to Yellowknife to observe Broken Hill Proprietary's negotiations with all of the parties affected by the mine. Nixon will report back to Irwin in Ottawa after next Monday, October 7, the sixtieth day.

Late yesterday we flew from Łutsëlk'é to Yellowknife on the sched, just hours after BHP left Łutsëlk'é on its chartered Twin Otter. It was a dirty, dark night when we got in, both grit and snow blowing in the chill air. Today and over the weekend, everyone working for or against Irwin's "significant progress" will gather in Yellowknife. The congress will not stop until there is, or is not to be, a diamond mine at Lac de Gras. This morning's stillness portends climax.

At Akaitcho Treaty 8's discussion last night, the chiefs asked, "OK, who is going to talk to this guy face to face?"

Chris, as our lead negotiator, will meet with Nixon. Nick avoided meeting with Nixon, saying that his expertise—the dollars and cents of any agreement—was not required. Chief Beaulieu suggested that Avi take his experience with business in the North along to the meeting with Nixon. At that, it occurred to me that the two men going to meet Nixon had experience solely with Akaitcho Treaty 8 leadership in Yellowknife, not with people on the land. Also, neither of them had expertise in the history of Treaties 8 and 11, nor in the conflict between the Dogrib land claims and the Treaty 8 land entitlement position. I wanted Nixon to understand that any agreement with private industry would eventually feed back into the Crown's way of honouring Treaties 8 and 11. I volunteered to go.

Chris looked discomfited. Avi liked the idea. Nick was relieved.

Chief Sangris was fine with it, Chief Beaulieu less so. Chief Lockhart had not come to Yellowknife. Since Łutsëlk'é had no chief, elder or councillor present, I had neither their support nor their direction. And the others all knew it.

Click, snap go my hard heels on the frosty pavement. We walk steadily, with a mission. We must make Minister Irwin's representative understand that Akaitcho Treaty 8's right to benefits from BHP is as valid as the Dogribs'. If Nixon, and thus Irwin, does not understand this, and if we cannot reach agreement on impacts and benefits with BHP by Day 60, the mine may well go ahead with only the Dogribs' agreement. After we meet with Nixon, we have two, at most three, more chances to meet with BHP. Chris also wants Nixon to intervene with the company, to pressure BHP to put money on the table before we discuss its impact and benefit agreement (IBA) template. For these issues, for all Akaitcho Treaty 8's concerns with mining diamonds on the Barrens, we have been allotted just ninety minutes with the minister's representative.

◆   ◆   ◆

WE enter the Precambrian Building, a sterile high-rise off 50th Street that is the bastion of the federal government in Yellowknife. The wind tunnels up cold from Frame Lake. This street is concrete, empty of life, although the Precambrian landscape is visible no more than a block away.

We wait only a few minutes until we are ushered into a meeting room where Peter Nixon sits alone at a large table with a blank pad of paper in front of him. His fine, understated sweater almost hides a tie. With his neatly trimmed hair and his quiet hands, he is the personification of neutral. Autumn air wafts into the carpeted quiet with us. After we exchange greetings, Chris begins with his usual long preamble. He stretches back in his big chair, basking in Nixon's attention. He reviews each meeting Akaitcho Treaty 8 has had with BHP, each time he has argued with the company to show us the money before we proceed on the template. Nixon does not respond as the minutes tick past. He waits until Chris peaks with "[BHP] just won't put the money on the table. How can we talk about anything else if they just won't put the money on the table? We can't work through their template agreement if they won't give us a number first."

"It is standard in negotiations like this that the money comes last. It is always the last thing put on the table, after all the other terms are dealt with," Nixon replies quietly. Chris looks nonplussed.

Avi takes over. Along with his business sense, he brings presence and size to this table (both traits that I lack). He explains at length the financial consequences if the money is too little to be of any good.

I watch the clock hands tick. Nixon is just listening.

Chris, Avi and Peter Nixon browse abstract solutions—if the Dogribs settle for x dollars, will Akaitcho Treaty 8 accept y?—like caribou fattening on a breezy August day. I am getting tense.

Finally, I intervene: "Here's what Minister Irwin needs to know."

They have been in a triangle of words from one to the other. The three men stop what they are saying and turn to face me.

I continue: "BHP's mine is on land that was not ceded to the Crown in either Treaty 8 or Treaty 11. The Crown recognizes it has not completed the treaty process, which is why it has entered into the comprehensive claims process or 'modern treaty' with the Dogribs and the treaty entitlement process with Treaty 8. Since neither the Dogribs' nor the Treaty 8 process has been completed, the Crown has the fiduciary responsibility to look after Treaty 8 and Treaty 11 interests in that land. We all know that the Crown's fiduciary responsibility conflicts with the Crown's responsibility to develop that land.

"If the Crown allows BHP to go ahead with the mine at all, the Crown is allowing part of the treaty to be settled through the creation of another third-party interest on Dene traditional lands. The treaty processes state that third-party interests are to be honoured in the 'final' settlements. So once BHP goes ahead on that land, neither Dogrib Treaty 11 nor Akaitcho Treaty 8 has any more claim to the land itself.

"If the Crown allows BHP to go ahead on the basis of an agreement only with Dogrib Treaty 11, then it is failing in its fiduciary obligation to look after the interest that Akaitcho Treaty 8 has in that area. The overlap between Treaty 8 and Treaty 11 traditional land use in that area is a long-standing boundary issue that needs to be resolved as Treaty 8 is fulfilled and the Treaty 11 comprehensive claim is settled. To allow BHP to go ahead without recognizing that overlap is to allow BHP's development to solve a historical boundary issue in advance of completing the claims process."

Nixon looks at me, silent. But his eyes are suddenly bright with interest.

I summarize: "The minister needs to ensure that there is equity between agreements that BHP makes with the Dogribs and with Akaitcho Treaty 8. The minister should not allow the mine to go ahead if BHP only reaches agreement with the Dogribs, but not Treaty 8." He's got it.

By now, we are almost out of time.

"One more question," I say, looking directly at Nixon. "What is significant progress?"

He backs away from the table as if hit by an air bag, then grins, shaking his head. Imitating his boss, the minister, he cups both hands in front of his sweater like a poker player and says, "The minister is keeping that very close to his chest."

"So we don't really have any way of knowing whether we are even coming close or not, whether the mine might go ahead if only the Dogribs get an agreement with BHP," I reply.

"Right."

I can't help it. I sigh, hoping it is under my breath. We are excused; we all shake hands.

Avi, Chris and I walk the four blocks back to the Dene Nation boardroom. We wait for the chiefs and the rest of our team. When they arrive, Chris reports Nixon's view that the money will come last, that we will have to negotiate on BHP's template agreement before the company will put a financial offer on the table. With little discussion, we agree to start working on the template at our next session with BHP. I summarize my argument to Nixon for equity between the Dogribs and Akaitcho Treaty 8. And, last, I add: "And Irwin isn't saying what constitutes significant progress."

◆   ◆   ◆

BY 10 A.M., our whole team—Chris, Avi, Nick, Darrell, me—is back at the Precambrian Building. This is to be our grand, penultimate session with BHP. But Jim Excell is not present. Die-vid Boyd is on holiday in Australia. Only Jerry Bair, the long tall Texan, is familiar from earlier sessions, along with Jim Bergelsman from San Francisco. There are seven of us around the table. On the periphery, Sarah takes notes and looks after coffee. Whenever the discussion heats up, she covers the several diamond rings that she wears.

Nick and I sit down at the table. He's worn a blazer, shocking me. In turn, he has noticed my city footwear.

"Are those your ass-kicking negotiating boots, Ellen?"

I kick him under the table and turn back to BHP's latest template for the impact and benefit agreement. Now that Chris is willing to lead on BHP's template, we can get down to business.

But first, BHP says that they will address this agreement not to all of Akaitcho Treaty 8, but specifically to the communities of Ndilo, Dettah and Łutsëlk'é. We protest the exclusion of Denínu Kųe. The Dogrib

Treaty 11 Council is made up of four communities. So is Akaitcho Treaty 8. But, they say, DIAND directed them to deal with all the Dogribs, but with only three of the Akaitcho Treaty 8 communities. We argue numbers. They are adamant. They insist on their wording in the agreement and argue that once we have the benefits, Akaitcho Treaty 8 can divide them among their communities as they see fit. This is true. We assent, giving in to the fear that we will have no agreement at all, not before the minister's deadline. After, maybe, not at all. I feel like I've been punched in the stomach. But we proceed.

Now it is Nick's job to close the financial gap between what BHP might offer and what might be fair to Akaitcho Treaty 8, just reduced to three of four First Nations. Fair, relative to what the Dogribs will get. Fair, for the Dogribs and Akaitcho Treaty 8, with reference to the minimal return indigenous peoples the world over get when natural resources are extracted out from under subsistence lifeways. We all know that Łutsëlk'é will receive pittance compared to the mine's profit, or even to the value of real estate BHP will rent or buy in Yellowknife. We know that BHP's intent does not include training Dene for management positions at its mines or anywhere else. We know that Akaitcho Treaty 8 will get less than the Dogribs.

But we don't speak these things. We speak as if, what if. The process works, slowly. Nick proposes formula after formula for Akaitcho Treaty 8 to increase the dollar return on whatever money, in whatever form, comes to the Dene from the mine. We discuss scholarships from BHP for Akaitcho Treaty 8 members, to increase the overall capability of the First Nations to work in the mining industry. We discuss unbundling, or allowing smaller, more narrowly focused construction and operations contracts. If BHP will tender less complicated service packages, small, young First Nation companies can bid successfully against large, experienced corporations that handle everything from catering to shipping heavy equipment across the country and up the ice road. We discuss giving preference to aboriginals over northerners or other groups when hiring. BHP argues that giving preference to northerners—without specifically citing aboriginal peoples—might be sufficient to ensure that Akaitcho Treaty 8 peoples get jobs. We argue for aboriginal preference and reiterate the barriers, not least geographic location, that First Nations people from the small communities, especially off the road system, face in getting to the point of hire. We discuss royalties specifically for Akaitcho Treaty 8. BHP goes to great pains to enlighten us about the heavy royalty regime it faces from the federal government. BHP answers virtually every request we make with another calculation of the high cost of getting the diamonds out of the ground. It is such an expensive process, they maintain, that they really don't have much of a profit margin to share with Akaitcho Treaty 8.

We request that BHP make working at the mine a more culturally rewarding experience by having boats and snow machines available for employees to use during their off hours. The company refuses, citing safety and security concerns. I wonder how the safety of the mine and the security of the diamonds matter so much more than the safety and security of partners and children in the communities.

The two-week-on, two-week-off rotation BHP is so proud of looks quite different when you are the parent holding a job back home in the village and looking after the kids. Effectively, you are a single parent for the duration of your partner's shift at the mine. There's no reliable childcare. What happens when your partner returns home from the mine? Especially if BHP flies him the long way home, back through Yellowknife? There he has to wait, usually overnight, to catch the sched flight home to Łutsëlk'é. Tired from the shifts, tired from the travel, most especially tired of living by another culture's rules and subtle but pernicious racism on the job, the mine worker is just as likely to hit the

Gold Range Hotel with his wages as the grocery store. BHP could avoid contributing to this kind of employment stress by making Łutsëlk'é, and the other small communities, the pickup point for its employees.

I remind BHP that Cominco's Red Dog Mine in Northwest Alaska, which has Alaska Native corporate investment and a "good" aboriginal employment record, has, after twenty years, not a single aboriginal person in a management capacity. I ask if there aren't benefits we could put into this agreement to help Akaitcho Treaty 8 people really become partners in the mining industry.

The answer is that it isn't BHP's responsibility to educate people for management in the industry. That's up to the First Nations and the government—who might, someday, establish a school of mining in the North. In the meantime, BHP offers "good jobs" to truck drivers and chambermaids.

At some point it gets dark outside. We break for some meal, a very late lunch or early supper. BHP's representatives promise that Excell will join us when we reconvene. Chris, Nick and Avi assure me that Excell will "bring the money." In other words, since we've been good kids and talked about the company's draft agreement, we will receive a financial offer.

Several people leave the building to smoke. They are gone a long time. It's the same as it ever was, I think, the old song "Smokin' in the Boys' Room" running through my head. They're working on the deal, no doubt. I find myself sitting on a civil servant's desk to telephone my sons. It is Friday night, and I am tired and discouraged. I face another weekend in Yellowknife, far from my children in Edmonton and my life near the land, with the people, in Łutsëlk'é. As always at times like this, I am just plain lonely.

About 8:30 P.M. we reconvene. Sarah has gone home, so we have no official record of the meeting. After we are all around the table, Bergelsman goes to get Excell. Minutes later, as Excell comes down the stairs from BHP's offices, my tired brain sees Jesus Christ descending to save us all. But it's only Jim, not a bad man, no saviour either. He's just a skilled mining engineer who, as the leader of BHP's project, is doing what must be the job from hell right now. I wonder what his reward will be if he pulls off this agreement by next Tuesday—this one and all the other agreements.

An unearthly quiet descends as Excell takes his seat. The hot air, the energy, has leaked out of the room. At first, no one speaks. The building is still around our small group at this table, united, at last, in a common purpose. We agree that we are in accord on some changes to BHP's IBA template, and that some of these changes will benefit Akaitcho Treaty 8. Each team will take this draft agreement to our principals over the weekend. We will meet again Monday morning to report on their response. Then (drum roll, I think) Excell lifts a piece of paper out of the single slim file he has brought with him.

There it is. A dollar figure. Not bad, but certainly not great. Especially when shared among all of Akaitcho Treaty 8. Next to nothing compared to the real money from diamonds, which will flow, like all sour deals, south. Our comments, and Excell's, are perfunctory. We follow the unwritten script now. "Thank you," we say. "We will take this offer to the First Nations for their review, rejection or acceptance." Likewise, Bair, Bergelsman and Excell will take our improvements—some scholarships, some preferential contract opportunities, some mine royalties—to their principals. We will meet again, on the sixtieth day.

Chris, Avi and Nick seem to think that we deserve a good, celebratory meal. We telephone the chiefs, then retire to the Factor's Club dining room at the Explorer Hotel. According to our strategists, it is as important to be here to advertise our success as it is to eat. For this I am glad, because while I can remain upright in my chair, I am far beyond hungry. Once again we are around a long, rectangular table. Instead of binders and briefs, the table is covered with a white cloth. Soft candle light makes us all look much more important, I believe, than we are. I muse on the historical meaning of our gathering, its ethical contradiction. We are a group of largely white negotiators working for aboriginal people. We are spending the money the Dene requested from its fiduciary, the government, to pay for negotiations with the private sector. The government will tax this same money. We dine in an edifice named for the explorers and company factors who first exploited this land for profit rather than material or spiritual sustenance.

On Saturday morning, I say goodbye to Nick, who is going home to Whitehorse. He feels that his work is done and that it is now up to the First Nations to decide on the agreement.

I am dismayed by the prospect of having to explain the financial points of the agreement to others without him here to continue explaining them to me. I am also concerned that without Nick's clarity and creativity at the negotiating table, we will not gain any further concessions from BHP. But he heads for the airport, and I join the rest of the team at the Deton'cho Corporation building in Ndilo for a long, smoke-filled reaction meeting. We try to redraft some of the agreement's language so that its eventual legal interpretation will be slanted in our favour. Nothing looks better or more clear when we adjourn.

From this congress, I go to meet Archie Catholique, who has arrived in Yellowknife to represent the Łutsëlk'é council at this weekend's meetings. He will also interpret for some of the elders we want to fly in on Monday or Tuesday to join, we hope, in reaching agreement with BHP. Archie and I phone over to Łutsëlk'é, where Chief Lockhart, Antoine Michel and other community members are gathered at the First Nation office. Archie and I go through the essential parts of the agreement, projecting our voices through the speakerphone, working hard to explain the financial concepts in plain English, then in Dëne Sųłin yati. The community directs us to continue with the current strategy. Try to increase the money up front and through the business and employment preferences, they counsel. Work with the Yellowknives.

Antoine will come in on the afternoon flight. He will try to meet with Premier Morin tonight. We are all concerned that there be fairness between what the Dogribs get and what Akaitcho Treaty 8 gets from BHP. We want the premier to pressure BHP toward equity between the Dogribs and Akaitcho Treaty 8.

After our phone call, Archie and I go to the crowded Dettah council chambers. There, Chiefs Beaulieu and Sangris are briefing their joint council, asking for their direction on the draft agreement. Also present are Yellowknives Dene staff, Land and Environment Committee members and other First Nation members. Chris Knight lectures on the agreement. Calvin Helin and Chris Lemon, two attorneys from Vancouver who have been hired by Treaty 8 to represent us at the final working session on the environmental agreement, comment briefly. Chief Sangris speaks for a long while in Dene yati. As with our conference call to Łutsëlk'é, no one is jumping up and down with excitement over BHP's offer. But no one is saying "Absolutely not good enough." The consensus is to go back to the bargaining table on Monday to try to do better.

I have the sense that a clock is ticking somewhere but I can't hear it because all the energy directed to these diamonds is interfering with the clock's signal. We know that all the BHP people are working this weekend, that the Dogribs are meeting, that the Northwest Territories government staff are at work on the socioeconomic benefits agreement that includes all northerners.

Monday, October 7 is the sixtieth day, but the actual deadline is, by consensus, October 8 at midnight. I'm gathering notes in my hotel room when the phone rings early in the morning. It is Don Morin, the NWT premier. I brief him on Akaitcho Treaty 8's progress, then ask his opinion. "Keep goin'," he says.

Before Akaitcho Treaty 8 meets with BHP again Darrell, Chris, Avi, Archie and I compare notes. Through various channels, we have learned that the Dogribs met with BHP last night and that the NWT senior legal counsel observed the meeting, as he is supposed to observe ours with BHP today. We know that the Dogribs have "a number," a dollar figure higher than ours. The NWT legal counsel told Chris to have Chief Beaulieu phone the premier for the number. When the premier phoned me, I asked him about the figure. He said he'd just arrived and didn't know.

At 9:15, we begin, again, with BHP. This is our last chance to make substantial changes to an agreement; if we meet again, it will be to accept or reject a deal. We still don't know how much money BHP is offering the Dogribs. Our efforts to find out are going nowhere.

BHP, and we, state tentatively, cautiously that our principals are "interested, maybe even intrigued" by the draft agreement we discussed over the weekend. It is enough to move forward, but rueful head-shaking all around the table communicates that we need more.

We know that BHP must finish this meeting with us by noon. Excell does not appear. BHP makes us a final offer on paper.

Peter Nixon, the federal minister's representative who has been observing this meeting, speaks briefly. The minister's decision on significant progress will be "subjective." Irwin is not going to state any criteria against which we, BHP or anyone else can measure progress on the agreements. None of the others show anything like the frustration I feel. If Irwin intends to approve the mine solely based on an agreement between BHP and the Dogribs, what is the best strategy for Akaitcho Treaty 8? Should we accept whatever we can get before the deadline, or should we hold out for more after the deadline, when the only leverage will be litigation against BHP and its mine? Or litigation against the Crown for failing to uphold its fiduciary obligation toward Akaitcho Treaty 8? Or should we resort to civil disobedience—blocking the ice road when BHP starts moving construction materials up to the mine?

As the meeting closes, it is left that Chris will communicate with

BHP to arrange a time tomorrow for one more brief congress. Then we will shake hands on a deal or walk away.

In the afternoon, Archie and I go over the numbers with Chris while we wait for Chief Lockhart and the Łutsëlk'é councillors to call. Again, we discuss this morning's meeting and strategy over speaker-phone. Elders Liza Enzoe and J.B. Rabesca will fly to Yellowknife for our meeting with BHP tomorrow.

◆   ◆   ◆

OVER at the Explorer Hotel, attorneys for the First Nations, the Crown, the Northwest Territories and BHP are finessing the environmental agreement. Christina Ishoj and Chris Lemon are our Akaitcho Treaty 8 representatives at this meeting. We've spoken frequently by phone over the past several days, but late Monday afternoon I walk to the Explorer Hotel to observe how things are progressing. Christina and Chris sit together on one side of this vast meeting room, which seems to be filled with bureaucrats and attorneys in white shirts and ties. On the table in front of each negotiator is a microphone. The formal atmosphere is a surreal shift from the cramped room where we were closeted with BHP.

I sit down in one of the empty chairs that line the walls of the big room. I listen, but it is almost impossible to pick up the gist of the discussions. Gradually, though, I realize that the negotiations are bogged down on a technical point about the flow of funding to the independent environmental monitoring agency that will watchdog BHP.

Christina leans back and gestures to me to pull my chair forward. She and Chris whisper cues to me so I can understand what is being said. It is good news. I ask, "You mean, you are back on the money?"

"Yes," says Chris. "We were getting really close, but things were moving a bit too fast . . . Nobody wants to see an environmental agreement initialled if none of our clients have signed their benefit agreements. We might have finished today, but after lunch everything just slowed right down."

He tells me that he and the Dogribs' legal counsel have actually worked in concert to stall this afternoon session. Soon enough, all parties agree that it is too late to finish the agreement today; they adjourn, agreeing to meet again tomorrow morning.

That evening, a curious lull ensues. It is as if everyone can see the finish line. We even believe that we are all likely to cross it. No one wants to break from the pack and sprint to the finish. What if we don't have the right clauses and royalties for that last gasp?

◆   ◆   ◆

ON Tuesday morning, October 8, I speak to Premier Morin one more time by phone. I press him on fairness for the Dogribs and Akaitcho's people.

He asks, "What are the weak points?"

I summarize them quickly. He is terse, then, because he, like me, is sure the Dogribs are getting a better deal.

"Keep going," he growls. "Just keep going."

Negotiations have their own momentum. Their ritual is as tightly scripted as a hockey match before overtime, encapsulating the same sleepy periods in the game and the same bursts of explosive energy. In overtime, nobody calls penalties and the action is sudden death.

Tuesday, Day 61, we wait. And wait. The building tension, this pushing to the limit, creates a strange mystique around reaching agreement. It seems like an unwritten rule that some secret aura will make the deals better if they are done in the middle of the night.

As the day wanes, I come to understand that we will not be done in time for me to catch the late-night flight to Edmonton to see my sons.

Chris Knight books and rebooks meeting times with BHP. First it is four, then seven, then eight, then nine. Akaitcho Treaty 8 is in BHP's queue after the Dogribs, perhaps also behind the Government of the Northwest Territories. By evening we place bets among ourselves on the value of the Dogribs' agreement and on when BHP will actually get around to us.

We are using the Dene Nation board room as our base. In these days before cellphones, Chris shuttles between us and the telephone to BHP. Archie comes and goes between us and the elders and other Akaitcho Treaty 8 members who are in town. Chiefs Beaulieu and Sangris go between us and their offices. Their crowded agendas leave no time for waiting.

News dribbles in by phone as the hours pass. Negotiators for Canada and BHP initial the environmental agreement late in the day. The representatives for the First Nations agree to an "implementation protocol" for the environmental agreement. It is obvious that the chiefs believe the First Nations will reach financial agreements with BHP by midnight. This is significant progress, even judged objectively. All that remains are the agreements between BHP and the Dogribs, Akaitcho Treaty 8 and the Government of the Northwest Territories. We are a step closer to the mine's approval.

Fatigue, then attrition, sets in. Archie tells me the elders are tired; it is getting late and they don't know about coming to a meeting. The Dene Nation boardroom is in the same building as the Discovery Inn, where most of us are staying, and the Red Apple Restaurant, which has become a second office. People slip away to eat, or to their rooms to rest. When BHP rebooks for nine, we all drift away for a bit.

When we return, it is to wait again. Chris Knight, freshly attired in a white dress shirt open at the collar, seats himself next to Chief Beaulieu. Calvin Helin, one of our new legal counsel from Vancouver, sits on the chief's far side. Avi sits to Chris's left. I'm left of Avi, at the end of our table. But as we wait, Avi and I move to an old sofa in the hallway, put our feet up and talk softly, going over and over the terms of the agreement. Through the boardroom doorway I can see Chief Beaulieu pacing and smoking. Chris swivels back and forth in his chair, talking to anyone who will listen. Archie phones to say the elders are not coming; it is too late for them.

In my notes, I've scrawled my best guess about what the final agreement will be. There is no question in my mind that there will be an agreement. We've known for several years that diamond mining is going to happen. The only latitude we've had is to try to get an agreement containing the best possible benefit, the least negative impact. What we don't know is how whatever we agree to will play out. What we don't know is if, this time around, through this kind of process, the impact of mining will be more positive, or at least less negative for Akaitcho's people. What we don't know is if the benefits will actually improve people's lives or just change them. What we don't know is if the rifts between the Dogribs and Akaitcho Treaty 8, and within Treaty 8 between Denínu Kųe and the rest, will ever heal.

It is nearly 11 P.M. when BHP's negotiating team phones to say it is on its way.

Soon Excell and Bergelsman and Boyd and Bair come up the stairs. They seat themselves quietly on the far side of the square of tables. We approach each other cautiously, dancing an awkward dance through the agreement one more time. After two hours of discussion, the stumbling blocks remain. This may be a deal for Akaitcho's people, but it is not a good deal.

Around 1:30 A.M. on October 9, BHP tells us that a deal has been made with the Dogribs. The cash component is "slightly higher" than ours, "based on the numbers [of First Nation members] that the Department of Indian and Northern Affairs gave us." Akaitcho Treaty 8, along with all the other key parties, has initialled the environmental agreement. The minister has his "significant progress." With the Dogribs in, with environmental monitoring above and beyond what current law requires, who could argue against a diamond mine? The only question is whether or not BHP will sweeten their offer to us at all. They don't have to. They've won. Does Treaty 8's "goodwill" matter to them? Not at all. They can proceed without Akaitcho's people, using the Dogribs as their poster children for good relations with aboriginal people. Canada can reward the Dogribs with progress in their land claim negotiations, even allowing them to claim, singularly, land that they have shared with Akaitcho's people since 1829.

At this moment, Akaitcho Treaty 8, already reduced by almost a third of its members in its effort to get this far with the miners and the Crown, can move ahead with what it has or walk away.

What would Akaitcho and his advisors have done? What would the elders do, especially the Dëne Súlin and Yellowknives elders if they were to sit down with the Dogrib elders?

I have nothing to say during this meeting. Jim Bergelsman says the "meeting in Łutsëlk'é was a waste of time," and I think perhaps I should say something. Perhaps I should state what is true—that from the beginning this has not been a fair process, one conducted on a level playing field. But I don't. Who would hear me, on the side of the table where I sit or across the room? It is too late for that. Chief Beaulieu and Chris continue to trade numbers and formulas for the timing of payments. These monies, slight increases to our benefits, will make a difference in interest earned at the bank. They will make no difference to the larger damage done—neither to the land nor to the people. I see something that has not come clear in my vision before this moment. I see the greed stretching from the time one hundred years ago when Cecil Rhodes annexed Matabeleland and Mashonaland for the British, when Rhodes's agents preyed on the indigenous conflict between the Matabele and the Mashona and on the Matabele king's trust in white missionaries. Canada has preyed on an age-old conflict between the Dogribs and Akaitcho's people. We negotiators, whom the First Nations trust, have done our best, but it is not good enough in the face of greed. We use methods less bloody than those of the past, but our motivation is no more pure.

Diamonds smell to me now. They smell of that room, that night. Of thick stale cigarette smoke. Of heavy men's cologne. Of human arrogance. Of greed. Of irrevocable change to the land.

In the middle of the night, no—later—in the early morning, we reach agreement about least possible damage and greatest possible benefit. By then, "least," "greatest," "possible," "benefit," "for whom" all defy definition. At 3 A.M., with nothing more than nods, we all stand. We move toward each other. Everyone on our team shakes hands with each BHP negotiator. Jim Bergelsman apologizes to me for his earlier derogatory remarks about Łutsëlk'é. I accept his apology, with this reply. "The worth of time all depends on who and what you are working for."

10. *Second Rapids*

◆   ◆   ◆

Do South African diamond miners suffer more from
poor mining conditions and racism than they benefit
from having jobs? If you really believe so, don't buy
diamonds. (Not a great sacrifice for most of us.)

—Linda Hasselstrom, *Land Circle: Writings Collected from the Land*

MINISTER Irwin's deadline has come and
gone. Nothing momentous has happened, at least nothing obvious to
the public eye. My concluding note says only "Out for coffee. Slept
4:30–6:00." The days following October 8 are eerily quiet. I am able to
spend them in Edmonton with my sons before returning north.

The following week when I am back in Łutsëlk'é, *News/North*, the
northern press oracle, runs a story on the agreements under the head-
line "Two Down, Three More to Go: BHP and Treaty 11 Reach Agreement, Miners Ready to Spend $750 Million."

No details have been released on either the BHP-Dogrib agreement or
the environmental agreement. The article states that negotiations with

Treaty 8, Metis and Kugluktuk Inuit are continuing. It is not the first time, nor will it be the last, that Akaitcho Treaty 8 is left out of the story. We know we have an agreement with BHP's negotiators and that they, and we, will discuss it with our respective principals. But our agreement doesn't make it into the news or into the public consciousness.

In Łutsëlk'é, Ndilo and Dettah, the chiefs and negotiators are working the agreement through each community. It cannot be signed until each council passes a resolution ratifying it. Before that can happen, all of the First Nation members must be informed, then they will vote to accept or reject the agreement. No one knows quite how long this process will take.

At the same time that the agreement is circulating, the chiefs write a reminder to Minister Irwin that Treaty 8 negotiations must be resumed expeditiously, especially now that Treaty 8 has met Irwin's deadline for agreements with BHP. When, Akaitcho Treaty 8 asks, will Canada appoint its new negotiator for the Treaty 8 process?

Day to day, life continues as it always does in Łutsëlk'é. It is Thanksgiving, and the holiday weather is perfect for fall hunting. Several of us stay in town to cook for most of the day while the hunters go out on the land in search of moose. By afternoon dusk, I walk across the village carrying a warm stuffed turkey in a cardboard box. It is perfectly clear, calm, cold. The rocky islands to the west are bare and stark against the sunset sky. The still lake is a watercolour palette. J.C. and Hanna's house on the point is warm and full of elders and children, all gathered for the feast. But the hunters have not returned. We wait for them during the long sunset. It is nearly dark, and still no boats return. Bits of conversation fill the air.

"Must be really cold on the water."

"They must have got some meat, else they'd be back by now."

"I hope his dad keeps my boy dressed up warm enough."

"The water's low in the river . . . hope they don't hit rocks."

"Hope it doesn't blow up."

Just as the last light fades off the water, we see the boats come around the point. By the time the hunters reach shore it is so dark we cannot even see them beach and unload the boats. Soon they walk up to the house, and cold air sweeps into the crowded room as they come in. Before we can ask any questions, J.C. Catholique, home from Fort Smith for the holiday, walks to the table where the turkey, salads, canned corn, mashed potatoes, cakes, fruit juice and pies are spread out. On his hunting knife, he carries an enormous shank of fire-roasted moose, which he plunks in the centre of the table.

"Now," he says, "it's a real feast."

We begin the meal with prayers. J.C. scoops hot coals from the wood stove into a small cast-iron skillet. He holds the end of a sweetgrass braid to the coals, then wafts the subtle fragrance to east, south, west and north with an eagle feather. Around him the blessings fall on his elders, wife, children, grandchildren, community and friends. Quietly, to myself, I give thanks for the public process, insofar as it works.

◆   ◆   ◆

On October 21 and 22, the Water Board resumes its hearing on BHP's licence application. Since the last public hearing, the Water Board's Technical Advisory Committee (TAC) has worked through BHP's application for two full days, on October 8 and 9. Most of us working for Akaitcho Treaty 8 were otherwise engaged on those days with the financial and environmental agreements, so we missed the briefing and the questions from government specialists in hydrology, aquatic environments, fisheries and so on. We do, however, have on the record the written questions that intervenors submitted to the Water Board plus BHP's answers. The paper record is piling up like waste rock. The unknowns deepen like a kimberlite pipe being mined. It is challenging to understand the project and its many implications, simply to grasp what we know and what we do not.

Today we gather in the assembly room of Northern United Place, a multipurpose ten-storey building that demarcates Yellowknife's small downtown from its hinterlands. This same room is used for church services, baptisms, weddings, funerals. The old Yellowknife Film Society used to show classic movies here. As I walk in, I remember seeing Charlton Heston projected on the tall white wall. He played a British military commander dying at the hands of the locals in *Khartoum.* Surely this is as good a story of the colonized exacting revenge as has ever been told.

The board members are seated high above the public on the dais. The public sits in the folded chairs normally filled with church goers, looking up in supplication, it seems. The room is as dim as a tomb, the atmosphere heavy. There are even more professional strangers here than there were at the last hearing, since the board has appointed its own independent experts to provide technical advice.

After board chairman Gordon Wray opens the hearing, the first speakers are three Dogrib elders, old men whose faces are as beautiful as their eloquent history of the land. Joe Mackenzie, Joe Migwi and Alexis Arrowmaker speak in detail about the land of Lac de Gras and what it has meant, and means, to the Dogrib people.

Joe Mackenzie: "I also know that there are not going to be jobs available for every person in our area. That is why our way of life has to be passed on to our kids . . . That is why I am pleading to you to make sure you take care of this land and also this water. The animals have to rely on the land and water as well . . . I want you to make sure that you do not contaminate or pollute the environment and the water as well."

Joe Migwi: "[The caribou] used to have their migration in the area of the Lac de Gras, so I am sure that they are going to change their route. I want that monitored . . . We are not only talking about the caribou migration, but other animals and fish. Even if I was given a job, I would walk on the land and monitor everything that is going on around that mine site. We have to also monitor the transporting of the oils on the winter roads in case there are any spills."

Alexis Arrowmaker: "What is going to happen to the land after [the mining companies] are finished with it? That land will be considered dead. There may be regrowth on the land, but still underneath the land will be dead . . . I am sure this is not the first diamond mine at all and we know the destruction that is going to happen on the land . . . What is going to happen to our people? What is going to happen if the migration route is changed? How are we going to survive? Our livelihood will be gone."

 No questions are asked of the elders.

After they speak, we take a brief coffee break. It is hardly long enough for me to shift world views from the elders to the Dogribs' technical experts.

Chris Mills, a professional engineer, addresses the board. He describes himself as having a rather specialized practice in "acid-rock drainage, water chemistry, and metal transport and aqueous solutions in the mining environment." Mills speaks with the speed and passion of a man possessed by his work. He is perfectly lucid on the uncertainty he has been asked to examine, the possible side-effects of removing rock to create the mine.

"The basic concept of acid-rock draining test work is that if you disturb the land, you test to see what the consequences of perturbation of the land are. Mining is considered to be a temporary use of the land in Canada, and restoration to its former self is not expected but mandatory in the mining industry in this day and age. Those items that would be disturbed by the Lac de Gras operation fall into four categories, which are common to all other projects:

1. overburden: the material that is removed prior to mining;
2. waste rock: the material that is removed as part of mining and left behind when the diamonds are removed (waste rock is usually stored on the surface);
3. the pit walls: the faces of rock that are exposed as a result of mining;
4. the tailings: the waste product from the ore-milling process, which in this case would be the kimberlites after the recovery of diamonds."

Even to the non-miner, he has made the maze of BHP's proposed mine elegantly straightforward. He continues, cautioning the board about the simple, direct connections between mine disturbance and lack of knowledge about the effects. Mills finds BHP's preparatory work "fundamentally deficient in six areas." First, BHP does not know enough about the minerals in the rocks it will move, therefore the company does not know the potential for acid to drain from the disturbed rocks to surrounding water and land. Second, BHP has not done any research on the possibility for acid-rock drainage from two of the kimberlite pipes it proposes to mine, the Fox and Misery pits. Third, the lack of data about undisturbed kimberlite compared to crushed and stored kimberlite makes it difficult, if not impossible, to understand the potential for acid-rock drainage. Fourth, the company's planning for neutralizing any acid drainage is inadequate. The final two deficiencies concern uncertainties about clay particles in drainage: How will the clay aggregate? What sediments will form in waters draining the mine operation? Without this knowledge, BHP cannot safely predict the quality of the water it will eventually discharge from its operating areas and water-holding ponds back into Lac de Gras and the Coppermine River drainage.

I am reassured when Mills tells us: "Some of you may unknowingly have some familiarity with smectites." Talc, as in talcum powder, and vermiculite, used for kitty litter, are cleansing agents, or smectites. These, along with naturally occurring smectites at the mine site, neutralize acid. In other words, there may be hope for maintaining a proper balance of acid and alkali in the disturbed area. Kindly, Mills has attached a layman's guide to acid-rock drainage, its meaning, chemistry, behaviour and treatment, to his written submission for the board.

It isn't even 11 A.M. and already one expert has revealed six technical deficiencies *in one area of concern*—acid drainage from the mine tailings. In our seats, the Treaty 8 environmental agreement negotiators, Christina Ishoj and Chris Lemon, and I share silent headshakes. What *did* BHP learn about its claim block before filing its Environmental Impact Statement?

After Mills's presentation, Dogrib legal counsel Arthur Pape asks him, "If this application were to go to other regulatory jurisdictions in Canada and North America, how would it be received?"

Mills answers: "I think that a project that is submitted without proper tailings evaluation might possibly be rejected . . . Certainly if one went to the permitting agencies and said, 'I have a gold deposit and all I am going to remove is a few grams of gold and I am not going to bother sampling the tailings, when the laughter stopped you would have an awful lot of work on your hands." Mills recommends that much of this work should be done within six to twelve months to "close some loopholes and close the knowledge gaps that currently exist."

Despite Chairman Wray's early admonition that we avoid both the language and behavior of a court, this hearing unfolds something in the manner of a trial. Wray is both judge and chair—he keeps tight control of the proceedings and does not suffer fools or tangents gladly. The board members sit as a jury, whose verdict we will not hear for some time. The defendant, however, changes from time to time.

Back on September 9 and 10, at the first round of Water Board hearings, BHP took the most criticism and "cross-examination," although Wray moderated all questions. Today, the accused, or at least the most likely to be at fault, are the federal government departments that regulate mining. These include the Department of Indian and Northern

Affairs, which is like Big Brother in the North, insidiously involved everywhere. The Department of Fisheries and Oceans is here, its lead speaker a manager from Winnipeg. The Department of Environment is also present and accounted for. As each party with an interest in the mine takes its turn before the Water Board, it is questioned by other intervenors. Wray questions everyone.

The topics flow in three streams: technical unknowns, procedures for regulating BHP, and consequences BHP's mine has had, and will have, on the First Nation relationship with the Crown. All through this day and evening and through the next day, these streams sometimes flow together, sometimes apart, and following them is every bit as confusing as navigating the myriad channels of the Slave River Delta. Still, this gathering of experts and intervenors sees questions and conflicts more clearly articulated than they were six weeks ago. This may be progress, but moment by moment, it is easy to get lost.

After Chris Mills's detailed primer on acid-rock drainage, consultant Tony Pearse summarizes three reports that the Dogribs have tabled with the board. Each one highlights a different technical issue. The first states that BHP's current studies on aquatic life are insufficient. No one really knows what is going on in the lakes the mine will affect, except that the lakes "will not be recovered within the thirty-year time frame proposed." For change on the claim block to be monitored as the mine is built and operated, we need to know something about the existing ecosystem, nutrient cycles, oxygen depletion and the makeup of water at different depths within each of the different lakes. At this latitude, the tiniest disturbance will affect already small populations.

A second submission reveals the lack of information about the frozen-core dams and the network of tailings ponds that will contain mining effluent. Some of the sites for the dams have been selected from *air photos*. In other words, BHP's construction planners have not even conducted actual site investigations. The report's conclusion reads, "The project is at its conceptual stage and, as indicated by the titles of the available reports, the design is in the preliminary phase. While the presented concepts appear to be technically sound, the lack of solid backup data and the extent of assumptions used, make some performance predictions questionable. The available database makes some of the closure scenarios uncertain." Assumptions. Scenarios. Conceptual. Preliminary. Lack of solid backup data. (What about solid primary data?) It is becoming clear to me, at least, that the mine is an experiment in progress.

The third report concerns BHP's plan for abandonment and restoration, that is, what the company will do with the landscape and waters when it has taken everything it wants and is ready to leave. This is the plan Jim Excell spoke of so proudly in Łutsëlk'é. The report states: "In general, the reclamation program lacks sufficient detail. Specifically, integrated mine operations and reclamation planning is absent and the reclamation strategy is poorly developed. The information that is presented lacks sufficient details and does not integrate adequately either the baseline data that were collected or general ecological concepts." The report also states, "In my experience, it is very difficult to undertake progressive reclamation when mine production equipment and operators are given the task of recontouring and site preparation." In other words, mining truck drivers don't make good landscapers without reorientation and training. Assuming, of course, that the landscape architect knows what to plant and where to water and has an adequate budget.

Before lunch, we also hear from fisheries expert Dr. Peter McCart. He reiterates points he made originally before the environmental assessment review panel nearly a year ago. Essentially, he says, the mine will cause major losses of habitat. He also notes that "this is a new kind of mining in the Northwest Territories . . . There is no useful model for predicting what complex impacts might occur with respect to habitat and the fish that depend on those habitats."

McCart recommends five related research efforts to improve the current "fuzzy" basis that we have for predicting fish habitat loss and calculating compensation for it. He is optimistic that these studies can go ahead while the mine is under construction and during its early years of operation. One study needs to describe the most basic fish biology, "their migration patterns, habitat preferences, and those habitat preferences which might limit their production." Other studies should experiment with "enhancing" fish habitat to increase fish populations near places where the population is destroyed by the mine. All of the studies should monitor what actually happens to water and fish at the mine site.

McCart introduces the problem of "acid pulses" in Arctic waters. These occur naturally, but may be exacerbated by the explosives to be used at the mine. Ammonium-nitrate fuel-oil explosives are a source of nitric acid that may accumulate in the snowpack. As the snow melts in the spring, the acids travel into water sources, causing peaks in acid levels that can kill fish. McCart explains that monthly stream monitoring can miss acid pulses entirely because they build up and decrease over a few days. When the ice breaks up on the lakes and rivers, BHP or its regulators will need to monitor streams every day.

He suggests routine monitoring for aluminum too, since his studies indicate that it looks as if there are appreciable quantities in the water. "Aluminum concentrates itself in fish gills," he reminds us, "and suffocates the fish."

McCart concludes by saying that a difficulty within BHP's environmental impact assessment (EIA) and the transcripts of the Technical Advisory Committee meeting is that "there is very little reference to the fish that might be affected and their biology . . . I think that there has to be a greater consideration of what fish are going to be in the waters around the mine and what they are going to be doing at the time that—for example—you release the water from Cell E of the Long Lake

Tailings Pond . . . This water will be going down a stream in the spring of the year . . . The fish that is most likely to be heavily involved in streams . . . is the grayling. It enters these streams early to spawn . . . as the water starts to flow. It moves upstream even while there is still ice in the stream. It is very common to see grayling skittering up over the surface of the ice where water is flowing over the surface . . . to be there when the temperatures reach the appropriate level."

At his words, my body remembers the thud of a fish I once tripped over on a brilliant spring day in the Arctic. I was leaping from rock to rock in a spring-swollen river, avoiding ice that looked stable but might give way at any moment. The midday sun and its reflection off ice near-ly blinded me. Then my big SnowPac boot hit the head of a fish that emerged just as my foot swung over its pool. I don't know if it or I was more surprised. But I recovered faster than the fish. I lifted its stunned, supple body from the frigid water and took it on to our camp. We ate it for lunch.

McCart says the fish need water about eight degrees Celsius to spawn. One of BHP's plans for draining effluent from Cell E means that water just below the ice cover will drain into the water the grayling navigate to spawn. Water just under the ice is the coldest, McCart states.

"So if you take the clear water immediately under the ice, you are taking very, very cold water, probably zero to one degree Celsius, possibly two degrees Celsius. Somebody has to think about what that means to the spawning success of fish. These fish are not going to start spawning until it reaches about eight degrees Celsius. If you continue to pump very cold water downstream during the period when they would normally be spawning, it might have some considerable effect on the success of their reproduction . . . There has to be more consideration of those kinds of things than I see in the deliberations of the Technical Advisory Committee or in the EIA itself."

We are less than four hours into the hearing. Our group eats lunch in the small meeting room off the pretentious L'atitudes Restaurant at the Yellowknife Inn. L'atitudes replaced the old Miner's Mess, where the entire town used to gather every morning before work to exchange information as a community instead of a bureaucracy. But we've grown up now. L'atitudes has very big plates and very fussy food. I watch the stock market quotes stream by in red lights along the meeting room wall. I wonder how many lakes and rivers, how many fish, how much acid and aluminum lie behind those numbers.

11. *Third Rapids*

◆ ◆ ◆

In a hundred or two hundred years no one will give a rip how many diamond rings were dug out of the ground at Koala, or how many electric dishwashers or remote-control channel changers the people of the North were able to purchase with the profits generated. What will be obvious by then is whether or not Canada had the foresight to preserve intact some shred of the immensity, purity and wildness that is here in the Far North.

—Dave Olesen of Reliance, NWT, in presentation to
environmental assessment review panel

AFTER lunch the dim hearing room is somnolent. Wray moderates a scintillating debate between the Dogribs' expert Chris Mills and BHP's engineer Don Hayley on the chemistry of waste rock dumps and mining pit walls. My mind wanders to the Big Pipe at Kimberley and to the chemistry of relations between blacks and whites in South Africa. Wray brings me back to mining pipes on the Barrens with "Thank you, gentlemen. Shall we continue—in English please?"

Legal counsel Arthur Pape concludes the Dogribs' intervention by answering a question from Alan Denroche, legal counsel to the Water Board, about how the Northwest Territories Water Act provides for compensation in cases where loss of water use affects people:

"Aboriginal peoples are a recognized entity in Canadian constitutional law . . . Aboriginal peoples are comprised of individuals who share a collective history in connection to land and other cultural and historical attributes. So there is no question in our mind, that section 14(4) applies to groups of individual persons as well as individuals." The distinction between individual and group compensation is significant in law. In 1993, for its decision on the Taltson case, the Water Board sought a legal opinion on whether or not compensation normally awarded to individuals could be extended to groups such as the First Nations. The legal opinion was favourable for the First Nations, but it has not yet been tested in application. Pape reminds the board of this decision.

The rest of the afternoon belongs to the Yellowknives chiefs and elders. Łutsëlk'é elders were due on the noon plane, but it is running several hours late. The elders once again bring their overriding concerns to this forum: Dene title to the land and Dene responsibility for keeping the land alive.

At the request of elder Judy Charlo, our intervention begins with her prayer in Dene yati. As is customary, the prayer is neither translated nor recorded. Chief Sangris also speaks briefly, in Dene yati, about completing the Treaty 8 land entitlement. He states, "Whose land are you on? In the back of our mind, you are in Akaitcho Territory."

When Fred Sangris, the young man responsible for the Yellowknives' Land and Environment Committee, addresses the hearing he reiterates this claim to the land as he eloquently shares the stories of his great-grandfather, who was born at Bloody Falls on the Coppermine River.

"Ever since they found the diamonds," he says, "a lot of people—everyone is claiming that area, even the Metis people. I wonder, why they are doing this? I think we should tell the truth about that. We can't just make up stories. We have to tell the truth about who really owns that area."

After Fred has spoken, elder Judy Charlo recalls the peace treaty between Chiefs Akaitcho and Edzo that settled the Chipewyan and Dogrib land boundaries: "When we talk about Akaitcho, he was a Chipewyan leader and he used to live around this area. Around that time Edzo and Akaitcho made peace, and KeTe Whii used to be the person that was in the middle and made them have peace between these two regions. They used to have war between these two tribes [the Dogribs on one side and the Dëne súłiné and Yellowknives on the other], and KeTe Whii was the one that made peace with the two tribes. My grandfather used to tell me stories about that. We say the Dogrib people hardly used to go out on the Barren Lands because they used to be scared of the Chipewyan people. So they lived below the treeline a lot. That is what they used to say. Since that time, the Chipewyan live in [the Barren Lands]. Ever since then, we [the Yellowknives] have been living among the Chipewyan people, the people that live on the Great Slave Lake here. All around this whole lake, Great Slave Lake used to be all Chipewyan people . . . even my great-grandmother used to talk about the Lac de Gras area."

Elder Joe Martin tells the story of the Dene woman who found the gold that led to Giant Mine right here at Yellowknife: "That rock she took from the Giant Mine area, and the gold was on a windowsill and the prospectors came and saw that rock and asked, 'Where did you get that?' The old lady told them that if she asked them for something and they gave it to her, she would tell them where she got the rock. She said, 'Look at my stovepipe. There is holes in my stovepipe and it is held together by wires. If you give me three stovepipes, I will tell you where I found this gold.' She went to the Giant Mine area with the boat and she told the prospectors that this was the area that she got the rock from and she left them there. Since that day, they have been taking gold out of the mine, out of the land. It is like that old lady has given millions and millions of dollars away just for three stovepipes."

Chief Bill Erasmus, a Yellowknives Dene who is also head of the

Dene National Office in Yellowknife, tells the legal history of aboriginal title to Dene traditional lands. He reviews the 1973 judgement in *Paulette v. The Crown*, in which sixteen Dene chiefs claimed that an interest in their traditional lands could be protected through a caveat under the Northwest Territories Land Titles Act. As well as recognizing this interest and the land protection it sustained, the judgement stated "that notwithstanding the language of the two treaties there is sufficient doubt on the facts that aboriginal title was extinguished that such claim for title should be permitted to be put forward by the caveators."

Erasmus also gives members of the board copies of the results from the Dene land use studies. When the Yellowknives realized that the mines were going to go ahead with or without settling the land question, they did an inventory of how people in Dettah, Ndilo and Łutsëlk'é use the land, and the caribou and fish it supports. He talks the board through these findings now.

But it is Chief Beaulieu who dominates the afternoon. Darrell is not a big man. He is on the young side of middle age. He speaks in quiet, measured tones, almost gently as he begins. Yet he commands respect. He wears a business shirt without a tie, his collar open and his sleeves rolled back. His hands are clasped on the table in front of him as he leans toward the microphone. Behind his quietude is an intensity, an iron will in a velvet voice. He speaks for a long time, his discourse building one small point at a time. He says he wants to place the diamond mine in the context of northern development and his people. He says that mining development is not new.

"The primary reason that treaties were negotiated—particularly in our territory here and further north in the Treaty 11 territory—is that there was mining exploration. There was a boom in 1896, 1897, 1898— there was a rush to the Yukon for gold . . . basically that is what initiated our discussions on treaty. The intention of that treaty from the government was to be able to clear the way for development. As indicated earlier by Chief Bill Erasmus, the land question and those treaties are still a point of discussion.

"But in 1896–97 there was a boom, and it seems like in 1996 there is another boom. Now that boom came and went and this boom will, as booms do. It will end. A little about what that boom did here besides initiate those discussions on the treaty. Our people prior to that were able to hunt, trap and fish anywhere on what they know as their traditional territory. In 1916 the Migratory Birds Convention was enabled [which restricted Dene take of waterfowl]. In 1928, there was a major epidemic that wiped out a majority of the First Nations in this territory. The Dene of this territory had consistently talked to the federal government . . . to relay their concerns about the legislation that was being enabled without their consent . . .

"Under Canadian law, Dene, or what is known as Indians, were not human beings until 1960. They were not considered capable of thinking and voting and deciding what they could do on their land or who could represent them in the House of Parliament. That is the context of how Dene have been treated over the last hundred years.

"The Dene were a hunting and gathering society. In some respects, they still are, but due to the impacts that have been here and developing more and more, that way of life has been disappearing. We are being forced into the information age. From hunting and gathering into the information age in less than thirty years, which took the Europeans five hundred years to do, going through the agricultural sector, the industrial sector and finally into the information age . . .

"In the application to the Water Board, it asks: 'Is there going to be any impacts on Native people? Was there any interest that the Native people had in that territory?' The answer [from DIAND regulators] was no. I think that has to be clarified. In 1966 the Government of Canada publication on treaties in Canada indicated that that particular area [Lac de Gras] was unceded Indian Territory, very clearly.

"A lot of our discussion in the community is about struggle and how the Dene have survived. Surviving the colonialism and persevering through the impacts of development . . . Is the board capable of taking the responsibility for anything that could happen in the future when there are no plans? If you are going to consider a water licence without any plans in place, are you prepared to take the responsibility? Or are you going to make the decision and later go on to retire in Kelowna while the Dene people have to live with the decision that this board makes or the recommendations that the Technical Advisory Committee makes to the board? Are you going to live and die here? Do you not think that the original people that are born, that live here and that are going to die here should have the decision-making capacity to be able to decide how this land is going to be taken care of?"

Chief Beaulieu reminds the board that one reason for extending the hearing was the elders' statement that the Lac de Gras drainage connects with lakes that drain into Great Slave Lake. He quotes the late elder Joe Charlo, who said, "The land is like our bank, it is like our fridge. Every time we are hungry we can go out and make a withdrawal. If you are cold, if you are tired. The land provided for the Dene for thousands of years, not for twenty-five years."

The chief continues, "Over the last month—in August there was no discussion on environmental agreements, there was no discussion on impact and benefit agreements, there was no discussion on protected areas strategy—in a matter of three and one-half to four weeks, all of those agreements all of a sudden became the focal point besides the Water Board hearings. Since September when the Water Board hearing was held, all these other processes took the time and energy of our resources here, took all the time . . .

"There is information—a lot of technical stuff that we do not know how to deal with. We tried to bring in some technicians. I think over the last few years we have had about fifteen thousand dollars for the environmental assessment review process to bring in our technicians, maybe fifteen thousand dollars for this process here. So over the last couple of years not much—thirty thousand dollars. I would like to know what the department has spent, in technicians or their other various departments in the government, on the technical data and trying to interpret what is happening out there and how do they make those interpretations? What are they based on when you are talking about air quality? There is no air quality legislation in the Northwest Territories—absolutely none . . .

"What we experience here is the dust from the tailings at Giant Mine which blows up across the lake. As a matter of fact about two and one-half weeks ago . . . it was like hitting a big thick wall. You will probably remember the day, it was September 29 or 30th, very, very strong winds. It was like hitting a thick wall and that is all dust coming directly off the tailings. How do you monitor that? How do you keep that under wraps? . . .

"There are concerns about the impacts of the lake dewatering and the diversion channel. As a matter of fact . . . what type of licence do you need to build a diversion channel? I think that is a question that should be answered here. What kind of licence do you need to build an airstrip?"

(BHP has already built an airstrip and part of what they call the Panda Diversion Channel, to drain the lake on top of what they call the Panda Pipe. Many observers have wondered how the company managed to build those while working under land use permits for "exploration" as opposed to development. BHP had applied for, and received from DIAND, amendments to its exploration permits for the airstrip and water diversion channel.)

"In this project there are five economic pipes identified," Chief Beaulieu states. "The last I heard, there were about ninety pipes but we don't know if they are economic or not. What if they are economic?

What if there is an amendment requested to this licence? What is your process for amendments? We have certainly found out what the process for amendments is for land use permits within the department. There is no process . . .

"I said earlier that if these things were clear and concise and the certainty was there on the land, that proponents such as BHP would not have to go through this—all these different agreements, all these different hearings, all these different things . . . Each First Nation across Canada has gone through this for over a hundred years. BHP has just been here for the last five years. We have gone through that and we continue to go through that, and the department is sitting back here. They are listening to this and they have listened to this for the last thirty years here in the Northwest Territories and they continue to listen. I think listening is the wrong word—I think they hear us, that's it. They are not listening, they just hear us . . .

"This board, the EARP panel, the minister, the prime minister, the media—all know that this project affects people. More importantly, it affects the Yellowknives Dene First Nation . . . The heaviest effect of any development in the North Slave or Akaitcho Territory, the heaviest impact is alway on the Yellowknives Dene First Nation, always. Not on the four communities over there, not on the other communities, not on the southern communities, not on the southern provinces. Chief Don Balsillie was very clear on that about Pine Point Mine when he indicated that the Queen got all the money from that, the government got royalties, the shareholders got their cash and the First Nations got the shaft."

◆   ◆   ◆

As Chief Beaulieu speaks, the restless room grows ever more still. Into the silence that holds when he stops talking, Wray finally speaks: "I think this would be an appropriate time to take our supper break."

We walk four blocks to a restaurant. When the server asks what I would like, I answer, "I'd like some Cell E effluent, please."

Chris Lemon, across from me, chimes in, "I'll have asbestos dust."

Then Christina Ishoj, "Aquatic habitat, please, with oxygen depletion on the side."

Others order crushed acid rock, smectites, even a defrosted ice-core dam, until we go completely around the table. The waiter, cheeky and on board, advertises the dessert special: diamonds in rough.

When our giddy laughter subsides, we talk quietly about the hearing, its tenor and likely outcomes. Everyone is of the opinion that BHP will get a Class A licence in time for mine construction to begin this winter. Chris Lemon feels that, because of the Dogribs' intervention and our own from the elders, the conditions attached to the licence will be suitably strict. Surely the potential acid-rock drainage will be closely monitored. The chiefs seem resigned to BHP's progress from exploration to production even though the Treaty 8 negotiations have not yet resumed.

Chief Lockhart and I take a few minutes to go over the material he has asked me to present at the hearing on behalf of Łutsëlk'é. He reminds me to emphasize his message to Minister Irwin that any licence issued must recognize aboriginal and treaty rights.

All too soon we are back at the hearing. Councillor and elder J.B. Rabesca has come in on the late plane from Łutsëlk'é. It is clear that, at seventy-four years old, he is worn out from the day. Still, he speaks cogently if briefly: "From Lac de Gras there is a river that flows and from there it goes all the way to Ptarmigan Lake. From there it flows into Artillery Lake and from there it goes down the Lockhart River and into the Great Slave Lake." Again, Łutsëlk'é puts on record that waterborne pollution from the mine may contaminate the sacred river.

It is my turn to speak. I present Łutsëlk'é's technical critique of BHP's research methods for assessing the environmental impacts of the mine. There is much I could comment on, but I confine my presentation to comparing the long time frame and thousands of observations that make up indigenous knowledge to the recent time frame and tiny sample of "scientific" data points that mines across the North represent. I note that we scientists and technicians actually know very little about the human and environmental consequences of diamond mining on the Barrens. I reiterate that lack of funding from the fiduciary and lack of time make it impossible for Łutsëlk'é to prepare adequately for this development.

On the question of the drainage from the Lac de Gras watershed, I try to show the scientists in the room how technical knowledge is at times as imprecise as their worst fears about the elders' knowledge. Łutsëlk'é had submitted written questions to BHP about the Lac de Gras drainage, but we received the company's answers only two days ago, by fax. The reply referred to maps that we did not receive. The only point I can argue is that BHP has interpolated the direction of water flow from large area maps that were drawn based on aerial photography. I remind every field scientist present how much room there is for error between such maps and "ground truth," or what we see when we walk on the land.

On behalf of Łutsëlk'é I recommend that, if a licence is issued, it be no longer than three to five years, with stringent requirements for more information to be provided during the first twelve months on the watershed question, addressed collaboratively with the elders; more population data on the fish; and more tailings data particularly relevant to the acid-rock problem. I request that aboriginal and treaty rights be recognized, and that financial security against damages to the land be given directly to the First Nations, rather than to the Crown. Lastly, on the First Nation's behalf, I request that First Nation members have priority in employment and training for environmental monitoring.

When I finish speaking, Wray directs questions to Akaitcho Treaty 8. He asks about the progress of our negotiations with BHP on impacts and benefits. We answer that the agreement is in the hands of the communities for review and ratification if they so choose. Alan Denroche repeats the question he asked the Dogribs regarding compensation for aboriginal groups. We answer that our position is the same: the First Nations, as groups of individuals with a shared interest in the resource, are eligible for compensation. A hydrologist from Indian and Northern Affairs asks elder J.B. Rabesca precisely where water flows south from Lac de Gras to the Great Slave Lake drainage. Chairman Wray answers that the board will specifically deal with that issue in its dealings with, and direction to, the Technical Advisory Committee.

The next presenters are from the Department of Fisheries and Oceans (DFO). The department bears two responsibilities: to regulate lake dewatering and to determine what compensation must be made for the lakes BHP will destroy. Compensation will take two forms: money that BHP will pay to the department and, if possible, habitat it will create to replace that which it destroys.

Every aboriginal speaker has already expressed concern that compensation will go to DFO, not to the people who lose use of the habitat and the fish it supports. This issue, like land entitlements, is a reef on which development in the North frequently founders. Yet the federal legislation for this practice remains unchanged. Jeff Stein, of DFO's Habitat Management Division, reports that BHP has already agreed to pay $1.5 million in compensation for lost aquatic habitat, between 1997 and 2001. DFO plans to form a committee that includes aboriginal people to consult on the best ways to use the dollars. Aboriginal communities will write proposals to apply for the money to enhance fish habitat near them.

I could cry in frustration. Haven't the Akaitcho Treaty 8 representatives just told the Water Board that the First Nations lack staff for these processes? Most First Nation employees work project to project—starting when a grant comes in, stopping when it runs out. Setting up another fund First Nations can apply to perpetuates the demand on First Nation administrators and financial staff to write proposals for small pots of money for short-term projects. The developer pays the Crown. The First Nations beg the Crown for bits of money. The system pays the Crown to keep holding the First Nations' purse strings.

The situation is no better when it comes to habitat replacement. DFO's Stein recognizes that "like-for-like" habitat replacement is not "technically feasible" for BHP's development, "for a number of reasons, most of which are unique to the Arctic environment." (Why, then, I wonder, are we letting BHP destroy this environment? Particularly when it is obvious that virtually no basic data about what will be destroyed have as yet been amassed.) The reasons cited include that no one has figured out how to replace whole lakes (really?). That even if artificial lakes are dug, they will not fill, since too little moisture falls in the Barren Lands and therefore precipitation evaporates too quickly for much accumulation. That although the natural lakes are likely supporting as much life as they ever will ("having not been previously disrupted"), the fish they produce amounts only to a few kilograms a year. Lastly, that "the development area is remote from communities that could access potential fisheries."

I wonder if Stein has been listening to the aboriginal people. The development area is remote, perhaps, if your view of the land is confined to what you can see from your cubicle on the fourth floor of the Precambrian Building.

BHP's approach to lake dewatering is even more obscure. According to Julie Dahl, Arctic habitat coordinator for DFO, "Although lake dewatering is a seemingly straightforward activity, it does involve a complex of physical and biological factors. We, DFO, have yet to see the hydrological, physical and biological characteristics of those streams to be inundated directly with the dewatering activities. DFO is requesting that BHP submit the details . . . including the timing and the duration of dewatering activities—how the natural flows will be approximated and how the dewatering will be monitored for flow rates and for any impacts on the stream habitat and the stream spawners."

Why, I wonder, are all of the human resources packed into this room—and all of the money to pay us—being spent on BHP's application for a water licence, when the company hasn't yet provided the bare minimum of information we need to make an informed decision?

Furthermore, in Stein's words, "In addition to altering, disrupting or destroying stream habitats, the BHP diamonds project will impact directly on twelve lakes within the claims block. Six lakes must be dewatered to gain access to and exploit the underlying kimberlite pipes; one is to be dewatered to access granular resources for construction; four will be filled by process plant tails; and one will be covered by a waste rock dump." Despite all doubts, however, DFO and BHP have already reached a fish habitat compensation agreement. There was not, nor will there be, any public comment on the agreement. Although the company is willing to release the document to the intervenors, DFO (our public government) is not. We do know the agreement—which includes the $1.5 million BHP will pay to DFO—compensates only for lost habitat, not dead fish.

Arthur Pape, legal counsel for the Dogribs, questions the departmental representative about BHP's projects to enhance fish habitat in the artificial diversion channel that is already under construction. Stein answers: "I guess the answer to the question is no, *we have not done any in-depth study that we can rely on* . . . There are no real knowns with what we are dealing with up here and . . . a certain amount of this—I will grant you—is trial and error" (italics added).

Further questioning reveals that neither the mining company nor the department counted the fish or measured the habitat before they agreed to amounts and procedures for compensation. To set compensation, DFO relied on BHP's maps of habitat it would destroy.

At 9:35, Dr. Ian Gilchrist of the Water Board poses the last question of the night. He is concerned that genetic diversity will be reduced among the fish populations on the Barren Lands. He asks DFO's Stein: "You are talking about closing out ten lakes or something like that. Does DFO have any intent to salvage representative populations from the lakes that will lose their fish?"

Stein: "No, we don't."

Gilchrist: "Has DFO looked at other living organisms in these lakes, or has it any intent to look at things other than fish in the dozen lakes that will be lost?"

Stein: "No, sir, we do not."

Well. So much for that. His flat, unapologetic, terminal response quashes what small faith I had in the federal environmentalists.

12. *"I Don't Speak for the Minister"*

◆   ◆   ◆

*Well, maybe it's not dead yet, merely ill, on its last legs,
about to kick the proverbial bureaucratic can, suffering
from chronic archaism and terminal outdatedness. I am,
of course, referring to the soon-to-be-late Department of
Indian Affairs. I would say, "Let us observe a moment
of silence," but I hear people out on the reserves cheering
much too loudly. No more forms to fill out or offices to
visit, or people to tell you what you can and can't do,
or who is a Native and who isn't.*

—Drew Hayden Taylor, *Funny, You Don't Look Like One:
Observations of a Blue-Eyed Ojibway*

At 9 A.M. the next morning, 75 days after
Irwin set his deadline, the Water Board hearing continues. The
Department of Indian Affairs and Northern Development (DIAND) has
replaced Fisheries and Oceans (DFO) at the intervenors' table. If not for
that change, it is as if none of us went home or to hotels for the night.
Facing the Water Board is Lorne Tricoteux, long-time assistant regional
director. To northerners who know DIAND, "long-time" and "assistant"
are the kiss of death. Tricoteux is accompanied by eight staff—a ninth,
an expert on mine environment neutral drainage, had to leave last night
for Albania. This seems a destination even more desperate than communities such as Łutsëlk'é, the "isolated posts" where DIAND frequently

sends its out-of-favour civil servants. Tricoteux's presentation is vintage bureaucrat. If I didn't know better, I could almost believe him when he states (halfway through what turns out to be an hour-long presentation), "All our work to date indicates that not only is this project attractive to the Northwest Territories and the rest of Canada in terms of its potential economic and fiscal benefits, but also that any adverse environmental effects are mitigable." He reviews everything the department has done to aid and abet Broken Hill Proprietary's movement through the regulatory process toward diamond production. He emphasizes that Canada wants to ensure "the BHP project meets sustainable-development objectives." He doesn't specify what these are or who agreed upon them. He encourages the Water Board "to fully exercise its mandate" to deal with the "important issues" of the security BHP will provide against damages from the mine: an acceptable acid-rock drainage management plan, a comprehensive frozen-core dam monitoring plan, spill contingency plans and effluent discharge limits . . ." He details the numerous "guidelines" Canada has presented to the mining company that pertain to the "important issues." Tricoteux drones on, answering the written questions that other intervenors submitted to DIAND through the Water Board since the first public hearing on September 9.

I listen intently as Tricoteux explains the Crown's fiduciary obligations to the First Nations: "DIAND's fiduciary responsibilities are characterized in the Supreme Court of Canada's *Sparrow* decision, as it relates to regulatory activities that may infringe on aboriginal and treaty rights. As we stated in our written response to this question, the key ingredient to meeting the Crown's fiduciary obligation is consultation." He describes "consultation" on BHP's application over the preceding months through "a variety of calls for comment." He says that "government has gone well beyond mere compliance with its fiduciary guidelines" by (among other things) "providing financial support to aboriginal groups for negotiation of impact and benefit agreements and involvement in environmental agreement negotiations and for preparing for and participating in regulatory processes including these hearings."

I am sitting with Christina Ishoj of the Yellowknives Dene environmental staff and Akaitcho Treaty 8 legal counsel Chris Lemon. Christina and Fred Sangris write the requests for funding to DIAND for the Yellowknives Dene response to development. Lucy Sanderson and I do the requests for Łutsëlk'é. Christina and I glance at each other, wondering what financial support Tricoteux is referring to. I whisper to her, "Didn't Darrell say yesterday that DIAND noted 'no land claims concerns' on its evaluation of BHP's application? Didn't he say you'd had maybe an hour of back-and-forth communication with BHP?" We both shrug in response to Chris Lemon's raised eyebrows, then all three of us go back to listening.

Tricoteux continues with a description of what the department is doing to prepare for the cumulative effects of many diamond operations on the Barren Lands. He cites an internal audit of the department that concluded "the NWT region is managing its land and water activities related to mining in an effective and compliant manner." (Complying with whom, I wonder—international mining conglomerates?)

On DIAND's preparedness for diamond mining, Tricoteux intones, "Once BHP's final approvals are in place, and the terms and conditions of these regulatory instruments are known, thereby defining our inspection requirement, we will have until the fall of 1997–98, when the major necessary construction begins, to make sure we have the major necessary resources in place." In other words, to prepare for the increase in consultation, site inspections and environmental monitoring that BHP's operation will require, the department is, well, *waiting*.

BHP's plan calls for mine production by fall 1998. Does DIAND intend to wait until production to monitor? What about the construction phase? Tricoteux states, "Our inspection standard for construction activities is biweekly inspections, but we will do what is necessary to properly monitor this project." What about the loads of construction materials already being assembled to go up the ice road this winter, subject, of course, to approval of BHP's licences?

After Tricoteux's presentation, Wray leads the questioning. "Yesterday when we heard from the Yellowknives and from the Łutsëlk'é, the Yellowknives indicated that they had received only thirty thousand dollars to participate in the review of the technical data as well as the regulatory hearings. As you know, earlier on in September there was a request by these same groups to postpone this hearing because of a lack of funding. Then last night on behalf the Łutsëlk'é, Dr. Ellen Bielawski said, and I hope I got the quote here, said Treaty 8 has been sadly under-represented and under-resourced by its fiduciary, DIAND. Could you comment on those observations and, perhaps, for the board's information, tell us exactly how much funding was given to the aboriginal First Nations for this process?"

Tricoteux agrees to provide specific details on funding in writing, as long as the Yellowknives and Łutsëlk'é agree.

Wray continues, "In the interim, would you be prepared to tell us, at least a rough total figure as opposed to specifics per group, in general, how much in total the department has spent to date?"

Even sitting several rows behind him, I can see in Tricoteux's back that he wishes he were in Albania, or at least Alberta. He replies: "I am trying to do some quick math. The difficulty that I have here is that funding has been provided for a number of aspects of what we generally refer to as 'resource development and capacity' to deal with those including, as an example, funding that we provide under the Community Resources Management Program . . . The number is substantially higher than the number that I believe was referred to the board yesterday, but in all fairness to everyone I would want to make sure that we are clear on the details so I would prefer to table this information, with their permission, with you."

Christina catches my eye. We struggle to stifle our laughter as Tricoteux avoids the question. The funding Tricoteux mentions is small change. It pays stipends for Land and Environment Committee members to meet in the communities so they can discuss every land use application that comes through on a First Nation's traditional land. These applications will grow in quantity and complexity as diamond hunger grows. The standard funding is sometimes enough to pay the wages of part-time clerical help. The larger amounts pay for community improvement projects, such as cleaning up abandoned fish camps. The First Nations usually have to apply to DIAND for specific, small pots of money for each project. Scientific experts, much less legal counsel, are way beyond the scope of this piecemeal funding.

I could kick myself for not having presented exact figures yesterday. But Lucy and our First Nation administrator hadn't found time to summarize exactly which bits of money we have cobbled together for our staff, elders and Land and Environment Committee members to "consult" and negotiate in the seventy-five days since the minister set his deadline. This is just another instance of the First Nations being overwhelmed by the speed and scale of this development.

Chris Lemon thanks Wray for "raising the funding issue." He assents, for Akaitcho Treaty 8, to having DIAND's financial allocations put on record. But he clarifies, "I am not talking about the other programs, the Community Resource Management Programs or any other funding that goes to the First Nations. We just want to know what was provided for participation in the Water Board hearings, and I think it would be useful to know what was provided to other aboriginal groups as well, so that the whole consultation process is transparent for the board."

Wray moves on to questioning about the draft environmental agreement. Tricoteux described it as an important part of DIAND's preparedness for diamond mining. Now Wrays asks, "Could you please tell me, first of all, why you felt it necessary to draft this type of agreement?"

Tricoteux defers to Chris Cuddy, chief of water resources in DIAND, who replies, "I believe the direction to prepare the agreement came from Minister Irwin . . . It really was to complement the regulatory process not to replace the regulatory process."

Wray counters, "Is this a one-off or is this going to become standard procedure for any new development in the Northwest Territories?"

Tricoteux answers, "I guess at this point in time I would have to say that it is a one-off."

Wray presses further, "Perhaps your legal advisor will have to answer this one, but I wonder, under what statutory or legislative authority has this agreement been enacted?"

Again Tricoteux defers to Cuddy, who explains, "The agreement will be a contract between the Crown and BHP."

Wray is concerned that the environmental agreement is solely DIAND's creature. He clarifies, "When we heard the presentation by Mr. Stein on behalf of Department of Fisheries and Oceans yesterday, it was obvious that they had only just become aware that this agreement was in place, and that really, they had not taken a look at it from the point of view of the Fisheries Compensation Plan . . ."

Tricoteux speaks about "interdepartmental consultation" but asks Cuddy to jump in because "one of the difficulties we would be facing here is the fact that DFO legislation is in fact distinct and separate and there may be some difficulty in coordinating some of these aspects." He pauses for a moment then turns to his colleague, saying, "Chris, did I get us into trouble?"

Cuddy speaks about "interdepartmental consultation on some drafts" but notes that the negotiations were "fairly fast moving."

Once again, haste. We are speeding, rushing to get these diamonds out of the ground. Even within the Crown bureaucracy, people seem to have been inadequately consulted and unprepared. At least, I think, they get paid for being so, while the Akaitcho Treaty 8 First Nations do not.

Wray probes deeper into the turbid depths of regulatory overlaps. Both financial security against mining damage and a company's reclamation plan are instruments the Water Board usually uses to ensure that a company complies with its licence. The usual reclamation plan also includes requirements set through land use permits. The first-time environmental agreement for BHP also requires a reclamation plan. He says, "My question is about coordination . . . The way I read this environmental agreement, it is the Water Board Reclamation Plan that takes precedence. If that is the case, then where does that leave the company as obviously, then, it is in breach of contract?"

Cuddy attempts an answer: "I am not sure that one would actually take legal precedent over the other, specifically in the case of reclamation plans—which is very much the way it is today."

Wray, holding his fierce energy in check behind his microphone, declares, "You have lost us . . ."

They've certainly lost me. I speak and read English and bureaucratese. I'm someone educated in science. I can even manage pidgin-legalese. Yet DIAND argues that it has met the legal requirement for consultations with the First Nations. DIAND argues that it has done this through hit-or-miss funding to the Land and Environment Committees, which are made up of hunters and trappers, many of whom don't even speak, much less read English. The question of what regulatory instrument—the water licence, a land use permit or the environmental agreement—will take precedence remains unresolved.

Wray moves on, saying, "I will have to think about that one." He asks BHP if it has questions for DIAND. They don't (and why should they?). It is obvious, I think, that DIAND is too confused to regulate or monitor the company effectively. BHP is just fine with this. The less said, the better.

Next, Chris Lemon takes on DIAND's contradictory mandate. He asks Tricoteux: "DIAND has indicated—with respect to acid-rock drainage—that BHP documents are preliminary documents. That with respect to the tailings management plan, DIAND has identified inadequacies and deficiencies in those plans. DIAND has indicated that it is concerned about the water balance plan, that the effects monitoring program is only an initial framework and that the reclamation plan does not have to be submitted until six months after the licence is issued. We know that we have a fisheries agreement where the compensation requirements were calculated by BHP upon the basis of—as I understand it—volume and area, and that there is in fact no guarantee that habitat will be replaced. And we also know that aboriginal peoples will be affected by this project, that fisheries will be lost and wildlife will be affected. I want to know why, given all of this, DIAND is still prepared at this time to support this application, and whether DIAND considers itself to be in a position of conflict of interest?"

Tricoteux answers that DIAND has already stated its rationale for recommending BHP receive a water licence. He continues, "In response to his question of whether we feel we find ourselves in a conflict of interest, the answer to that is in fact, no."

Tricoteux asks Lemon to explain his concerns with respect to fiduciary. Chris responds, "We know that aboriginal rights will be affected by this project, we know that. The fiduciary has an obligation to protect those aboriginal rights, and I want to know why DIAND is prepared at this time to support this project when it knows that aboriginal rights are going to be affected?"

Tricoteux states DIAND's understanding of its obligations with respect to fiduciary: "Canada does in fact have a special relationship with aboriginal people but in fact that relationship does not always automatically trigger a fiduciary obligation." DIAND has already provided the Water Board with a written statement on this topic. "I suspect without putting words into Mr. Lemon's mouth that where we are headed in this discussion is associated with the unfulfilled commitments arising out of treaties, but I will leave it stand at that."

"That is exactly where we are not headed," Wray snaps. "If I allow this debate to continue, we will be here for the next week."

And we should be, I think. Because those unfulfilled commitments, the question of aboriginal title to this land, are the heart of the matter. All of BHP's superficial research into the impact of a mine, all of DIAND's pitiful appearance at "consultation" with the First Nations is just overburden.

I know Wray knows this. But resolving these issues is not his job as chair of the Water Board. He holds other powers that may slow the headlong rush to mine diamonds. He's going to keep his focus on using them.

Back and forth again goes the exchange between Chris and Tricoteux. Chris enters into the public record Akaitcho Treaty 8's evidence that DIAND has not, indeed, consulted meaningfully with us. Tricoteux defends the department, saying, "We have tried, given the limitations and challenges that all of us are facing on this project, to try and consult and to respond in a manner that was available to us."

Chris notes, "We know that the process was pushed along very fast by a sixty-day deadline set by the minister and we just want to know what was the effect of the deadline? What happened after the deadline that justified it?"

Tricoteux shakes his head. "I don't speak for the minister or the cabinet in terms of justifying deadlines." He speaks instead of "good faith" and "best effort" toward reviewing the BHP project. Then he states, "In terms of the effect that it had, again I am not sure that I understand the question, but in an effort to answer it honestly and fairly, what it did—at least for some of us in the department—was to sort of take stock of an approach or approaches that may be helpful to use to try and make progress on each of these fronts . . . We developed a matrix which sorted out what were the likely issues . . . That is what it triggered for us as a start and then we carried on with the process and we have already reported on the results as of October 8."

Wray requests a copy of the matrix.

Chris Lemon turns to the question of reclamation after the mine closes and asks whether DIAND is now prepared to guarantee that reclamation will be done whether or not the security deposit is adequate.

Chris Cuddy responds, "I guess it is a conditional guarantee on there being funding available, appropriated for that purpose by the federal Treasury Board."

Chief Beaulieu joins the questioning. He notes that Minister Irwin has called the North a "quagmire" of land and water regulation. Chief Beaulieu is curious about where and when the Crown applies legislation. Specifically, he asks, "Does the Indian Act apply in the Northwest Territories to the fullest extent?"

Tricoteux grasps for legal straws, eventually concluding, "So I guess the answer is yes and no, depending on which provision of the act."

Wray cautions Chief Beaulieu to keep his questions pertinent to BHP's application, to which the chief replies: "I was trying to bring some context in relation to the Inland Waters Act and other acts or legislation that would govern activity in the Northwest Territories." He continues, "Now when you go back to the treaties, the Department of Indian Affairs' position has always been that First Nations have surrendered . . . If they are surrendered lands, then the Indian Act should apply fully. But that is not the case. Now there is a situation of uncertainty here . . . Land has not been settled in what we call the Akaitcho territory. That leads me to the question I asked of the proponent: Has any land in the immediate area been identified as Native or Crown land . . . and withdrawn pending Native claim settlement? The answer was no . . . During the caveat days in 1973, there was 450,000 square miles of land that was identified, and that particular area, as again mentioned through the Department of Indian Affairs' own maps, identified that land as unceded Indian territory." He states again that the Crown has not appointed a negotiator for the Akaitcho Treaty 8 land entitlement.

Then he goes on to describe the Lac de Gras area, "Now this particular area was selected prior to anybody knowing there was diamonds there."

Wray directs the discussion away from land claims but asks Tricoteux to clarify the Crown's position of land ownership in the Lac de Gras area.

Tricoteux: "With all due respect to Chief Beaulieu and his concerns with respect to Canada's position on claims and what has transpired with respect to negotiations—which I personally can't speak to because I was not directly involved—the concerns that are associated with claims are a matter of ongoing dialogue with the department, including with the minister. The department remains open and available to discuss those issues."

Wray: "Mr. Tricoteux, I really don't want to go here. I do not want to get into a discussion on land claims. The question is, what is the department's position on the lands with regard to the Lac de Gras project?"

Tricoteux: "The department's position is that there is no absence of certainty with respect to the lands that are in question, that in fact these lands were ceded and surrendered under treaty. Thank you."

Chris Lemon, elder Judy Charlo and Chief Beaulieu keep after Tricoteux. They ask questions on land, on consultation, on where the water flows from Lac de Gras. Finally Chief Beaulieu picks apart Tricoteux's bureaucratese: "We don't understand on one hand if the position of the minister is that we ceded and surrendered our lands, then the Indian Act fully applies here. On the other hand, the minister is saying that the Indian Act does not fully apply, again due to the court cases that say that these lands have never been surrendered. That is the uncertainty and that is the quagmire that the minister keeps on referring to. So if one piece of legislation in relation to people here and development is uncertain, the question to Mr. Chairman and members of the board is: What legislation does apply? Are they all selectively applied in the Northwest Territories? Is the Bank Act selectively applied? Is the NWT Act selectively applied? . . . Mr. Chairman, our intention is to clarify these issues, not to hold up development, not to hold up land claims, but to clarify and resolve and move ahead with our lives."

Wray states, "With the greatest of respect, that is a very important question and it is deserving of a comprehensive and full answer, and I will ask then that perhaps the department could respond to Chief Beaulieu in writing with a copy to the board with regards to the specific questions that he has asked?"

Tricoteux remarks, "We will certainly review the matter through the transcripts, and I am going to take our best efforts to provide an appropriate response."

After lunch, Kevin O'Reilly of the Northern Environmental Coalition questions DIAND. The coalition represents several local and international groups that work to conserve land, water, air quality and wildlife. O'Reilly presents evidence that DIAND has not yet developed its objectives for sustainable development. How, he asks, can the department say the BHP project meets them? The coalition also raises the possibility that fluctuations in the price of diamonds will affect BHP's profit. Are the board and DIAND certain that the mining company will have the financial wherewithal to restore the mine site? To repair accidental damage during its operations?

The Inuit of the Coppermine River drainage express their concerns with river pollution and compensation for lost fisheries. Arthur Pape summarizes for the Dogribs. Chris Lemon summarizes for Akaitcho Treaty 8. Dan Johnson, John Searle and John Witteman summarize for BHP. Gordon Wray summarizes for the Water Board, for himself and for the North as he sees it.

Wray concludes, "Many of the issues that we heard are the same ones that we were dealing with twenty-five years ago. I eagerly await the day—and this is my personal opinion—that a northern government elected by northerners and accountable to northern people is making these kinds of decisions, and maybe we will see the changes that most of us feel are necessary."

As Wray closes the public hearing, I sum, divide and average the various recommendations. BHP wants a licence with a long term. DIAND concurs. The First Nations have argued that if BHP is licensed now, the term should be very short, between one and three years. If the Water Board simply averages the possible licence lengths, BHP's first Class A water licence will have a seven-year term. But I check myself. Is there any chance that the Water Board will decide BHP should not receive a licence until the flaws in its research are corrected? Until DIAND does a better job of acting as a fiduciary to the First Nations? I doubt it. I'm quite certain that BHP will have a Class A licence, and begin to build its mine, before the end of the year.

◆   ◆   ◆

THE next day, before the plane leaves for Łutsëlk'é, I sit in on two separate meetings of subcommittees to the Water Board's Technical Advisory Committee. From one I take the Chamber of Mines' representative's refrain: "It isn't in the Aquamin report, so we can't regulate it." Aquamin refers to the national standards that regulate water quality from mines. A process to modernize them has dragged on for five years already. But diamond mining is new in Canada. Some of what BHP wants to do has not yet been considered by miners or regulators. The industry's approach to the unknown is "there is nothing we can say about that." A government hydrologist tells me, "Water is always short-changed in these deals . . . just 'sold down the river.' " We share a painful laugh over his bad pun. The other meeting is on effluents. How is it possible to make small the entry of toxic chemicals into a pristine Arctic watershed? We spend the afternoon debating "safe" amounts of aluminum, copper, ammonia, cadmium. Should each element be monitored, regulated or ignored? The discussion is framed by dull walls, fluorescent light, binder upon binder of numbers from laboratory tests, and recommendations from studies of mines and water across Canada.

In the back of my mind flows always a picture of the Coppermine River in summer: bright, hard, clear, the brilliant water reflecting the endless sky and light of June days and nights in the Arctic. With the vision comes the feel of spongy tundra under my boots as I walk across the greens, browns, pinks and yellows of the Barrens, of the twenty-four-hour sun burning my face and of the wind unbroken by trees. In the depths of the river, I picture fish swimming freely, unaware of the insidious arrival of ammonia and the gill-clogging particles of aluminum. In pockets of fine gravel along the shore, grayling lay their eggs, unaware that cubic tonnes of additional water will come down the river when BHP dewaters its chosen lakes. This artificial flood will scour the gravel patches, destroying the eggs and the future of the grayling.

I picture too the caribou as they begin their return from the Bathurst calving grounds. First a few, then more and more, move toward the narrow passage between Lac du Sauvage and Lac de Gras. Only six kilometres west, enormous trucks haul kimberlite out of the pit the miners call Misery. Artificial light in the late summer night, noise, fumes, dust—all deter the caribou. Their migration is disrupted, the herd deflected around the diamond fields.

These images—bright Barrens water, migrating caribou herds—flow through my mind as the meeting facilitator polls the committee about regulation for each effluent to come from the mine. "Ammonia," he says, raising one healthy, muscled arm to get the group's attention. I think, that arm was nourished with clean water.

"Regulate at two to four," comes one response.

"Monitor," someone else says.

"Regulate, between two-point-five and three-point-five," answers a third.

On around the small stuffy room the discussion goes until something approaching agreement emerges from us few representatives of our arrogant species, deciding the future of the water and its life.

Xaye

Winter

13. *Waiting for ʔetthén*

◆　　　◆　　　◆

*The missing caribou of this and other years heighten
my appreciation of the true character of this land, its
harshness and unpredictability. And when they arrive,
if they do, we will greet them again with wonder.
Where did they come from? Where will they go?*

—Dave Olesen, *North of Reliance*

*T*WENTY-EIGHT hours later, October 24/25, I
find myself on a red-eye flight to Ottawa with Chief Darrell Beaulieu.
Chief Balsillie of Denínu Kų́e has secured a rare meeting with the treaty
negotiations overseers, and Chief Lockhart sends me along. I am wakeful on the jet, mindful of all the First Nations people, all the chiefs, who
have made these hopeful expeditions to the capital from their far-flung
communities for the past century and longer. The courage of their
convictions about their land is almost unfathomable to more comfortable souls.

The meeting time is inversely proportional to the long travel time.

Once again, Chief Balsillie lays out the urgent need for Akaitcho Treaty 8 negotiations with the Crown to proceed quickly. We are told that the feds are in the process of picking their new negotiator, and that he will be appointed soon.

Afterwards, we meet our member of Parliament, Ethel Blondin-Andrew, briefing her quickly on both the meeting with the feds and on BHP's progress toward diamond mining. She suggests that the chiefs might be able to catch Minister Irwin at the Liberal Party convention, although his staff refused Chief Balsillie's request for a meeting. All of us grab a taxi to the convention. The chiefs manage a very few minutes with Irwin, reiterating their single point: third-party interests, such as BHP, are eating up the land before Treaty 8 has been settled. Treaty negotiations must resume.

As Irwin disappears down a crowded staircase, I wish I could have asked, "Why? Why sixty days for all the people are giving up, for so little in return?" But I already know the answer. As one person in the sixty-day fray put it weeks ago, "They are just waiting for the diamond royalty cheques at the Treasury Board."

Late Friday afternoon, we turn around and make the long journey home.

◆   ◆   ◆

THE next day, I find myself in a still, white world. This Saturday morning the diamonds, the Water Board hearing and technical discussions, the money, seem not to exist. Nothing but falling snow is visible beyond the village, not even the shore across the small bay. The snow muffles all sound. I was lucky to get in before the snow came; no planes will come until this weather lifts. Ice on the small lakes is thick enough for snow machine travel. The big lakes are still open.

During the weeks of freeze-up, we have been pretty well town-bound. "Starting to be good winter travel," people say now. But no one is going anywhere fast. There are no caribou.

The hunters go farther and farther from the village each day, as the ice hardens on the lakes and the snow deepens on the trails. *"Dudee,"* they say when they come back to town. "We saw nothing, not even tracks."

Something is wrong. When the caribou take this long to come, or don't come at all, there has to be a reason. It is all people talk about. In the old days, people would have picked up and moved their winter camps until they found the caribou. They would have spread out in smaller and smaller groups so as not to starve, living on rabbits and fish. Sometimes they were very, very hungry. Sometimes they did starve.

These days, people turn to the community freezer, where the supply of meat from the fall hunt on the Barrens is dwindling. All the boats are out of the water, the motors drained for the winter. The local Co-op store raises prices on its meagre stock as people turn to store-bought food. If they have the money for it. People who have had steady jobs for a few years draw on food they ordered in on the annual barge. Many haven't worked steadily enough, or have earned too little, to pay for a barge-order supply of staples. Trips to Yellowknife—for medical or business reasons—are in high demand. If one family member buys a ticket to Yellowknife or, better yet, gets flown to Yellowknife at their employers' expense, he or she buys groceries for many. Even with the cost of air freight, this is cheaper than it is to buy at the local store. It will be weeks before the big lake freezes hard enough for snow machine travel to Yellowknife.

Frank Marlowe, sometime diamond claim staker, and Stephan Folkers, Łutsëlk'é's jack-of-all-trades, are telling bullshit stories while we drink tea down at Stephan's, on the quiet north shore of Łutsëlk'é. Radio chatter in the background is from *The House*, CBC's weekly radio program on Parliament. Its topics become one with the stories. I tell a few big-city tales from my day in Ottawa.

None of us is moving quickly this morning. The guys, both wearing grease-stained coveralls, are about to return to the corpse of Frank's snow machine, which lies outside. It broke down several kilometres out in the bush last night. Frank walked back to Łutsëlk'é. Then, in the snowstorm, he and Stephan went out. It was late last night before they returned, hauling the broken-down transport in a sleigh behind Stephan's snow machine. As for me, I'm procrastinating on an application to the Department of Indian Affairs and Northern Development (DIAND) for development-impact response funding. I'd rather watch a dead skidoo than write another funding application.

A snow machine roars down the shore outside. Then another. Hunter Sammy Boucher's dogs begin barking. Stephan's neighbour—who is Sammy's brother-in-law—speeds by in his truck, stops briefly, then drives over the rise into town. Something's going on. I volunteer to find out what, while Stephan and Frank return to the machine. Frank might need it.

I trek through soft snow to the rise behind Sammy's house. From here, I can just see across the lower slope of the village. Purposeful activity is everywhere. Hunters are loading sleighs with grub boxes. Parents are bundling kids into gear beside snow machines. I go no farther than Bernadette and Joe Lockhart's shed, where the Lockhart clan is gearing up to hunt. By now the answer is obvious, but Bernadette fills me in. "*7etthén*. Caribou. At Snowdrift River, going to that side," she says, gesturing south then southwest toward the invisible line of hills that is our horizon in clear weather. I can picture the route, a series of lakes that parallels the Macdonald Cliff.

I hoof it back to Stephan's as fast as I can with the news. He's already loading his sleigh, then lashes the canvas cover down over the essentials—grub box, axe, tools and spare parts. His shell bag hangs on the handles. Frank is looking plaintive. His machine isn't going anywhere for a while. Suddenly he declares, "I'll see if I can borrow one from Georgie." He takes off with his unmistakably swift stride. Stephan takes pity on me, knowing I haven't had time to find the used snow machine I want to buy this fall, and offers me a ride.

◆   ◆   ◆

WHAT the buffalo were to people of the Great Plains, caribou are to the Dëne súɬiné. So much so that European explorers identified the Dëne súɬiné as "caribou eaters." To the Dene, caribou are "walking people" who, pragmatically, take special care with their feet. Like humans, like all things organic and inorganic, caribou embody a spirit. They talk to each other over long distances, which helps them come together for their migrations. (Scientific observers say the caribou are silent except after calving, when cows grunt at their calves, or during the rut, when males bellow and snort.) Groups within a herd have leaders. I have seen a small band of caribou, perhaps eighteen animals, cross a road where a truck tractor trailer begrudgingly slowed as the bulls climbed the road embankment. While the driver laid on his horn, several cows shepherded the calves up and across the road after the bulls. Several more cows and two bulls stood between the calves and the semi until all the calves were across the road.

Some Dene get their medicine power from the caribou, and share their dreams. If people accord proper respect to the caribou, the animals will provide for the Dene as they have forever. Before fur traders brought metal implements, rifles and cloth, caribou provided almost everything the people needed: meat for food; hides for shelter and clothing; bone grease for lubricating sinew and skin, and for cooking; bone and antler for tools; sinew for dog harnesses, bows and lashing. The tender caribou fetus kept the elders alive after their teeth had worn away and they could no longer chew dry meat.

These days, "providing for the Dene" may mean being the object of a Dene enterprise, such as a guiding business that takes tourists to see the caribou migrations. Yet caribou still provide most of Łutsëlk'é's meat. In winter when the caribou are within the forest and the meat is fresh, Łutsëlk'é Dene eat two to three caribou meals per day; in summer, when the caribou meat is frozen, fish and moose may be a larger part of the diet. Still, caribou meat, dried or frozen, is part of the daily diet. Caribou hides are still made into exquisitely beaded jackets, gloves, shell bags, moccasins. Bleached white by the spring sun, the hides make soft and supple wedding dresses.

In contrast with their relatives to the west—the Dogribs and the Dene of the Mackenzie River Valley, who rely more equally on moose, mountain goats, woodland bison, woodland caribou and even bears for meat—Dëne sųłiné depend almost exclusively on caribou from the Barren Lands, where several different herds range. Although their calving grounds are discrete, while roaming and migrating the herds overlap each other's ranges and mingle. But when the pregnant females begin their determined trek toward calving grounds far out on the tundra, they stay the course to the calving ground where they were born.

Caribou biologists named the herds after their calving grounds, and these names are now used by the people who "manage" the herds, including the Dene who serve on caribou management boards. Łutsëlk'é Dene rely on caribou from the Bathurst herd, which numbers around 350,000, and, somewhat less heavily, on the Beverly herd of about 276,000. The Bathurst calving grounds are north-northeast of Łutsëlk'é. The Beverly calving grounds are northeast.

No matter what time of year, Dene are always thinking about caribou. The herds are enormous when massed to migrate during the spring and fall, but the land is much bigger. Finding the animals, or being in the right place at the right time for them to find you, is survival. When the herds are dispersed, in the winter forest or the summer barren grounds, they are much harder to find. It is a fact of life in Dene culture that if the animals and your hunting decisions fail you, you must have relatives with stronger luck to turn to.

In the past, Dene would kill not only enough caribou for themselves, but enough to cache for others who would almost inevitably join them from somewhere the caribou hadn't been. In winter, Dëne súłiné used to spread out in small groups, each moving around their territory as successful hunting required. If caribou did not pass right through their hunting territory, people moved closer to relatives who had been able to kill caribou. In those days, even before radio, communication among the small groups was remarkable. Then, as now, people visited each other's camps, constantly exchanging information gleaned through close, daily observation of the land.

The land and the caribou are still the first topic of conversation in Łutsëlk'é, where binoculars sit on every windowsill. In late July or early August, Łutsëlk'é Dene watch for an insect with a long segmented body, with yellow-on-black markings. When it appears at the people's bush camps near the treeline, they say: "It's from the caribou. Look, the caribou are coming back." When the animals come, people follow them and each other, using tracks in the snow. They watch the patterns of birds in flight, which are good indicators of activity on the ground. And they listen for sounds—of caribou hooves clicking, ravens cawing over a kill, people speaking—which carry remarkable distances over water and in the winter cold.

When their ancestors first followed the caribou into this land, Dene must have learned the most reliable places to intercept the migrating herd. On the labyrinthine lakes and rivers of the Barrens, caribou come together to swim across water at narrow passages. They are strong swimmers, and though they sometimes cross long stretches of water, the animals more commonly traverse where the water passages are short but not necessarily smooth.

Dene have always hunted caribou at such crossings, both from the land and from canoes. While waiting for caribou at narrows, Dene fished the nutrient-rich currents where the big lakes flow through these narrow, rocky gaps. Today, Łutsëlk'é Dene still hunt where Artillery Lake narrows at its southwest end and keep a communal hunter's cabin there. Taltheilei Narrows is the only narrow crossing along the north shore of Great Slave Lake. Animals cross there to the Pethei Peninsula, which leads them on to Desnéthché and the lake's southern shore. Łutsëlk'é Dene do not hunt near there much any more because a fishing lodge and its guests dominate the narrows. Traditionally both Dogribs and Akaitcho Treaty 8 people hunted caribou at the big crossing between Lac du Sauvage and Lac de Gras. Now this place is famous more for the diamonds that will come from a pit Chuck Fipke named Misery, just west of the crossing, than for its caribou.

No one knows, yet, what the caribou will do while Misery is mined. The diamond fields straddle the Bathurst herd's migration route between Łutsëlk'é, Wekweti (Snare Lake) and Bathurst Inlet. In Łutsëlk'é this fall, people think that the migration has diverted, or split, around the diamond explorations at Lac de Gras. If the herd, or most of it, has turned west around the exploration site, it will drift south and west. The herd will move closer to Gameti and Wekweti and eventually toward Tsoti and Rae-Edzo. To come closer to Łutsëlk'é, the caribou will have to cross McLeod Bay, or Taltheilei Narrows and Christie Bay. This will not happen until late December or January. It will likely be a hungry, and irritable, time in Łutsëlk'é.

One thing is for sure. The caribou we are tracking today have come just for the Łutsëlk'é Dene. The Dene believe that the caribou give themselves to people. Their meat is a gift, and must be shared. It is not for individual gain. If young people hunt caribou carelessly, the elders chastise them. When bad things happen in the community, it is said that someone has been harassing caribou. Liza Enzoe calls this "suffering the animals." These caribou are the first sign that some of the herd may have come east of Lac de Gras, across or around Artillery Lake, and continued southwest toward Łutsëlk'é. When caribou are west of Artillery Lake, coming off the Barrens down the Barnston and Hoarfrost Rivers, they are on ground that both the Treaty 11 Dogribs and the Treaty 8 Yellowknives as well as the Łutsëlk'é Dene hunt. When there's plenty of caribou, no problem. But this year so far there have not been.

Nor have many caribou come, yet, on their eastern route toward Łutsëlk'é. This becomes obvious as soon as we wind our way out of the woods onto the first long lake that leads to Snowdrift River. Any tracks are quickly erased by the steady snow, but there are no animals here. We've seen several people, some leaving town in the same direction we did. Others went the opposite way. By now they will be circling toward us. The caribou should be between us and them. We see nothing until a headlight emerges through the falling snow. We brake to a stop, as do the two machines coming toward us. Stephan says, "Nothing yet this way." The hunter on the other machine replies, "Larry saw two on his lake, he went after them. Not too many. Ernest went toward his cabin, Snowdrift River there, says no tracks that way. Going to try up on that side." His big mitt swings up toward the Macdonald Cliff.

But we are lucky. Frank, who did manage to borrow a snow machine, sees and shoots one animal at the end of the small, thin lake that is the winter trail to where the Snowdrift River enters Stark Lake. When he reaches it, he breaks its neck, then ties a rope around it. He tows the animal toward the shore so we can make fire. When we stop, Frank removes the rope, then cuts off the caribou head. He places it right side up on the snow. Is its spirit watching the proper dismemberment of its body? The animal lies on its side. Frank lifts first a foreleg, then a hind leg, splitting the hide in a line from the neck down the belly of the animal. Then he stands to one side and peels back the hide in short, strong tugs.

I sometimes help with butchering, and I have been with Dene women who hunt and butcher caribou themselves. Usually, however, when men and women travel together, butchering is exclusively the men's job. I've learned to stay well back and approach cautiously when men are butchering. Women are prohibited from stepping over anything, anywhere—the rope that ties the sleigh to the snow machine, an axe lying on the snow—and we must be especially careful never to walk over caribou blood. We are also not allowed to touch men's gear, especially not anything used for hunting—parkas, shell bags, rifles, knives. Even in a "modern" context, loading or unloading a boat or sleigh or pickup, women observe this proscription. It might be relaxed, but one always asks.

When hunters butcher caribou, blood droplets sprinkle the snow, so I walk up the shore to find a sheltered spot. I toss a handful of snow into the air, where the wind carries it north. Stephan cuts down a dry tree, which I use to make fire. Once I get the fire going, I melt snow in a blackened teapot. I've cut a small birch, which I force into snow banked around the fire. Two thick spruce branches make an A-frame support under the birch when I angle it over the fire. Soon, Frank brings two racks of ribs to the fire. I skewer a rack onto the sharpened end of the birch, being mindful not to walk over any blood that drips from the meat.

The ribs cook slowly, the very lean meat dripping only a little onto the fire. The fresh meat and woodsmoke smell primal, a rich aroma in the cold absence of all other scent. That absence is the smell of winter, at least until I cut ʔĕl, or spruce. When my axe blade severs the evergreen boughs, the trees release a tiny sharp scent that reminds me of turpentine. With the branches, I make a spruce tapestry on top of the snow we pack down around the fire. On these soft boughs we'll be warm sitting by the fire to eat.

The light is half gone by the time Stephan and Frank finish loading the fore and hind quarters, the head and all the organs into the sleigh. They walk up from the ice, warm from the work of butchering, stripped down to snow pants and hooded cotton sweatshirts. They carry choice pieces of meat and put them on the grill I've laid over the fire. As darkness falls, we sit by the fire, drinking hot smoky tea with sugar. From time to time we turn the ribs, testing them for just the right doneness. Finally Frank takes the rack off its roasting hook and cuts it into three- and four-rib pieces, passing one to each of us. He stacks the rest on the edge of the grill. *"Dedhay,"* Frank says. I pass him the salt shaker. The fresh meat is tender beyond belief in my mouth.

We hear two snow machines approaching. The drivers head toward our fire, kill their motors at the edge of the lake, follow our trail into the trees. We make room for Felix Lockhart and his brother Alfred on the spruce. I dig mugs out of the grub box for them. They help themselves to ribs and tea, and Alfred reports, "Not many caribou. Joe and James got two over there [gesturing east] but nothing on Duhamel Lake."

"They are mostly over on the north side," says Frank. "Plenty caribou over by Rae." He'd been out to Rae-Edzo the previous weekend to visit family. In fact he lives there most of his time now. "Plenty meat over there, for those Dogribs," he adds. "The caribou, they're going around that mine. It's right in the middle. They come down from the north, to come this way or down to north shore, they run right into that BHP. That noise, that dust, they're gonna have to do something about that, or else the caribou won't come this way."

"Hard enough when they are on the north shore, even on McLeod Bay," says Alfred. "I was going north one day, fast up around Barnston River, and this trail crosses and here's these Dogrib guys just givn' her on this trail coming from west. Almost smashed up. Don't like it, all them guys coming all this way out east to our territory."

"Lots, now, really lots, so many people in Yellowknife," Frank answers. "All coming this way when the caribou are over here. But now those caribou go west around that mine, straight into Dogrib country, easier for the Dogribs over there anyway."

"Maybe that's what the mine and the Dogribs agreed to. Maybe that's why they are being so friendly with each other," Stephan says.

"Well, the government set that up, too," Felix says. "The Dogribs are doin' their land claim like the Sahtu and Gwich'in did, a comprehensive claim, not the treaty. That is what the Crown wants up here, the same land and water rules for everybody. They don't want comprehensive there, treaty here. The Dogribs are negotiating the way Ottawa wants. The feds told BHP to negotiate with the Dogribs. Treaty 8 had to say, 'Hey, what about us?' Łutsëlk'é is closer to that mine than any of the Dogrib communities except Wekweti." A pause. Then he goes on, "Back when we were all one, the Dene Nation, we could all work together against the feds. Now we're split, it's like the feds just take us one at a time. That's how they get what they want, one claim at a time now."

"Fallin' like dominoes," Stephan mutters.

"Yeah, right up the Mackenzie Valley," adds Felix. "Once the Dogribs sign their agreement, it'll just be us and Deh Cho who are holding out against extinguishment . . . I wonder if the Gwich'in and Sahtu think very much about what they did."

"They had to extinguish their title to all their land. That's what the Dogribs will have to do, too," I murmur, staring into the fire. To diamantaires, "fire" is the light that diamonds refract and flash in colour. "Brilliance" is the white light that shines through the diamond crystal. The Dene always tell me not to stare at the flames. When I look up again at the darkening forest, I am blind. "Surely my government can work to negotiate a 'modern' treaty that doesn't require extinguishment," I continue. "Why doesn't it? Why don't we?" We are silent for a while. Snowflakes melt above the fire, but the snow deepens in the darkness behind our backs.

"I wonder if a hundred years from now, I wonder if the Gwich'in and Sahtu will be arguing with the feds that they didn't extinguish their land title," Felix muses. "How can what people do 'extinguish' what people have with the land?"

Practical Frank starts picking up mugs and knives in the firelight. "Gonna have to look after the caribou, anyway. Make sure the land stays healthy for them. Gonna have to make sure we don't end up fighting the Dogrib over the caribou, too."

"Bad enough, arguing over those diamonds. Doesn't help with the treaty negotiations," Felix says, pulling on his parka.

"Do you think the Dogrib communities are happy with the impact and benefit agreement they're getting from BHP?" I ask him.

"We'll see, they'll see. I guess they figure they can go ahead and sign it soon, maybe even next week," he replies, then shrugs, turning away toward the lake. He and Alfred head down the trail.

"When do we have to decide?" Frank asks as we collect salt shakers and jars full of tea bags packed in sugar from our spruce floor.

"Not until you're all satisfied that the agreement'll do. We'll have some more public meetings about it this week, see what people think," I say. "If people want to sign it, we'll invite BHP to the community so Felix and BHP's guy can sign it together."

Stephan and Frank go down the trail. I hear the rumble as they crank their machines. I feed the fire with pieces of cooked meat, empty the kettle around it, douse what remains with handfuls of snow. As the firelight dies, I shoulder my pack and wait for my eyes to adjust to the darkness. Snowflakes melt on my cheeks as I too turn down the dark trail.

14. Excell's Moccasins

 ◆　　　◆　　　◆

The hunting societies of the world have been
sentenced to death.

—Hugh Brody, *Maps and Dreams*

I T is time to face the community. No one else's needs—not the miners', not the government's, not the diamond profiteers—matter in Łutsëlk'é right now. What matters is this land, these people. Is the impact and benefit agreement (IBA) good enough to meet with their approval?

Tuesday evening, October 29, Łutsëlk'é people meet in the community hall to discuss the agreement. Nick Poushinsky and I, with Archie Catholique's explanations in both English and Dëne Súłin yati, present the agreement. This part of my job is nerve-racking. There is so much uncertainty about BHP, the agreements have been reached under such time pressure, that I know they are flawed. Yet I firmly believe the

IBA was the best we could get given the resources—financial and human and temporal—we had available. We knew that Akaitcho Treaty 8 was swimming upstream throughout the negotiations, that Minister Irwin would most likely approve BHP's mine on the basis of an IBA with the Dogribs alone. That we have managed to reach an agreement at all is no small achievement. But what agreement would be, would have been, good enough? If Łutsëlk'é and Ndilo and Dettah don't ratify this agreement, what are the chances of getting something better now that the minister has his significant progress? What is the probability of getting nothing at all?

Progress through the agreement is slow. People absorb the information, ask questions. It is important that everyone understand because the community must ratify the IBA. If it does, the First Nation council will pass a resolution supporting the agreement. Then the chief, and BHP's appropriate representative, will sign it. However, Chief Lockhart is in Yellowknife working with the other chiefs on tribal council business that was set aside to deal with BHP, and Łutsëlk'é will not make any decisions until the chief is here to go over the agreement with First Nation members. As this evening ends, people simply agree to discuss the IBA with each other and their families.

The next evening, we hold a similar session about the environmental agreement. The First Nations are not signatories to that agreement, but the Land and Environment Committee will review it. The committee must provide its direction to the chief, who will then sign an implementation protocol to establish the Independent Environmental Monitoring Agency (IEMA). Slowly, the information moves through the community.

Not quickly enough for some. Minister Irwin is coming to Yellowknife in two days, on Friday, November 1, to sign the environmental agreement. At the same time, the Dogribs will sign their IBA with BHP. Akaitcho Treaty 8 is under pressure to sign its IBA at the same

time, although the communities have not yet ratified it. Łutsëlk'é
wants another public meeting with Chief Lockhart before he signs.
People also want BHP to come here for a signing in the community so
the First Nation members can take part, rather than have the chief sign
it as part of a show for Minister Irwin.

The media notices, suddenly it seems, that Akaitcho Treaty 8 and
BHP did reach agreement but that our IBA must go through community
ratification before the chiefs sign it. Reporters keep phoning to ask
what's in the agreement. What they really want to know is how much
money Akaitcho Treaty 8 will get. But the agreements are confidential.
Other than leadership and staff, only the First Nation members are to
know exactly what is in them.

All day Thursday, October 31, the pressure builds for Akaitcho
Treaty 8 to sign with BHP in front of Minister Irwin in Yellowknife on
Friday. The Land and Environment Committee is bogged down in the
environmental agreement and in a land use application from Canamera
Geological Ltd. This company, connected somehow, we know, to
DeBeers, is busily exploring kimberlite finds only eighty kilometres
north of Desnéthché.

Chief Lockhart calls to request that the First Nation councillors
gather at the office for a meeting by speakerphone. He needs to consult
the councillors about Łutsëlk'é's readiness to accept the IBA. Several
members from the Land and Environment Committee listen in on the
meeting. Opinions fly back and forth. It is decided that two councillors
will go to Yellowknife to join Felix and the other chiefs. Apparently,
some of the pressure is coming from parties who believe that BHP may
renege on its agreement with Akaitcho Treaty 8 if the chiefs do not sign
on November 1.

I finally manage to leave the office, especially the constantly bleep-
ing telephone, about 6:30 P.M. I head home to the log house on the
point. The waves I hear in the dark on my left will turn the shore to ice

sculpture overnight. The rising sun will light the ice when I walk back to work. Inside, I put wood in the stove and stand with cold hands over it in the darkness. I am drained from another day of lobbyists and lawyers, but it is Hallowe'en and I want to go to the community dance. I want to be with the people I am working for, especially the elders and children, whom I never seem to see these days.

I am just getting out of the shower when I hear the phone ring. Switching on the reading light by the phone, I answer in local dialect: *"Anh?"* It is Chief Sangris phoning from the restaurant in Yellowknife where the chiefs are meeting. We review the events that have led the First Nations to this point. Should Akaitcho Treaty 8 sign the IBA? Signing gives BHP permission to change the land irrevocably. It is this larger consequence rather than the timing or the location for the signing that has people concerned.

"Jonas," I begin, "it's the covenant clause that really worries the elders. All the benefits aside, we know that in the covenant clause you agree that Akaitcho Treaty 8 will never protest against or block any of BHP's actions. People understand that once the chief signs, no one can sue BHP, and we can't block the ice road to the mine site." He waits. I wait. Dene are so damn good at silence. Eventually, I continue, "Come on, my friend, you know I don't tell people what to do. The elders want another meeting, and they want their chief here for it."

We are both quiet for a moment. I wish him good luck as we hang up. I stare into the darkness, thinking.

The phone rings again. It is Chris Lemon, calling from Vancouver. He's probably the only one of the coterie of lawyers I don't mind talking to on overtime. I ask, "Hey, Lemonhead, what's up?" He replies that BHP just called from San Francisco. We discuss their message at some length—they do not seem concerned that Akaitcho Treaty 8 sign by tomorrow. Their board of directors hasn't even ratified our agreement. In other words, both parties, them and us, are at the same stage: taking the negotiated agreement back to the principals for assent. At this point, BHP's board of directors could still pull out—although I do not think this is likely—and our First Nations could also do the same by voting against ratifying the agreement. Chris doesn't think it is crucial that the chiefs sign tomorrow. I agree. I am reassured by his opinion. I think it would be a big mistake to rush into signing by tomorrow, simply to meet the minister's and BHP's media timetable. Here, in Łutsëlk'é, what matters is community consensus. Chris seems glad for my assent from out here in the wilds of Akaitcho Treaty 8 land. We sign off.

I am cold in my bathrobe and go to get more wood for the fire. Before I reach the woodpile, the phone rings once again. I pick up.

"Ellen, what ya doin'?" comes an unmistakable, gravelly voice that goes with the blackest eyes I've ever seen. It is Don Morin, the Northwest Territories premier, and his senior legal counsel on a speakerphone.

"Donnie," I reply, "I'm sitting here on my sofa, trying to get to the Hallowe'en dance, answering calls from men all over the continent. No one wants to dance with me, but it seems like everyone wants that agreement signed."

We discuss the IBA and what we know about BHP. Then the premier asks, "Ellen, do you think they'll pull the agreement?" I ponder the question. The silence lasts as long as the 180 kilometres of winter darkness between us. I hear logs fall in the stove and notice that my feet have gone cold.

Finally I answer, "No, Donnie, I honestly don't think so." He waits for my certainty. I have none. We talk about hunting caribou when he comes for his constituency visit in January, then we hang up. I remain frozen on the sofa. What if we are wrong?

Barely a minute later, the phone rings again. It is Jim Bergelsman of BHP calling from San Francisco. I remember his impatience with Łutsëlk'é, then his 3 A.M. apology to me a few weeks ago. We talk, tonight, because we have come to a better understanding of each other's commitment to the people we work for—and to a mutual respect. He doesn't think that his board will pull the agreement if Łutsëlk'é waits to sign it. I believe him. We hang up.

I think fleetingly of phoning the premier back, but I do not. His line will be busy. The phone does not ring. I dress up as a lawyer and go to the dance.

◆   ◆   ◆

On Friday, November 1, Minister Irwin; Stephen Kakfwi, Northwest Territories minister of resources, wildlife and economic development; and Jim Excell, vice-president of operations for BHP, sign the socioeconomic agreement that will give employment preference at BHP's mine to Northwest Territories residents, among other benefits. BHP and Dogrib Treaty 11 Chief Joe Rabesca sign their impact and benefit agreement. The Akaitcho Treaty 8 chiefs join in the ceremony and sign the implementation protocol for the environmental agreement. But the Akaitcho Treaty 8 chiefs do not sign their IBA with BHP. Ndilo, Dettah and Łutsëlk'é are moving steadily toward ratification, but the chiefs won't sign until their people have voted.

By Tuesday, November 12, Łutsëlk'é people are familiar enough with the terms of the IBA to hold a last public discussion meeting in the community hall. Nearly all the adults in the community attend. As always, the meeting opens with a prayer. Then one of the elders reminds everyone that they are here to "try to bring our minds together, in a good way." The meeting begins almost as scheduled, with Chief Lockhart chairing and leading the discussion, largely in Dëne Sųłin yati. Business is conducted expeditiously, with fierce but polite debate. Some people feel there should be no mining and it is a mistake for Akaitcho Treaty 8 to agree to anything with BHP. Others want more mining, sooner. Everyone else is on a spectrum between the two extremes, accepting diamond mining with a certain fatalistic inevitability, deeply concerned that it will not yield much of good for them and the land. When the young people speak in English, those fluent in both languages jump into the discussion, using both to make sure everyone understands. When everyone has had a say and all points have been discussed, Chief Lockhart asks about consensus on the agreement. A few people clap. Slowly the applause grows, then spreads throughout the hall. The people of Łutsëlk'é have accepted the IBA. I am torn—relieved, but saddened. The land will never be the same after diamond mining. But over and over again, in my daily conversations with people here, I have said, "We can't turn back the clock, nor make development go away. You have to make informed choices, and they are hard choices." People have made a hard choice here. I hope it is a good choice. Only one more step—a formal council vote—remains before the agreement is ratified.

Wednesday, November 13, dawns cool and clear. The balance between fall and winter is definitely tilting toward winter. I walk to the First Nation chambers to join council members who assemble, gradually, for a 9 A.M. meeting on urgent items. At one end of a work table, I sit drafting one of these—the First Nation resolution stating the community's assent to the agreement with BHP. Around me, the councillors move around sorting out unforeseen delays. Someone goes looking for coffee and tea because there isn't any. Someone else tries to find a person to take minutes because two staff members are sick and others, including the First Nation administrator, are doing jury duty. Finally, there is a quorum and a recorder.

Council dispenses with the first and second items quickly. Then attention turns to the agreement with BHP.

The discussion takes less than half an hour. George Marlowe, one of the most experienced councillors, is concerned about the percentages of royalties from the mine in relation to the rise and fall of the diamond market. It is the only question discussed in any detail at this last moment. People have accepted the other flaws and risks. The agreement seems such a done deal that council moves on to another item, until someone reminds us that they have to pass the motion to accept the agreement. Councillor Emily Saunders moves that Łutsëlk'é First Nation accept the impact and benefit agreement with BHP. Ron Desjarlais seconds the motion. It carries unanimously.

I don't have much time to think about the significance of what has just happened. Now that the agreement has been ratified, the signing with BHP, tentatively scheduled for this evening, will go ahead. I leave the meeting about 11:30 to look after details for the signing. BHP will arrive, as usual, on a chartered aircraft. The media will arrive on the sched a bit later. We will all attend a ceremony and feast in the community hall.

I leave the resolution with Cheryl Desjarlais, who agrees to type it onto the official First Nation council resolution form. Then the chief and councillors will sign it.

In my office, I squeeze past Nick Poushinsky, who is working on a business plan for one of the First Nation's small businesses. We speak by phone with the Yellowknives about their ratification and signing, which took place yesterday. I draft a press release, ask Nick to edit it, then telephone David Boyd, manager of human resources at BHP, to confirm the number of people who will arrive on their charter. I ask, "Die-vid, one of my Treaty 11 colleagues assures me that at their signing, you brought diamonds. And people got to hold them. So we are wondering if you are bringing any."

He answers, "Ellen, even I don't get to see or hold diamonds."

"So you aren't bringing any?" I counter.

"No way," comes the reply.

By 3 P.M., Nick and I have cleaned up and faxed the press release. A copy of the signed council resolution is in an envelope for Chief

Lockhart to present to Jim Excell. Liza Enzoe delivers the beaded moccasins the First Nation will present to Excell. Two weeks ago I phoned BHP's Vancouver headquarters to find out Excell's shoe size. The call went from the front desk to some more specialized sanctum and finally to Excell's wife. Then his secretary phoned me back. I walked the information up the hill to Liza's house. Now I gift-wrap the moccasins in one of the large binders holding part of BHP's Environmental Impact Statement. The cover reads NWT *Diamonds Project: Tailings Management Plan and Preliminary Design of Retention Structures* over a pretty, out-of-focus picture of Barren Lands lakes. On closer inspection, the lake in the foreground turns out to be a tailings pond. When I finish, I join Felix and Nick in the office to go over the signing program. All that remains is for our guests to arrive.

Nick and I jump into the four-by-four pickup we have commandeered to ferry the BHP guests from the airstrip to the hall. The snow of early afternoon is turning to freezing rain as I stick-shift the heavy truck over ice, up the hill and out of town. Neither the heater nor the wipers seem to be working. When we reach the airstrip, it is empty. BHP's charter is due to land thirty-five minutes ahead of the sched. We sit in the truck and wait as it gets dark.

Time passes. Ten minutes. Twenty, then thirty. We walk around once or twice, standing outside until the dampness drives us back into the truck. We manage to get the heater working, then the wipers. BHP's plane is late. Finally, out of the dark, a face appears by the window. I roll down the window. The sched agent has come outside to find me. She says, "BHP's plane turned back to Yellowknife. You're wanted on the phone." I laugh, shake my head and walk into the tiny terminal building to answer the phone. By the time I call down to the office, BHP has called to rebook our signing for the next day, weather permitting. (Later, Jim Excell will tell me they turned back because the freezing rain was "turning the plane to a block of ice.")

Moments later, the runway lights come on and the sched lands, bringing the media and all of the food BHP has had catered for the feast. As she disembarks, CBC's new reporter says, "The flight was really scary. Ice was peeling off the plane." We load her and the cameraman and all of the food into various trucks, then drive down to the hall. There, with BHP's assurance that it will bring more the next day, people eat jumbo shrimp in cocktail sauce, fresh fruit sliced on crisp lettuce, salmon mousse with almonds for scales, fresh buns and garden fresh vegetables with dip. These are all foods we never see in the local store. The new CBC reporter is upset because she can't file a story and the sched has already gone back to Yellowknife; she has to stay overnight. The cameraman, wearing moccasins that have seen long service, calmly eats cocktail shrimp with the locals.

Chief Lockhart asks interpreter Archie Catholique and me to explain to everyone gathered why BHP hasn't arrived but the food has. In English and Dëne Sųłin yati, we say, "BHP will come at the same time tomorrow, and they said they will bring more food. Now you can't say any more that you never got nothing from a mine."

◆   ◆   ◆

TWENTY-FOUR hours later, on November 14—98 days after Minister Irwin's initial announcement, Zah Lockhart Hall is packed. Old people and young people sit on the benches built into the natural wood walls. White ceiling fans spin on high speed. Bright lights between high blond ceiling beams contrast with the dark winter clothes of those seated below. No one is at the signing table at the front of the room, yet. Above and behind it is the eight-by-ten framed black-and-white photograph of Zah Lockhart, the elder for whom this new hall is named. In this big room we have drum dances, fiddle dances, feasts, playschool, healing workshops and bingo.

A crew of twelve young people—mostly men—who have already graduated from pre-employment training for the mine carries boxes of fast food (apparently, we went through our allotment of shrimp and mousse last night) and cases of pop from a truck to tables at the rear of the hall. They are trying to impress the BHP men. Then they sit down, a solid row of black hair, black jackets, big boots crammed together along one of the wall benches. Waiting. Waiting for the signing, the jobs and a future of something other than unemployment, welfare, clerical jobs, small-time trapping, sewage-truck driving and selling wood to white professionals who work for them.

Nick stands outside on the hall porch with Jerry Bair and David Boyd of BHP. They're smoking, chatting under the light at the edge of winter darkness.

Inside, people drift gradually to the rows of black chairs in front of the signing table. Archie discovers that there are no batteries in the interpreter's microphone. We move a small table for him to one side, find paper and pen so he can take notes for consecutive interpretation. Zepp Casaway, one of the oldest and best teachers among the elders, sits small, stooped and immensely dignified next to Chief Lockhart at the front of the hall. Honoured guests—all the elders, premier and MLA Don Morin, Chief Jonas Sangris—take their seats. The CBC cameraman stands ready by his tripod, the reporter with her tape recorder. The local Mountie stands at ease at the back of the hall, in dress boots, striped breeches and red serge.

Councillor Emily Saunders, as chair, opens the meeting. Elder Morris Lockhart says a long prayer in Dëne Sųłin yati. Then his son, Chief Lockhart, takes the microphone and asks the standard ice-breaking question, "Does anyone have a pen?" It is quintessential Felix.

The actual signings seem like the calm water after rapids. The only sound is the slight shuffle of paper and the quiet, polite words Excell and Felix exchange along with copies of the signature pages. From my seat along the wall, I can see the faces of many in the crowd. Interest, skepticisim, anticipation, cynicism, detachment—all play there. A peculiar mixture of uncertainty and relief leaves me drained. Then Felix and Excell look up at the crowd, stand, shake hands. And again, the Łutsëlk'é Dene applaud.

After the signings there is much warm handshaking and visiting. We share that good feeling for the night. Excell opens the tailings plan binder, laughs and holds up the moccasins for applause. He puts them on. They almost fit.

As we stand around talking, Jerry Bair points down at my moccasins and says, "I want those."

"You can't have them," I reply. "They aren't on the table."

"But I want some. Just like those," he persists. "Where did you get them?"

"You mean, who made them? Liza Enzoe."

"Would she make some for me?"

"Sure. But she'll need your foot measurement. Stand flat in your socks, trace your foot, then fax it to our office. The tracing, not your foot. What colour beads do you want?"

"Like I said, I want those. Just like that. How much?"

I bend down for a closer look. "Probably ninety."

"Ninety!"

"You got big feet." But he looks pleased.

Before too long, the elders are driven home and people drift away. By the time Nick and I truck several people up to the charter aircraft, snow is blowing around the nose of the Twin Otter. With honoured guests on board, BHP takes off. Łutsëlk'é is once again alone in the winter night.

15. *Sharing Accord*

◆ ◆ ◆

Commitments made by the Crown, by officers of
Her Majesty, whether in 1854 or 2000, are not
to be regarded as empty promises.

—Thomas R. Berger, *One Man's Justice: A Life in the Law*

"Where's the money?" As soon as the agreement is signed, everyone, it seems, wants to know the answer to this question. As lovely as the signing ritual can be, no matter how sincere our efforts, paper is only paper. Dene have signed many pieces of paper. Signing is nowhere near trust. True agreement grows out of practice. Trust grows out of good experience.

No one believes me when I say "I don't know where the money is." So I divert the question, reciting the legal and financial steps that must be taken before BHP actually pays its first instalment to Akaitcho Treaty 8. Once the payment is transferred, Akaitcho Treaty 8 Tribal Council will bank it in a First Nation financial institution on a reserve down south, where it will remain tax-free. I direct all questions about the money's disbursement to the chiefs.

To the First Nation members I say, "You guys have to work it out now." I've done my very best to get an agreement, but I know better than to try to tell the Łutsëlk'é Dene what to do with it. Oh, I have an opinion. I'll even express it, if asked, couched in the phrase "This is only my opinion." I believe that all parties within Akaitcho Treaty 8 ignore equity at their peril. The Yellowknives, Łutsëlk'é and Denínu Kųe First Nations need to work out among themselves how they will share the money from the diamond mines. It is my opinion that inequitable agreements now will haunt their children and grandchildren just like unfulfilled treaty promises from the Crown.

I cannot help with the sharing decisions. Instead, I concentrate on the parts of the agreement that are not in cash. Akaitcho Treaty 8 needs to hire someone to manage implementing the IBA. That person will look after the details of training and hiring First Nation members for BHP. Until then, even the administrative work remains with the chiefs, who are far too overworked to look after the day-to-day minutiae. I gather information for the chiefs to help with a job description and contact First Nation members, encouraging them to apply. Some people tell me I should take the job.

My reply is incredulous. "*ʔesjiá!* Take it easy," I say. "You can't have someone like me representing you on implementation. This is long term. It has to be a First Nation member. That's not the sort of stuff I know how to do, not to mention that I don't want to be working with a mining company for the rest of my days. No way." The rep will also oversee the unbundling of the mine construction contracts so that First Nation companies can bid on manageable pieces of the mine development project. But interpreting the agreement and implementing it is all new ground for the First Nations. Decisions are made very slowly.

◆   ◆   ◆

In the third week of November, at last, Canada resumes treaty negotiations with Akaitcho Treaty 8, even though Canada has not yet appointed its chief negotiator. Those present on the new federal team—most of whom are civil servants from Ottawa—assure us that "he will be appointed soon." An initial three-day workshop is intended to break the ice dam between Akaitcho Treaty 8 First Nations and the Crown. And so the feds have brought in a mediation team specializing in international conflict resolution all the way from Cambridge, Massachusetts. The shared goal is finding enough common ground from which to launch negotiations of the very contentious issues, such as extinguishment. The chiefs attend, along with two First Nation councillors from each community, the negotiators and legal counsel. We meet the federal team in the rabbit's warren of rooms underneath the Yellowknife Inn. The venue mirrors the state of negotiations.

Over lunch in the meeting rooms, it becomes clear exactly how much work we have to do. One of the Crown's senior people—a very bright, personable woman who wears exactly the same size and make of corduroy jeans that I do—asks me, "How did someone like you end up in a place like Łutsel—" before she bites her tongue, albeit with a smile. "That's not really what I mean," she continues, but all of us at the table shake our heads, laughing gently at her discomfort. Here again are the Dene, opposite people who simply don't know or appreciate what the Dene have. Or had.

I reply honestly, "People. Land. Water. I'm from the North, that's part of it. I find the people amazing. I really, really admire what they are trying to do. And I find living here a lot more interesting than conversations about the value of real estate in southern suburbs."

After lunch, our efforts to find common ground—where treaty entitlement negotiations can begin again in earnest—start with internal sessions. Each team is given a flip chart and a set of markers. Then we are asked, within our teams, to write on the flip chart not our own interests, but those of the opposite side. After an hour we break for coffee before everyone convenes in one of the larger meeting rooms. We present our lists to each other.

Akaitcho Treaty 8 lists some of Canada's interests as:

- "to achieve finality through extinguishment";
- "to only negotiate parts of the treaty";
- "to deny the Dene version of the treaty because the implications—sharing the land—are unacceptable"; and
- "Canada wants royalties from minerals, mining, oil and gas."

But for furious note-taking, the federal representatives hardly react to our list.

Canada lists some of Akaitcho Treaty 8's interests as:

- "to avoid extinguishment of future and existing political, aboriginal and treaty rights";
- "to recognize that the treaty is an emotional and spiritual document that embodies the belief in a nation-to-nation understanding"; and
- "to receive equitable treatment compared with Dene groups—the Gwich'in and Sahtu—who have already reached agreement with Canada."

Canada says Akaitcho Treaty 8 wants to maximize benefits from both of the existing claims policies: the treaty entitlement policy and the comprehensive claims policy. A reasonably accurate assessment, I think.

Discussion begins. We take each other's lists and correct them in front of each other. The mediators resolve spikes of tension with painstaking work on language and clarity. Humour helps. Laughter even ensues. Canada says that the extinguishment policy is under review. The federal representatives correct Akaitcho Treaty 8's contention about "only negotiating parts of the treaty." Akaitcho Treaty 8 omits the words "future" and "political" from Canada's interpretation of what Treaty 8 wants. The final lists read:

- "Canada wants to reach agreement on a new relationship, building on the treaty."
- "Canada wants to settle under existing DIAND policy framework."
- "Canada also wants a share of the royalties from minerals, mining, oil and gas."
- "Akaitcho Treaty 8 wants to maintain a bilateral relationship with the federal government especially on treaty, fiduciary and financial matters."
- "Akaitcho Treaty 8 wants to avoid extinguishment of existing aboriginal and treaty rights."
- "Akaitcho Treaty 8 wants a unique settlement appropriate to our needs, circumstances and treaty entitlements."

We then discuss improving communication and relationships. The chiefs ask that senior government officials come to the communities, not to talk about policies but to hunt, fish, camp and learn about the land. The feds request that each First Nation chief appoint a negotiator, rather than handle negotiations himself, so that the process might move faster. Akaitcho Treaty 8 is adamant that Canada's representative in the North, DIAND, "should involve Treaty 8 Dene in decisions which affect them ... "This," the chiefs say, "was *not done* for diamonds in Dogrib Treaty 11 and Akaitcho Treaty 8 territory."

To allow diamond mining on the Barren Lands, Canada has continued what it started with Treaty 8 in 1899. In 1899, 1900 and 1920, Canada drew arbitrary lines on paper maps and signed up aboriginal peoples as if sorting the cattle it promised in return for land. To this day, Canada adheres to those lines. Canada pursues extinguishing aboriginal title. It disguises this fixity of purpose under the guise of "changes in policy."

When Broken Hill Proprietary (BHP) partnered with Chuck Fipke's DiaMet Minerals to mine diamonds near Lac de Gras, BHP became the most recent catalyst in centuries-old conflicts. Not simply between Canada and Dene First Nations, but among Dene groups—Dëne súliné, Dogribs, Yellowknives—and Inuit. The land, its life and the diamonds are probably all that is older than human conflict, on the Barrens and universally.

A century ago, the Northwest Territories (NWT) included what are today the provinces of Saskatchewan and Alberta, all of Nunavut and the present NWT. Ottawa wanted the southern reaches of the old North-West Territories ceded, released and surrendered by the First Nations in 1899. Ottawa didn't get the First Nations farther west and north to cede, release and surrender their land until 1920–21.

When the treaty commissioners came north, the Yellowknives—Dëne súliné and the Dogribs had been at peace since 1829. (Of course, in written accounts by white explorers of the time, white people are said to have brokered the peace. I have seen this in print, but never heard a word about it from Dene elders.) Their leaders established a place, Taïke Deh, approximately midway between present-day Yellowknife and present-day Rae, as the permeable border between their respective territories. (In English, people call this border "Boundary Creek," but it is well west of the Boundary Creek on the Rae-Yellowknife road.) The Dogribs, led by Edzo, thereafter stayed more to the northwest of Great Slave Lake; the Yellowknives and Dëne súliné led by Akaitcho, to the east, on both north and south shores. Their activities overlapped until the great flu epidemics of the early twentieth century reduced the Dene populations from "many, many teepees along the shore" to few.

Enter the Crown. Commissioners divided the Dene along the lines Canada drew for different treaties, following a schedule set only by Ottawa's need to control resources in the North. The fixed border between Treaty 8 and Treaty 11 lands was drawn along the south shore of Great Slave Lake, northeast up the Lockhart River and Artillery Lake, then back northwest toward Wekweti (Snare Lake). The arbitrary division of First Nations into different treaty memberships haunts all the Dene along the arc of the treeline, the caribou migration routes and across diamond fields. For administrative convenience, Ottawa further divided the North into colonial regions. The border between the "North Slave" and "South Slave" regions is the same one Canada drew between Treaty 8 and Treaty 11.

Although this line made perfect economic and political sense for Canada, it did not take into account how Dene actually lived and used the land. Dëne súɬiné and their relatives and compatriots, the Yellow-knives, were divided. Łutsëlk'é is in the South Slave region. Ndilo and Dettah, along with all the Dogrib communities, fall in Ottawa's North Slave region.

At this meeting, we request that Canada correct its maps so that the public record shows Akaitcho Treaty 8 lands accurately. Akaitcho territory includes Ndilo and Dettah and all the land east of them on the north shore of Great Slave Lake. It includes Łutsëlk'é and Denínu Kųe, and long-used territory south, east and north of the present communities. Canada's maps show much of Akaitcho territory overlain by the boundaries of Treaty 11 and the North Slave administrative region. By the end of the week, we have agreed on issues we can start resolving together. But we also have "show-stoppers," issues that could cause negotiations to rupture yet again. The most contentious of these is extinguishment.

♦   ♦   ♦

BEFORE treaty negotiations are actually underway, and well before IBA implementation, Diavik Diamonds comes calling on Łutsëlk'é. Diavik has been requesting a meeting with us for almost a year now. The company's correspondence is chummy. They want to get to know us, be our friends. "We regard BHP as the worst-case scenario," they say.

Diavik has been around, with staff at every public meeting, and as many others as it could get into, during BHP's environmental review. Now Lucy Sanderson schedules the company to meet with the Land and Environment Committee in Łutsëlk'é on December 12.

Until a few months ago Diavik Diamonds went by the name of Kennecott. Mining companies have family trees every bit as exotic as the kinship systems anthropologists love to map. I have no illusions about Diavik's heritage. In Alaska, my birth home, Kennecott Mine is a ghost town. American millionaires J.P. Morgan and Daniel Guggenheim acquired silver and copper deposits there through their Alaska Syndicate, displacing the indigenous Ahtena people of Alaska's Copper River drainage. The syndicate ran a railroad, salmon canneries, a trading company, coal mines and two steamship companies. Kennecott yielded $287 million worth of copper and silver between 1911 and 1938, when the ore body was exhausted. The Ahtena received no benefits or land until the Alaska Native Claims Settlement Act passed in 1971. Well before then, Kennecott merged with Standard Oil of Ohio, and then with British Petroleum. Now Kennecott's patriarch is a global conglomerate, like BHP, named Rio Tinto plc. Kennecott's direct descendant will be Diavik Diamonds. Like a rebellious child, Diavik will deny any similarity between its approach to mining in the North and that of its parent and grandparent companies.

The day before Diavik comes to town, Nick Poushinsky, who continues to serve as a financial and mining consultant to Łutsëlk'é, is scheduled to arrive. We will review what we already know about Diavik's plans and what we want to learn from them. But the flight from Yellowknife is weathered out, and Nick hitchhikes in on Diavik's charter the following morning. The winter day is as clear and bright as they come.

Diavik has brought its president all the way from Salt Lake City, along with the mine designer, who is the likely future manager. He is moving from Salt Lake City to Calgary. He and I talk kids, schools, livable neighbourhoods. A slew of other people, all white, all men, also come along. Their northerner on staff is Doug Willey, a long-time Yellowknifer.

The Diavik men hang numerous maps and diagrams on the walls, then speak slowly, in careful language, illustrating their words with gestures across the displays on the walls. It is hard to see what they mean through the glare of bright winter light off their laminated displays. But it is obvious that they have rehearsed non-technical analogies for their engineering plans. One might be led to believe that they will do nothing more innocuous than set fishnets. When they finish, we have a clear, concise, if superficial description of their plans. The diamonds they want to mine are underneath Lac de Gras. They will build a dike into Lac de Gras, drain water from one arm of the lake, then mine the drained area behind the dike. Repeatedly, one or another of them says, "We are interested in minimizing the 'footprint' of our project." Déjà vu, I think. How can draining part of Lac de Gras, then mining what you've drained, be "minimized"? Diamond mining and "small footprint" seem an oxymoron to me. But I don't say this. Instead, I ask, "How big is your claim block?" The answer is something akin to "Whoa,

Nellie, we don't need to go there." As far as I can tell, we do. BHP's land lease covers 10,960 hectares. But their claim block—the area they've staked and will continue to claim as long as they continue exploration there—is 344,000 hectares. They advertise the large claim block to shareholders and potential investors. The claim block casts a broad shadow on the land, of third-party interests in the making. If I've learned anything about these diamonds, it is that they are plentiful and the miners won't stop until they have mined them all.

After their polite presentation, to which the Land and Environment Committee simply listens without much comment, I want Diavik's representatives to see the village that has been my home these diamond years. I want them to see it through my novice eyes, at least, if not through the eyes of the Dene. I climb into the cab of the pickup with the president and the future mine manager as they prepare to leave. I guide the driver slowly along the shoreline, now cast in the pale hues of mid-winter sunset. Only the weathered plywood sheds and smokehouses along the shore delineate land from frozen, snow-covered lake. At first glance, I am sure what they see are ramshackle, second-hand "junk" piles and structures. What I see, what I want *them* to see, is the well-organized, well-cared-for footprint of living from land and water that sustains the community. I explain the snow bumps far out on the ice, the nets set below them, the fish collected every day, cooked, smoked, consumed all within our visible range. Smoke rises from teepees and small plywood smokehouses with holes in their low roofs. I show them the neighbourhoods of Łutsëlk'é, what family first camped where and how the government housing has grown up in the same pattern. I point out that the trails are used more than the suburb-modelled roads that the government builds for the village, how the dogs are kept up in the woods or out on Dog Island in the summer. I explain where the trails we can see fanning out across the ice go, who travels them, the caribou and moose they bring home for us all.

Where the main road leaves the lower village for the airstrip, I ask to be let out of the truck. I skid down the slope to the First Nation office as they drive away. I slip between two worlds, I think. I know what the miners are about. I respect their competence, even, grudgingly, their single-minded drive to get the minerals of their desire out of the ground. I know with certainty what they will do. I believe I also understand something about the people here. I know what Łutsëlk'é's experience will be with the miners. If not in detail, then generally. This is an old story, one about to be retold with only minor variations on the main theme.

But Diavik's story in Łutsëlk'é will play out over several years, as does implementing the IBA with BHP. Not long after Diavik's visit, Russell Banta, the new federal negotiator, visits Łutsëlk'é for the first time. These negotiations, delayed by design or by the Crown's neglect throughout BHP's environmental review, are at last underway. Łutsëlk'é hosts a week of negotiations in January 1997, when we begin, with hope, to build on the common ground established in November's "ice-breaking" session. Yet we still struggle with contemporary rules of engagement for implementing Treaty 8 almost one hundred years after it was made. Canada has at least pretended to examine alternatives to extinguishment in both its government report, *A New Partnership,* and through the report *Treaty Making in the Spirit of Coexistence: An Alternative to Extinguishment,* the latter the result of work for the Royal Commission on Aboriginal Peoples. However, the Crown is imposing the comprehensive claim model on the entire Mackenzie Valley by enacting legislation that applies to all the Dene areas, even though Akaitcho Treaty 8 and the Dene of the Deh Cho region have declined to enter into these "modern treaties." When third-party interests, such as diamond miners, enter the scene, Canada furthers the situation of those who play by its preferred rules. In this case, those players are the Dogrib, who embraced the comprehensive claim policy and its requirement for extinguishment.

To the north and west of Akaitcho Territory, the Inuit of Nunavut also chose a comprehensive claim. When the Nunavut Act came into effect in 1999, the Northwest Territories was divided once again. A new border was drawn on the map. The permeable boundary that fluctuated for centuries between the Dëne súłiné and the Inuit is fixed now. Because the Inuit chose the comprehensive process and extinguished aboriginal title, because they reached agreement with Canada before Akaitcho Treaty 8, they claimed, and got, land and resources that were arguably shared with the Łutsëlk'é Dëne súłiné. The same thing happened at the southern border of Nunavut, the sixtieth parallel north of Manitoba and Saskatchewan. In those provinces, Dëne súłiné are pursuing the Crown, their fiduciary, through the courts for giving away Dëne súłiné caribou-hunting territories to the government of Nunavut.

All of these paper agreements are flawed. Rigid boundaries across land that has been shared, home to a resource as mobile and important as caribou, do not work. The land and resources should be shared, not parcelled off like body parts to conquerors seeking souvenirs.

◆   ◆   ◆

"Oh, I'm so tired of this," Dettah chief Jonas Sangris says finally, pushing his chair back about three in the afternoon in the council chambers, where we are cooped up with these perennial differences. "I want to go hunting." His frustrated emphasis is on the word "hunt."

Łutsëlk'é chief Felix Lockhart agrees, stretching his arms up over his head.

"Why can't we?" I ask. "We can keep on talking when we are out there."

With an energy completely opposite to the lethargy that has descended on the meeting, the Dene chiefs and negotiators organize the hunting party. Of course, they invite Banta, who says he'd love to, but he doesn't have any gear. No problem. In minutes, everyone has gear, borrowed or shared, requested by phone and delivered by snow machine. We have enough machines to drive or seats for riders. It is about minus thirty degrees Celsius, near sunset, and the winter winds have swept the snow of the big lake into dunelike swales. When Jonas guns the machine over them, I bounce up and down like a yo-yo, anticipating tomorrow's pain. He teases, "Ahh, can't you ride with someone else? I really wanted to just give 'er out there." But all the other machines are full, so he is stuck with me once again.

As they often do in windy winter, the caribou are hanging out where the three islands come together. We are quick to find them, quick to shoot them. I go to shore to make fire. Banta collects sticks while I cut ʔɛ̃l, and Clayton Balsillie, now our negotiations coordinator, cuts dry trees.

Felix comes up with the rib racks and looks at Banta's pile of little sticks. He says, "Who brought these?"

"Russell," I answer.

"Oh," he replies, "thought maybe it was you."

"Nope, Felix, I'm beyond that," I respond wryly. "I am, finally, way beyond that."

When we return to meet again that evening, Banta has learned something about big wood and big fire. Most of all we are full with the richness of the land. We are, in a word, satisfied.

Xaluka
Early Spring

16. *The Healing Journey*

◆   ◆   ◆

The land is my pillow.

—Liza Enzoe, Łutsëlk'é elder

JANUARY passes with its deepest cold but grow-
ing light. The miners move smoothly from "exploration" to mine construction, with a seven-year water licence in hand. Truck tractor trailers
haul steadily up the ice road to Lac de Gras. People seem to forget,
overnight, the tense questioning, the sustained effort of the fall—to
voice objection to the mine, to participate, to set conditions for it and
monitor changes to the land. No one speaks any regret. People take jobs
at the mine but return home with talk of poor wages and racism on
the mine site. Caribou are all around Łutsëlk'é. We eat well. Women's
knives are always busy, opening the rich thick muscles of caribou into

parchment-thin sheets of meat to hang for drying. They scrape the caribou hides in preparation for spring, when the hides will hang outside like laundry, bleaching white in the sun.

In February (*dzirinéth*, or "longer days") the miners make the first payment to Akaitcho Treaty 8, just as set out in the impact and benefit agreement (IBA). People argue about the money, in the way of people everywhere. Some favour investment. Some want immediate, individual payment. Others want planning. Consultants offering assistance flock like birds returning with the light. The chiefs, the Crown and the treaty negotiators continue to lay down common ground for fulfilling Treaty 8.

In early March, on a quiet Saturday morning at home, I see two caribou walking upwind across the frozen lake outside my window. It is only minus twenty degrees Celsius, warm for this time of year, but the wind off the Barrens is bitter. If it weren't early morning, those caribou would be eaten for lunch. But they pace steadily northeast and disappear into the forest. They are the beginning of the spring migration to the Barren Grounds.

Six weeks later, I am going the same way. From the highest point on the portage I look north. Far below, Great Slave Lake glows with the last light. We left the ice at dusk. Caribou, trailing northeast, stood out against the snow and a sunset sky shot with pastels—pink, peach and lavender. Entering forest darkness, we toiled through thick brush on a steep, wickedly twisted trail. Up here, snow holds twilight among stark spruce, burned black three summers ago. A cold east wind off the Barrens chills my sweat. For this moment, I am alone, resting astride my snow machine, breath slowing with relief.

People well enough to travel, and some very ill, make this journey each spring. This year, we carry with us the grief of two adolescent deaths in January. Cancer continues its work in Łutsëlk'é. Conflict over the benefit money and what to do with it is taking a toll now, along with the usual poverty. The load I pull over these steep portages between the icy inlets of Christie Bay is a bittersweet amalgam of doubt and grief. Not to mention the fatigue that has dogged me since October. While Irwin's sixty days flew by, winter got ahead of me. By mid-November, it was too late to get ready. Some winters are like that. You learn to mop up the floods when frozen pipes burst, sew a new ruff on your parka long after your cheeks have gotten frostbitten, buy your used snow machine and tune it up in bitter January instead of mild October. You just hang on until spring. I love winter, but it needs a fall, and I'd lost mine to the diamonds.

Which are having a pernicious effect on the community. All winter the diamonds have outrun the land in importance. The stones and the miners continue to drain the First Nations' energy away from Treaty 8 negotiations.

In Łutsëlk'é, an election for chief and council looms. The election will be close. The issues are money, how the IBA and treaty negotiations have been handled, and sobriety. I work for a chief and council committed to sobriety and recovery among the leadership and in the community. Another faction is not. They believe that more money could have been gotten in the negotiations. Perhaps they are right. When time slowed down after the deadline passed, I wondered. I wonder still. Doubt. If the "money" faction is elected, they will have their turn negotiating, with Diavik Diamonds. I will not be here. I know that my days in Łutsëlk'é are numbered. My friends know this. Grief.

I am a woman broken by diamonds. With twelve others, I am on a healing journey to the sacred falls.

The descent will be easier, but for my fatigue. My right throttle-thumb cramps, my upper arms ache as if yoked. My sleigh, heavy with gas and winter gear, will jackknife on the hill. The trail heads down around a steep open slope, then into trees and darkness again. New frost on the snow will make the trail slippery.

I start slowly, easing the throttle. The full moon rises over my right shoulder. By the time I reach the lake, the others, their machines and sleighs, are silhouetted ahead of me in the moonlight. Bumping across the shore ice ridge, my machine comes to an abrupt slanting stop as the skis hit flat ice. I don't stop, but slide ungracefully down the seat and fall off, ending up in the snow with one leg still on the seat. I swear under my breath and hope my companions don't see me. Quickly, I jump back on, edge forward and join them.

I cut the motor, lift the hood to cool it. I haul a thermos of sweet tea from under bungee cords on my rack and galumph forward in huge boots to stand with the others. We wait there, talking quietly about the portage, identifying the people behind us by the timbre of their engines. The red pinpoints of cigarettes trace our route ahead against the sky. Steam rises from mugs, soft voices speak in the immense night. The silver moon lights the huge world around us. In the hush, I feel night spirits, granting us their presence as we take in this moment.

Then, signs of imminent departure: motor covers and thermoses replaced, parkas zipped, sleigh ropes and hitches checked. Adults gather children and seat them in warm crevices between larger riders. I walk back to my machine, work the dreadful pull-cord start and idle, waiting for Henry Basil and Jackie Coulter, whom I follow. Quickly we spread far apart on the huge lake. Soon headlights bounce way ahead and behind.

We head east, arcing away from land. The wind rises and blows stinging snow across me. I wish I'd pulled on my heaviest parka, with the wolf ruff, but I don't stop. I am warm enough with the peace of knowing where we are. I have travelled this ice trail many times by boat. The full moon lights our way, hanging above the cliffs to the south. Above them and east, the aurora dances lightly, ribboned mint along the edge of the sky. North and centre stage of our world this night, Comet Hale-Bopp flies in a sky even deeper, more mysterious than the deep lake below us.

All winter I studied the stars brightening and fading each long night. Orion walked on the ice across our horizon, Sirius following. Ursa Major stood on its handle, turned the dipper upside down through the night. Auriga squared the southern high sky, and as spring came red Mars visited Leo. The stars kept me sane, showed me time, and the tininess of human folly in the galaxy.

Tonight our world is numinous. I do not name the stars or study the sky but let it blanket me. The comet's tail scatters light across the blackness like phosphorescence on a night sea. Beyond, deeper and deeper in space, stars burn, palpable energy vibrating taffeta blackness. Gases and flares, planets and moons are almost, *almost,* visible in this clarity.

No diamonds ever glowed so.

I am entirely blessed to be here, suspended on ice between water and sky. For the first time in months, I am free from the pain and noise and filth of development, of my species at its greediest. When Hale-Bopp comes again, will Earth remain anything like she is now? Will this lake exist, this clean water, this piled ice, the pressure ridge now coming into view ahead of me? Surely the air will not be this clean, nor the water. Some of the rivers filling this tenth-largest lake on the planet will be dammed, perhaps even the sacred river we travel toward tonight. Spillways will change the rivers to the north, reservoirs replace lakes. And toxins of one form or another, air- or water-borne, will be here that are not now. One hundred years ago, even thirty, the noisy smoking machines we drive were not here to shatter the peace or foul the air.

But I am here now. The Creator, by anyone's name, has given me the gift of travelling through this lush and remarkable night. We turn north to find a crossing through the pressure ridge, then curve away south again. I wonder why we swing so far offshore until I see the dark stain of soft ice and open water beyond. Silently I thank my companions for their knowledge, gleaned from those who have gone before us to the bottom of the lake. This is not a journey I would venture alone.

◆   ◆   ◆

IT is midnight when we reach Noel Drybone's cabin at Reliance—just over the peninsula from the old weather station, all its "Property of Canada—No Trespassing" signs reflecting our headlights as we approach the buildings from the lake. The station has been closed for years. Łutsël'k'é has tried, and tried and tried again, to have the buildings turned over to the community, but the bureaucracy in Ottawa is recurrently stunned by the complications such a transfer entails—although the government made the rules. So the buildings sit, a decaying third-party interest, complete with rusting forty-five-gallon drums. We speed on to Noel's, then crowd into his cabin, but there are too many of us for the small space. We stay only a few minutes, then we are on our way.

I stay close to Henry's taillight now because we are moving with swift purpose. I sense that there is a plan, but that it might change at any moment. We are headed toward Ha keth Cho, the summer field of infinite blueberries. This place is full of memories. Here, Chief Lockhart, Henry and I were once stranded with a broken outboard. Here DiAnn and Raymond and Stephan and I once came to swim, on the rumour that this water might be slightly warmer than where we were camped. Tonight I can't see the opening in the hills in the darkness, but I know their shape. Here Liza and Annie, Vicky and Mary Rose and all their families, the men too, and I have harvested more berries for more years than any of us can count.

Just as I sense Henry gunning his motor to pull away, my headlight picks up the brownish stain of overflow. Again I hear every word everyone said to me last week: "If you see overflow, just gun it, just go, don't slow down," so I just gun it and roar through brown slush in the black night until I reach shore and momentum carries me right past everyone stopped by the trail, looking back down to the lake, dreading the moment when someone gets mired in the slush.

No one gets stuck. When all the machines are through the overflow and on shore, we start again, fast, up the forested trail. It is much wider, more heavily used than the brushy trails we travelled earlier between Christie and McLeod Bays. Suddenly, Henry stops. I stop behind him on the trail. Already, uphill, others are pitching their canvas-wall tents. Henry and Jackie have ours out of my sleigh moments after I brake. Henry borrows my headlamp, hangs it on a spruce tent pole so that Jackie can see the Coleman stove.

It is the middle of the night—no, well into early morning—and I am colder than I have ever been. Surely so cold that I might die. My whole body, especially my exhausted shoulders, is wet with cold. Jackie looks through the grub box for the tortellini she planned for supper tonight, as if she hadn't noticed that "tonight" passed hours ago in the wind on the big lake. I think how ridiculous tortellini is right now. I just want to get into my sleeping bag, to get away from the awesome, awful cold now squeezing me. But I stand still, keeping a tent line taut for Henry. Moving behind the tent, I get stuck in deep snow and fear that I might freeze to death right there before anyone notices I am missing. The northern lights dance on.

Finally, after a meal of hot soup and dry meat, I slide into my frigid sleeping bag. The tent isn't much warmer than outside. I murmur that I have a bad headache.

Henry's voice comes from the pitch blackness on the other side of the tent: "It's the gas. It's from your engine fumes and from what you are hauling in the sleigh."

Almost as soon as I fall asleep I wake up. I am alert, bladder full. I curse the cold, sure it can't be later than five o'clock and that we didn't get to sleep until after three. I pull on my parka, my huge boots, not much else. Then I unzip the tent door, shivering, and take only four steps to the packed trail so that I will not sink into the wet spring snow.

Then I gasp. I look through majestic green-black spruce, down a grey rocky ridge, to the white expanse of Great Slave Lake far below. The moon—glowing ivory still, enormous—is setting toward the northwest horizon. To the east, above the portage summit, the sacred falls and the Barrens, the rising sun pours gold over the snow-covered granite.

Once in a lifetime, I remember. I breathe thanks to the Creator. She knew that only one thing could have gotten me out of my sleeping bag, out of the tent, out to the clear space and air, into this perfect dawn.

Late that afternoon, after one sleigh gets mired in overflow for several hours, and after I, in the briefest moment of inattention brought on by fatigue, drive my own machine into a deep soft drift and Gilbert Abel has to dig and tow me out, we all reach the small lake where we will camp for ten days. On our first day there, we rest and improve our camp. On the second day, we travel some hundred kilometres out onto the Barrens searching for caribou. One small skittish herd startles and sprints into white land and sky, vanishing where there is no horizon. Only one animal turns our way and gratefully we take her, for dinner and breakfast and dry meat. This is land food for the spirit as well as for the body.

"Oh, ptarmigan in the morning in the spring," sighs Henry happily as he stretches out of his sleeping bag. It is our third spring day camped on the edge of the Barrens. He and Jackie share the wide side of the tent. My thick spruce and down bed is angled across the short side, where the barrel stove sits in the corner. I've already been out of my sleeping bag (only from the waist up) to start our fire. The heavy canvas-wall tent, set in deep snow, warms quickly. Outside brilliant snow melts from Precambrian granite, its convex planes catching south sun. Sparse short spruce line the ridge above the lake. Spruce poles mark the water holes we chopped through ice still two feet thick. Lilting ptarmigan carouse on the far shore where the sun warms them. Today we will break trail to the sacred falls.

Hours pass in hard labour, thick brush and heavy wet snow. We break the trail with snowshoes and axes, for snow machines with passengers less able than ourselves. Now we are on the flat above the river canyon. I recognize this place. My feet know its rock and summer blueberries, my lungs its rich crisp air, my eyes its early autumn colour. My body remembers hiking here four summers ago with Henry one evening in misting rain. We didn't have enough food in our bellies to keep us warm in the damp weather. Today it is spring-warm, windless, the light flat, grey, white.

We leave the snow machines above the gorge. Checking the rope fixed along the trail, we traverse the snow slope hinged on the steep wall. Below, Desnéthché is open, spring running, the current strong but deep. Ice chunks accelerate toward the falls. The water looks dense, like polished viridian glass we could walk across. Even hiking with the wind, we hear the falls.

Soon we reach the rough, broad precipice. Dark water funnels over the first small drop, boils white in the shape of the Old Woman's head, then foams and thunders over the brink down the folds of her dress. As always, people come here ready with their prayers. Speech stops. Each of us is now with our own demons and failings, pain and desire, in search of our own grace from the land. I don't watch the others. I've brought my offering.

Later we gather where the current is strongest above the falls, to collect sacred water for the camp. Henry, brave, old and scarred, ropes his thin waist with cheap nylon line. Carefully he steps down to the edge of snow-packed ice overhanging the water while we anchor him from above. I loop the line around a young spruce. I feel its needles against my cheek, smell its green retsina cold. Black spruce, hardly a tree in the rest of the fertile world, so precious here. I thank this tree for its winter green, for holding us. Henry dips thermos after thermos into the water, passing each one up to young Kris, who passes them up to me. I lift each one to Ruben, above me on the trail.

By late afternoon we are ready to leave. I am last. I look back. Pale yellow light bleeds through cirrus clouds. I turn back into the wind rising upward from the falls. To the sheer cliff sheathed in ice, a winter's worth of frozen spray. I drop to my knees in the deep snow. The wind and spindrift freeze my face. I crawl again to the precipice where I threw my offering over the falls—locks of my children's hair and a silver ring, wrapped in a worn bandanna my mother gave me. I crawl into that wind, that snow, that thunder of the falls, and I pray.

Epilogue

◆   ◆   ◆

Canada is a newcomer to the world of diamonds,
but it is already one of the largest producers of top
quality stones. Its mines are remote and its diamonds
are clean. Or are they?

—Ian Smillie, *Fire in the Ice: Benefits, Protection and Regulation*
in the Canadian Diamond Industry

In February 2002, five years after Broken Hill Proprietary (BHP) was granted the land and water permits to build Ekati Mine, I find myself in a pickup truck driving north up the ice road. I am with two Dene companions, both of whom wish to remain anonymous. Diamonds are that controversial, still. Both men have hunted and trapped on this land for their entire lives. Tonight, we are headed for one of their cabins. Tomorrow, weather permitting, we will reach the diamond fields.

It is creaking cold, probably below minus forty-five Celsius, when we reach the cabin about 10 P.M. and unload our gear from the truck. The ice snaps beneath us; the stars crackle in the absence of moon and aurora.

Soon the dull roar of an airplane motor cuts through the still night. "Damn BHP," one of my friends curses, "they always come right over, just this time of night now." Once all our gear is inside, we make short work of building a big fire in the barrel stove and head for bed.

At 4 A.M. I wake up, sweltering in my upper bunk. I can hear the truck running outside. Across the cabin, I can just make out the shadow of a raised hand holding a remote car starter. This method beats having to get up a few times in the night to start the truck, or burning fuel all night long so the battery doesn't die. In a few minutes, the truck stops. The hand disappears back into a sleeping bag, and the snores begin again.

In the morning I am eager to get going. I have wanted to make this trip since Łutsëlk'é signed its impact and benefit agreement (IBA). Not everyone shares my enthusiasm, however. When I mentioned my desire to drive up the ice road to Jerry Bair not long after the signing, he groaned, "Oh, so slow. So boring . . ." Some perverse part of me remains fascinated by the ways our species overcomes nature. We are very good at it, at least in the short term, and I want to see first-hand how this whole supply line to the mines works.

Although it is not really private, the route is not exactly open either. When planning the trip, I learned that to travel along the road one needs permission from the managers. BHPB and Echo Bay Mines Limited manage the ice road. BHP became BHP-Billiton, or BHPB, when Australian corporate giant Billiton plc merged with BHP in May 2001. BHPB then bought Fipke's company, DiaMet, so BHPB now owns eighty per cent of Ekati Mine. Prospectors Fipke and Blusson each still hold ten per cent.

The corporations don't own the land or the water the road traverses. But shortly after one of my companions proposed the trip to them, I got a call in Edmonton from Denise Burlingame, BHPB's current manager for external affairs. Our initial pleasantries covered, as they so often do in the North, where we'd met previously, but the conversation quickly turned serious.

She began, "We are still talking about whether or not this trip can happen, from a safety perspective."

"Umm," I countered.

"I understand you are working on a book," she continued. "Are you coming up to interview people at, or about, the mine?"

"Not really. The book more or less takes place back in 1996–97," I replied. "This is just something I've wanted to do, to see the outcome of the work we did."

"What work?"

"I worked on the negotiations for Akaitcho Treaty 8's IBA with you, back in '96. I never got to see the result."

"Well, we have safety concerns," she reiterated.

"Umm," I replied again.

"Well, I'll be talking to people back in Yellowknife about whether or not this can happen from a safety perspective."

"OK."

Apparently the company resolved its concerns. We were given some sort of clearance, or at least a memo was faxed from BHPB Yellowknife to mine security at Ekati to say that we would be driving the road.

We leave the cabin about two hours before dawn. On the lakes, high snowbanks line the road, which is graded wide; in places it is even two divided lanes. Signs tell us which track to take, northbound. Across the portages the icy tracks are narrower, sinuous. The greatest danger seems to be encountering a truck tractor trailer on a tight curve or a hill. Through the darkness of one wooded stretch, my friend says, "If anyone really wanted to block this road, here's where to do it." He gestures right, left. "There, and there." The headlights pick up rock outcrops that the road threads between.

We reach a place called Lockhart Camp just before sunrise. Like other modular construction camps from Prudhoe Bay to Arctic Quebec, this bland maze of portable buildings has a distinctive plastic sound, smell and feel. The entranceway is startlingly bright under fluorescent light. It's quiet; most of the drivers must be sleeping. Rest stops are mandatory during the twenty-four-hour-a-day trucking season. Ice-road truckers usually catch a shower and a meal here too. A few drivers stand at a check-in counter, where a manager writes down their time in or time out. Clipboards holding the traffic lists hang on the wall below signs for each of the stops along the road: Ekati, Diavik, Snap Lake, Kennedy Lake, Lupin.

Echo Bay's Lupin Mine, on Contwoyto Lake, is the longest haul; supplying Echo Bay is the reason the winter ice road for heavy trucks first came into existence. From Tibbet Lake, where the gravel of Northwest Territories Highway 4 ends about seventy kilometres east of Yellowknife, it is 567 kilometres to Lupin. My friend signs us in for Ekati, 377 kilometres over ice and portages from Tibbet Lake. While I wait, I read a small memorial on the wall to a trucker "lost during opening" a few winters ago. No details are given. I imagine the drivers of the heavy, hazardous rigs don't need to be reminded of the risks they take. We use the bathrooms and then help ourselves to coffee in a nearly empty cafeteria, surprising a couple of the Akaitcho Treaty 8 teenagers who staff the kitchen here. We exchange greetings but we don't stay long.

Outside, it is now light enough to see a field full of semis parked with their engines running. I try to photograph this acreage of trucks, but it is impossible. I would need a filmmaker's crane. I imagine shooting this scene: I would start with one weary driver climbing down from his cab in the cold, then draw back and up, high and higher, to show this migration of big trucks. The herd exhales diesel exhaust. Its unmistakable rumble is unlike any sound in nature. We clamber back into the cab of our pickup and settle in for the long day's journey out onto the Barrens. "No seatbelts," one friend reminds me. "No seatbelts on the ice road." Just in case we break through and have to jump.

It will be hours before we see anything of the mines. While the long shadows of northern light play slowly through another winter day, the terrain changes gradually from treeline scrub forest to sweeping white hills of tundra. The drive is anything but boring, although my mind is preoccupied with diamonds and the consequences of mining them. Sometimes we cross small lakes; other times, as on McKay Lake, we roll over the ice for nearly 150 kilometres. The trucks haul everything big and heavy for a year's operation: tires for the gigantic ore trucks at Ekati; machine parts, fuel tanks and all the diesel fuel to run Ekati and Lupin, the construction camp at Diavik and the exploration camps at Snap Lake and Kennedy Lake, or Gahcho Kué, as it's known in Dëne Súłin yati. We watch, and listen to, the lights and thrum of the diesel trucks, which travel four at a time in convoy every twenty minutes. We count each truck in the convoy as we go by; if we pass three on the ice, we know the fourth will be crawling up a hill over the narrow portage. We spend our short daylight hours watching for the long plumes of diesel exhaust that hang in the air behind the trucks.

As we drive over the bumpy portages, I learn about John Denison, the man credited with mapping out the ice road. One friend says, "These are all our old trails, you know." Now this seasonal road is another third-party interest. Denison and his friends learned about the portages and the currents and the longest lakes by hanging around with Dene trappers, going out on the ancient trails with them. My friends are good guides: they tell me the stories that go with landmarks they know well. We watch for caribou.

◆　　　◆　　　◆

THE land and water we drive over this February day on the way to the diamond source is still hotly contested. In its 1996 report, the environmental assessment review panel (EARP) recommended not only that the Crown settle outstanding land claims in the region quickly and equitably but also that it review the processes and policies by which it does so. To date, no policy has changed, nor have Canada's maps. As the Dogrib Treaty 11 final agreement nears completion, Akaitcho Treaty 8 has instituted legal proceedings to resolve the boundary dispute between the two groups. If Dogrib Treaty 11 is able to include the land between Rae-Edzo and Artillery Lake in its final agreement, it will cut the heart out of Akaitcho peoples' land.

We cross the almost imperceptible height of land between McKay Lake and Lac de Gras, into the Coppermine River drainage, which will bear the water-borne effects of Ekati and Diavik Mines. The road looks like a ribbon of ice through boulder-covered plains blown clear of snow. We pass a makeshift sign with a spray-painted arrow pointing along another graded track veering off to the west: Diavik. We drive twenty-three kilometres further north. At the sign for Ekati, the truck swings left, climbs off the ice and up onto the frozen tundra. We have arrived at the southwestern boundary of BHPB's claim block, the place Chuck Fipke named Misery.

BHP began mine construction in the winter of 1996–97, with a water licence allowing seven years of operation and comparable land use permits. The Ekati Mine opened in October 1998. Ekati rough, its uncut diamonds, is of the high quality that the prospectors anticipated—it is truly pure ice—and Yellowknife is booming again. The city that paved the gold under Dene land with streets has become the "Diamond Capital of North America." No deadline since Minister Irwin's sixty days has slowed the inexorable progress of diamond mining across the Barrens—or the permeation of the mining companies' power into every aspect of life in the Northwest Territories.

In the short term Akaitcho Treaty 8 is, perhaps, fortunate. A hydrologist from the Department of Indian Affairs and Northern Development (DIAND) and elders from Łutsëlk'é, Dettah and Ndilo have visited several locations southeast and east of Lac de Gras and its sources. At this point, no water is flowing out of Lac de Gras into the Aylmer Lake–Lockhart River system. However, Akaitcho Treaty 8 will have a much larger problem from the mines that DeBeers proposes on the lakes and rivers between Great Slave Lake and Artillery Lake. All of that land drains directly into Great Slave Lake.

The environmental assessment review panel (EARP) recommended back in 1996 that the Government of Canada "define when lands are considered to be at a stage of *advanced exploration* and the effect of this on their availability for selection by an Aboriginal claimant group" (italics added). Canada has not yet stated the difference between "exploration" and "advanced exploration" or whose interest takes priority when a corporate claim block overlays aboriginal land.

Through treaty negotiations, what remains of Akaitcho Treaty 8's traditional lands finally received some deterrent to development on June 28, 2001. Canada agreed to "interim measures" that protect aboriginal interests during the period that an agreement (a treaty or comprehensive claim) is being negotiated.

Neither Canada nor the Government of the Northwest Territories (GNWT) has yet established protected areas on the Barren Lands. The EARP recommended that a protected areas strategy be in place by the end of 1998. It took until September 1999 to produce the strategy; selecting and setting aside conservation areas did not begin until 2000. No land that will ensure the long-term survival of the caribou herds is at this time protected indefinitely from industry.

◆   ◆   ◆

AT the top of the rise above Lac de Gras, we pull up to a portable building like the ones at Lockhart Camp. From here, the tundra looks flat. But it is gently rolling, its undulations softened by the winter's drifted snow. Off to the north, I can see the slash of the Misery haul road. In the distance, a flat-topped horizon interrupts the rolling tundra. It is the base of what will become a behemoth, the Misery waste rock dump. It, and others at the mine, may rise fifty metres high.

Once inside the security trailer, we sign in and wait for our guide, one of the on-site managers of a Dene-owned company that provides ore hauling at Ekati. We have two reasons for this trip: one to see the ice road, the other to inspect new heavy equipment. The people of Ndilo, Dettah and Łutsëlk'é have partnered with the Dogribs in this company, called KeTe Whii Ltd. It is named for the man who mediated the peace between Akaitcho and Edzo in 1829.

While we wait inside for our guide, the two young security staff fill us in on their work. "We have to inspect every truck that comes in. You'd be surprised what some of those truck cabs are like. What we're really watching out for is drugs." Two semis pull into the yard outside, and the young woman dons her parka, safety vest and hard hat. Through the window, I see her climbing into the cab. Occasionally the radio blurts traffic, disembodied voices tracking the movement of trucks and personnel around this outpost twenty-nine kilometres southeast of Ekati proper. There's no fence, no wire—no need. In winter, the cold will stop anyone. In summer the mine is guarded by water, rock and hordes of insects.

Tom Unka strides in, taking a break from building a winter survival snow shelter not far from the security site. He's a Dëne sųłiné college grad employed in environmental monitoring at BHPB. We got to know each other when working on the Nánúlá túé research in 1993. Back then he was doing what northerners do to get higher education—leaving for a long period in the south. Now he works for John Witteman, the former DIAND employee who is still in charge of environmental affairs for BHPB. We ask about the snow shelter. Apparently it is to demonstrate winter survival skills to BHPB staff new to the North. Tom thaws out a bit while waiting for Witteman to join him before he goes back outside to dig into snowdrifts.

At last our guide arrives. The security guards outfit us with hard hats and safety vests. We head toward the equipment lot in KeTe Whii's pickup truck, leaving ours running at security. We are touring the equipment parked inside a warehouse when, at last, I see my first kimberlite. I've wanted to know for so long: is it really blue? A few loose grains are caught—at eye level—between the metal treads of a giant tractor. I reach out and rub the loose ore between my thumb and index finger; it is blue-grey, perhaps, and greasy. I've barely touched the stuff before our guide stops me, saying "Don't touch it. Don't touch anything. It's not allowed."

They are true, I think, all the stories I've been told by people who work here. You can't bend over anywhere on the mine site, much less pick anything up. Said one employee of the mine, "It's like a prison there." The company provides a gym, sauna, games rooms, twenty-four-hour TV, health benefits, even a diamond purchase plan. But the people employed here can't do anything outside but work.

◆ ◆ ◆

AH, the diamonds, the diamonds, the diamonds. My lament echoes Major Scobie's complaint in Graham Greene's classic novel of West Africa, *The Heart of the Matter.* I finally saw diamonds one day last summer when I got a tour through Deton'cho Diamond Works in Yellowknife. Ten per cent of the Ekati diamonds are cut and polished in Yellowknife now. There are three cutting factories—Deton'cho, a Yellowknives Dene operation; Arslanian, partly owned by the Dogribs; and Sirius, a Canadian-owned company. BHPB sells just over half of the remaining rough through its Antwerp, Belgium, marketing office. Until the end of 2002, the rest went to DeBeers for sale through its marketing agency in London.

About seventy people are employed in Yellowknife cutting diamonds. Most work at small, dim stations, shoulder to shoulder with each other. Computers determine the cut for each stone. The workers follow the computer's directions. You need four months' training to be a Yellowknife diamond-cutter, and you can get the training now at Aurora College in Yellowknife. Working indoors at a cutting bench is not for everyone, say some of the workers, but some people like it. When Diavik Mine begins production in 2003, Tiffany's will open its own cutting factory in Yellowknife to process some of its share from Diavik Diamonds.

Just after I saw the cutting factory, I hitched a boat ride across Great Slave Lake to the Łutsëlk'é Spiritual Gathering. There was no drumming that summer. "The drummers are all at the mine or working in Yellowknife," people said. Back in 1996, we asked for a provision for "cultural leave" in the IBA. No way, BHP said, it's too hard to keep to a mine production schedule. It seems it will be impossible to schedule Dene culture in keeping with mine production. Will there be any drumming left when the diamonds are gone?

It is nearing the early sunset when we finish at KeTe Whii. Since our truck is staggering occasionally in the minus fifty-two-degree Celsius cold, we decide to head back to the cabin, knowing we can always stop at Diavik for hot soup if we need to. If one is standing still, the wind chill factor makes it a frigid minus sixty-eight. The effect on the moving pickup is not good. Besides, once we are off the claim block, my friends can hunt caribou to take back to their families.

Just after we drive back downhill to the ice of Lac de Gras, we slow to talk to a flooding crew. My friend rolls down his window while two young Dene walk toward us. Their job is to drill through the lake ice and release water from below the road so it will thicken for the heaviest trucks. The young men wade through a low fountain of water spewing up through the ice. They and my friends speak the simple words of greeting in Dene yati. I hear the words for "cold" as the workers shift from side to side and beat their bundled arms against their chests. Because they are not employees of the mine, but rather of a firm sub-

contracted to the miners, the men on the flooding crew are not outfit-
ted with Arctic parkas as warm as the one BHP's negotiator Jerry Bair
wore in Łutsëlk'é during our negotiations in October 1996. As I watch
these young men shiver in their thin jackets, I remember BHPB's pro-
fessed concern for our safety. For my friends, who have hunted and
trapped here all their lives? For me, an interested member of the public,
who is making the trip at my own risk and with my own good gear?
These young men we speak with wear boots encased in ice, and their
brown faces are burned black with frostbite.

In the winter light of late afternoon, driving south, it seems the
mine has had no effect on the Barren Lands. I know only what I read in
the paper reports, primarily those from the Independent Environmental Monitoring Agency (IEMA) established under the environmental
agreement negotiated back in 1996. Unfortunately, I remind myself,
this agency is not so independent. Even before Ekati Mine opened, the
federal and territorial governments, with BHP, advised the IEMA on what
it should and should not emphasize in its work. They reminded the
agency of its funder's priorities—the agency's money, of course, comes
from BHPB.

Not surprisingly, nothing in the environmental agreement that created the agency provides money for First Nations to be directly
involved in monitoring the mine. And five years after the agency's first
report it is still encouraging, but not mandating, BHPB to use Dene traditional knowledge in its environmental management programs. I talk
with my friends in Łutsëlk'é, but they say the communities still have
difficulty understanding the written reports the agency produces about
the mine. The agency reports on Ekati Mine in careful, discreet language. Few numbers and test results are included. For those, one has to
read BHPB's original reports. Over the years, the IEMA has diplomatically
encouraged BHPB to report test results in a consistent and clear format.

What else is the agency saying about Ekati Mine? In the winter of

1997–98, even before the mine had opened, the IEMA reported that "a severe winter oxygen deficit" developed under the ice of Kodiak Lake in the centre of the mine site. BHP remedied the problem by moving its sewage discharge to the Long Lake Tailings Containment Facility. Kodiak Lake shows signs of recovery, but the IEMA predicts it will not return to its natural state while the mine operates.

For the first few years, mining operations—the open-pit excavation of several kimberlite pipes, a new and improved airstrip, the ore-processing plant and the mine "camp"—were concentrated near Kodiak Lake. Tailings were dumped just west at the Long Lake Tailings Containment Facility. In 1999, however, BHP began to expand its mining activities. To develop the Misery pipe, the company built an all-season, twenty-nine-kilometre road southeast from Ekati to Misery. Although BHP incorporated some gentle slopes from the tundra up to the roadbed so caribou can more easily cross the road, this route cuts at right angles across the caribou migration path. The long-term effects on the animals are not yet known.

At the same time that BHP began to develop the Misery pipe, the company applied for permits to expand mining to three new kimberlite pipes in its claim block. (DIAND had previously refused to treat BHP's planned expansion as "amendments" to its existing licences, which allow mining five pipes.) While the company waited for the minister to grant its new licences, BHP began constructing a second road, which DIAND had already approved. The Sable haul road, as it is known, will support northward expansion of mining in BHPB's claim block. Permits for this expansion await only the minister's signature in late 2002. Akaitcho Treaty 8 exercised the clause in its IBA for a five-year review, in keeping with BHPB's planned expansion to three new pipes.

BHPB's environmental record for handling kimberlite is not encouraging. Five years after BHP received its original water licence for the Ekati Mine, the IEMA recommended, as it has each year in one form or another, that BHPB research and develop a better geochemical and mineralogical understanding of each one of the pipes it mines. The latest IEMA report stated that "an emerging concern is the rising concentrations of nutrients (e.g., nitrate), metals (e.g., molybdenum, aluminum, arsenic, cadmium, chromium, copper) and major ions (e.g., calcium, magnesium, sodium, potassium, chloride) being discharged from Long Lake and King Pond into downstream waterbodies." New federal mining regulations introduced in August 2001 set stricter limits for acceptable levels of some of these elements. However, limits for arsenic, copper, lead, nickel and zinc remain the same, and potentially toxic elements such as cadmium and mercury are still unregulated.

Furthermore, kimberlite toxicity, defined by the IEMA as "the ability of diamond-bearing rock to cause harmful health effects to plants, animals and humans," has, the agency says, significantly adversely affected aquatic life in the lakes on the mine site. This vague language disturbs me. It seems that no one yet knows just what diamond mining means for land, water and life downstream. Downstream are Lac de Gras and the Coppermine River.

One animal I know I won't see near Ekati, winter or summer, is the wolverine. Animals from the sparse Barrens population were drawn to the food waste at Ekati. BHPB finally cleaned up its food waste disposal in 2000. By that time, several of the fierce creatures had already been killed, and the area population is now depleted. Ironically, the IEMA uses the wolverine as its logo.

The quality of government monitoring remains a major problem. We pass a DIAND employee, towing a snow machine behind a pickup truck. "Well, at least they get up here once in a while," my friends say. The mining companies offer better salaries than government does. In contrast, DIAND has at times been so shortstaffed it has been unable to inspect the mine sites for compliance with regulations as often as the law requires. At least one case—in which a government land use inspector caught Diavik Diamonds in an illegal quarry operation in late 2000 and for which Diavik was fined three thousand dollars—suggests the possible consequences of having too few staff to do the work.

Something of a "brain drain" has hit the small First Nation communities too. Experienced heavy-equipment operators have moved from community maintenance to jobs at the mine; people with administrative skills have taken jobs providing security at the mine or working for Yellowknife businesses that support diamond mining.

Even the Dogrib language has been affected by diamond mining. Since 1997, when BHP trademarked the word Ekati (which translates as "fat lake"), Ekati™ has become the company's signature on diamonds and T-shirts, and on plastic water bottles from the mine. The water bottles also say, in red letters, "Environment Matters." I wonder about Dene rights to their intellectual property. How can diamond miners trademark a Dene word? I see people wearing Ekati™ jackets, shirts and hats shopping in Yellowknife and at the big-city malls down in Edmonton.

I have begun to think of Ekati diamonds as black ice, the most dangerous kind. The kind you can miss seeing when your eyes are blinded by the pure light of sun on snow. Of course, BHPB takes the opposite view. Ekati diamonds have been very well marketed as "pure ice," untainted—like the Barren Lands they come from—by conflict, blood, criminals, dictators or terrorists.

In the late nineties, the London-based non-profit group Global Witness released its account of diamond mining. The report, called *A Rough Trade*, brought "blood diamonds" or "conflict diamonds" to world attention. Such diamonds are mined, often by women and children, under the guns of rebels in Angola and Sierra Leone, and marketed illegally. These blood diamonds are a major revenue source for African military dictatorships, which use the profits to buy guns and larger weapons. By late 2001, the blood diamond trail led to the financial coffers of Osama bin Laden and the Al-Qaeda terrorist network. And on August 23, 2002, the Canadian Security and Intelligence Service warned that organized crime may have targeted the Canadian diamond trade too.

Consumers looking for alternatives to blood diamonds have fuelled a boom in the Canadian trade. The marketers of "Canadian" diamonds would have us believe that our diamonds travel from source to seller on a domestic route. Not so. At this time, *all* Ekati diamonds leave Canada at least once. After a valuator contracted by DIAND inspects it, the rough is shipped to Europe for sorting. Only then does the ten per cent to be cut and polished in Yellowknife return there.

Security for Canadian diamonds is good, but not perfect. Theoretically, conflict diamonds could be mixed with Canadian diamonds, either at Ekati or abroad. According to the Diamonds and Human Security Project in 2002, mixing at the mine site is a common way of laundering conflict diamonds in other countries. At the Ekati mine site, no government security inspection exists. Likewise, procedures guaranteeing that diamonds from Ekati return for cutting and polishing in Canada are stringent, but there are gaps.

Several government agencies, including the Royal Canadian Mounted Police, DIAND, Canada Customs and Statistics Canada, are responsible for diamond security. Whether these agencies are checking for theft, collecting royalties, verifying import and export requirements or comparing rough product with gem sales, diamonds can and do go missing. Statistics Canada has difficulty reconciling rough units with gem sales. So much so that industry observer Ian Smillie reported, "There are two possible explanations: The first is that there is something wrong with the statistics. The second is that a lot of rough diamonds are disappearing from the statistical radar. Whatever the answer, the Canadian diamond industry and the Canadian government should be interested in finding a solution."

How can one tell a Canadian diamond from a blood diamond? The word "Ekati" is laser etched onto the girdle of every diamond cut and polished at Arslanian Cutting Works in Yellowknife. Other Canadian diamonds are marked with a polar bear or a maple leaf, but even these symbols are controversial. The GNWT and Sirius Diamonds, another cutting firm in Yellowknife, are at odds over ownership of the polar bear symbol. And HRA Investments in Vancouver marks its diamonds—purchased overseas and polished in Canada—with a maple leaf. But there is no guarantee that the rough it purchases comes from Ekati.

◆   ◆   ◆

THE three of us are quiet as we drive south late in the day. Near the turnoff to Diavik, the yellow cab of a road grader juts up through the ice. I wonder how long it will remain there, how much fuel and transmission fluid will leak into the lake before it is pulled out with yet more heavy equipment. I wonder too whether or not an environmental impact report is filed on such an incident, or if it is just too small in the grand scheme of diamond mining for anyone to pay attention.

Then, above a drift of windblown snow, we see caribou silhouetted against a cerulean sky. The animals are magnificent. As I watch them I can't help but think about the toxins that mine dust deposits on the snow. I can't see them, but I know they are there. The toxins spread across the landscape with the water of snow melt or summer rain, onto and into the lichen. Caribou eat this lichen.

As darkness falls, we near the treeline at the south end of McKay Lake. My friend murmurs at last, "Well, you could say this about the diamonds." He pauses. I wait. He breathes out softly, "Ahh . . ." and pauses again. Then speaking each word carefully, like a hunter taking aim, he says, "Some of the chiefs had the heart taken out of them when this mining started. The elders too. Lots of people have passed on, and the treaties weren't settled before they died." I wait again, but he says no more. There is certainty, I think, in the lifeless, mined-out pipes and the waste-rock piles. Aboriginal title is extinguished practically, if not legally.

Diamonds no longer surprise me. But I am still mystified by what people do. Who will want this desecrated land? It is no longer the land and the life that Dene signed their treaties to preserve. I am, most of all, deeply, finally, saddened. My friend speaks again, and it is as if our minds have come together, just as the elders describe. "The way they say it in our language," he says, " 'the elders' hearts are broken over a white stone.'"

I reflect on his words as the last light glows faintly along the horizon. The scene reminds me of the Ekati diamonds I once saw gracing a woman's neck. The model was faceless; only her jaw and lips and neck showed in the photograph. Her flesh was rendered entirely in shades of grey. A cool pale blue, the hue of Arctic water pooled on the melting ice of a sunny day, coloured the diamonds with the slightest gleam. We are hostage to diamonds, I think, like the frozen beauty of that nameless woman. We are bound by the notion that these diamonds—their mystique and beauty and power—will fill the void in our spirit, the places of our imagination, left empty when this land is finally gone.

Sources and Source Notes

◆   ◆   ◆

MUCH of this story is in the public record. The Canadian Arctic Resources Committee in Yellowknife provides a true public service by maintaining an archive on environmental matters and allowing access free of charge. I am grateful for their assistance. In addition to reports from the Independent Environmental Monitoring Agency, government reports and public hearing transcripts, I relied on the following published works for background on Treaties 8 and 11, on Dene, on diamonds and on the land.

Bastedo, Jamie. *Shield Country: The Life and Times of the Oldest Piece of the Planet.* Red Deer: Red Deer College Press, 1999.

Berger, Thomas. *Northern Frontier, Northern Homeland: Report of the Mackenzie Valley Pipeline Inquiry.* Rev. ed. Vancouver: Douglas & McIntyre, 1988.

Camsell, Charles. *An Exploration of the Tazin and Taltson Rivers, Northwest Territories.* Ottawa: Department of Energy, Mines and Resources, 1916.

Canada. Royal Commission on Aboriginal Peoples. *Treaty Making in the Spirit of Co-existence: An Alternative to Extinguishment.* Ottawa: Government of Canada, 1995.

Dene Cultural Institute. *Dehcho: "Mom, We've Been Discovered."* Hay River, NWT: Dene Cultural Institute, 1989.

Dene Nation. *Denendeh: A Dene Celebration.* Yellowknife: Dene Nation, 1984.

Frolick, Vernon. *Fire into Ice: Charles Fipke and the Great Diamond Hunt.* Vancouver: Raincoast Books, 1999.

Fumoleau, René. *As Long as This Land Shall Last: A History of Treaty 8 and Treaty 11, 1870–1939.* Toronto: McClelland & Stewart, 1973.

Government of the Northwest Territories. Department of Education. *Dene Kede: Education, A Dene Perspective.* Yellowknife: Government of the Northwest Territories, 1993.

Hamilton, A.C. *Canada and Aboriginal Peoples: A New Partnership.* Ottawa: Government of Canada, 1995.

Hart, Mathew. *Diamond: A Journey to the Heart of an Obsession.* Toronto: Penguin Books Canada, 2001.

Krajick, Kevin. *Barren Lands: An Epic Search for Diamonds in the North American Arctic.* New York: Henry Holt and Company, 2001.

Oleson, Dave. *North of Reliance.* Minocqua, Wisconsin: North Word Press, 1994.

Smillie, Ian. *Fire in the Ice: Benefits, Protection and Regulation in the Canadian Diamond Industry.* The Diamonds and Human Security Project, Occasional Paper #2. Ottawa: Partnership Africa Canada, 2002.

◆   ◆   ◆

Permissions

Author's Note and
Acknowledgements

♦　　　♦　　　♦

Every person involved in this story would tell it differently. I speak only for myself, not for Łutsëlk'é First Nation or for Akaitcho Treaty 8. Despite their best efforts to teach me well, I have no doubt made mistakes of fact and interpretation.

It was a difficult decision to use real names rather than pseudonyms that might have protected people's privacy. But almost everyone in this story played a public role as well as a private one. Nevertheless, when the story unfolded, no one around me knew I would write this book, because I did not know myself. To those who would prefer not to be in it, please accept my heartfelt apology. I decided to write because I feel the public story is larger than all of us, and needs to be told.

Aspects of community life, however, are and remain confidential, as does the impact and benefit agreement.

For assistance with language, special thanks to Sabet Biscaye, Stella Desjarlais, Jonas Sangris and Mary Rose Sundberg; and to Naomi Pauls for her dedication not to one language but two.

My fine editor, Lucy Kenward, patiently worked hard to make this complicated story readable. She suggested, gently, that not all of Akaitcho's people could be named in the book. In part because aboriginal people have been largely anonymous in the written and photographic record, more because they made me feel at home, I would like to name and thank virtually every person in Łutsëlk'é, and many in Ndilo, Dettah and Denínu Kyę. The following unfortunately omits almost all of the children, some now young adults, who are close to half the communities and close to my heart.

I must thank some very, very special friends: Henry Basil, Jeannie Basil, DiAnn Blessé, J.C. and Hanna Catholique, Archie Catholique, Stella Desjarlais, Liza and Billy Enzoe, Dora Enzoe, Stephan Folkers, René Fumoleau, Felix and Sandra Lockhart, Evelyn Marlowe, Frank Marlowe, George and Celine Marlowe, Jonas Sangris and Lucy Sanderson.

Out on the land, I had uncountable marvellous times with Raymond Abel; Gilbert Abel; Alizette and Louie Abel; Alfred Boucher; Ernest, Emily and Damien Boucher; Mary Rose and Modeste Casaway; Pierre, Lawrence and Joseph Catholique; Doris Catholique; Lorraine Catholique and Tommy Desjarlais; Vicky Desjarlais; Cheryl Desjarlais; Ron and Shirley Desjarlais; Dennis Drygeese; Mary Rose and August Enzoe; Peter Enzoe; Irene and Ruben Fatt; Jerry and Addy Jonasson; Angie Lantz; Kris Lantz; Alfred and Alizette Lockhart; Bernadette and Joe Lockhart; Tom and Rosa Lockhart; James and Sandra Lockhart; Pierre and Toby Marlowe; Freddie Nitah; Marie-Louise Nitah and J.B. Rabesca.

I thank all of my colleagues and friends in my life with Akaitcho Treaty 8. You each taught me so much: Clayton Balsillie, Don Balsillie, Darrell Beaulieu, Jackie Coulter, Debby Dobson and Ed Hall, Deby English, Avi Isackson, Christina Ishoj, Chris Lemon, Barney Masuzumi, Don Morin, Chris O'Brien, Kevin O'Reilly, Brenda Parlee, Jerry Paulette, Magloire Paulette, François and Lesley Paulette, Nick Poushinsky, Susan Quirk, Marilyn Sanderson, Jerome Slavik and Tom Unka.

I could not have managed critical logistics without the Romano-Lax clan, or without Tracy Butler, Doris Sabatine, Ian McConnan, Jan Young and especially Kay Bielawski. Thank you.

I thank Frank Kense, without whose parenting our boys would not be the young men they are. To Connor and Adrian, thanks for growing up beautifully in Łutsëlk'é and in Alaska, despite having a mother well off the centre of the bell curve. In Edmonton, I cannot thank Mark, Ronnene, Matthew and Neil enough, from the beginning to the end; Michele, Yvonne, Denise for walking me through this; the Collinson-Fleming clan for a writing retreat that simulates Łutsëlk'é, without plumbing and with wood heat; Debbie Topinka for finding me diamonds in a dark place; Joyce Burnett, the Schlossers, the MacIvers, the Macdonalds and the Topinkas for nurturing me and my boys while I wrote this book.

As always, I thank my mother and the rest of my family; all of my sisters, especially, for the music; and my other sisters, Sarah Cooper Cole, Kristen Kemerling and Judie Halenko. Special thanks to Mom and Jean for looking after my Alaska home during the "diamond deadline" and for sharing life with me and the boys in Łutsëlk'é.

Carolyn Servid, Dorik Mechau and all the members of the Sitka Symposium, especially Ted Chamberlin, Julie Cruikshank, John Daniels, Peter Fleischer, Bill McKibben, Dan Morrow, Deb Robson, Marianne Spitzform and Steve Thompson, gave me untold lessons for writing this story; very special acknowledgements to Linda Hasselstrom and Vernita Herdman who know why. Bill Wilson and Jamie Bastedo both assisted with research and language. Mike Robinson, colleague and kindred spirit, read the penultimate manuscript for me. Thank you, all.

Most of all, I thank my writing colleagues for their patience and inspiration, especially Andromeda Romano-Lax and Bill Sherwonit, without whom this book would not exist; also Jim Adams, William Ashton, Nancy Deschu, Dan Henry, Jon Nickles and George Bryson—you are a writers' group to die for, whether we are laughing, arguing or retreating from bears.

One morning over coffee in the Łutsëlk'é First Nation office, someone said, "White people. The good ones—never stay long enough. The bad ones—you can't get rid of." I know that for a few people, I stayed too long in Łutsëlk'é; for the rest, I hope that for you, as for me, it was not quite long enough. *Marsi cho*, always.

Index